JEWISH REACTIONS TO THE HOLOCAUST

Yehuda Bauer

JEWISH REACTIONS TO THE HOLOCAUST

MOD Books   Tel-Aviv

JEWISH REACTIONS TO THE HOLOCAUST
by
YEHUDA BAUER
Institute of Contemporary Jewry
The Hebrew University of Jerusalem
English translation by John Glucker

No part of this publication may be reproduced, stored in a retrieval system, or transmitted in any form or by any means, electronic, mechanical, photocopying, recording or otherwise (brief quotations used in magazines or newspaper reviews excepted), without the prior permission of the publisher.

Copyright © 1989 by MOD Books
All rights reserved

English Series Editor: Shmuel Himelstein

ISBN 965-05-0482-6

Computerized phototypesetting & printing: Naidat Press Ltd.
Printed in Israel

MOD Books — P.O.B. 7103, Tel-Aviv 61070, ISRAEL

Contents

Preface		7
I.	The Jews in Germany and their Fate, 1933-1937	9
II.	The Transfer Agreement	25
III.	The Evian Conference and its Consequences	41
IV.	*Kristallnacht* and After	50
V.	Aliyah B and Emigration from Germany at the Beginning of the War	58
VI.	Jewish Leadership in Poland and German Policy, 1939-1940	66
VII.	Rescue Attempts	77
VIII.	The Sanctification of Life	86
IX.	The Decision to Murder the Jews — First Reactions	96
X.	The Western World and News of the Holocaust	110
XI.	The Warsaw Ghetto Uprising	119
XII.	Jewish Fighting	129
XIII.	Kovno, Vilno, Lodz and Minsk	138
XIV.	Western European Jewry	150
XV.	Jewish Reaction and Resistance in Other Countries	159
XVI.	The Reaction in Palestine and the Slovakian Affair — The "Plan"	164

XVII.	The Mission of Joel Brand	173
XVIII.	The Kastner Train	182
XIX.	The Bombing of Auschwitz	191
XX.	Too Little, Too Late	200
XXI.	Negotiations with the S.S.	208
XXII.	As Sheep to the Slaughter?	217

PREFACE

The reader has before him the revised edition of two courses of lectures delivered as part of the Broadcast University series of Israel Army Radio, dealing with the Holocaust — or, to be more precise, with Jewish reactions to the Holocaust and in it, and the attitudes of the Jewish and non-Jewish worlds to the Holocaust of the Jews. I have not pretended to provide an overall survey of the Holocaust; my intention was to provide my listeners with two popular series of lectures dealing only with specific aspects of this broad subject.

I have not tried, in this book, to alter the lecturing style, and I have therefore abstained from providing the reader with footnotes or references to sources. At the end of the book, I have given a bibliography which might, perhaps, help the reader who wishes to broaden his knowledge. There are now a few departments in Israeli universities which provide courses in this subject. Much experience in teaching this subject has been acquired by the Institute of Contemporary Jewry of the Hebrew University of Jerusalem, which provides very extensive courses on the Holocaust as part of its M.A. studies, but also has an introductory course for B.A. students, open to all students of the university.

Yehuda Bauer
Kibbutz Shoval

I.

The Jews in Germany and their Fate, 1933-1937

The antisemitic ideology of National Socialism had a quasi-religious character. The Nazis made use of the trappings of religion, and their ideology was an expression of a political religion on the one hand, and religious politics on the other hand. Thus, for example, the colossal rallies of the Nazi Party in the 1930's before the Second World War were designed by architects (including the famous architect Albert Speer) in the pattern of ecclesiastical ceremonies. Instead of walls, which did not exist, of course, in the huge open spaces where these rallies took place, they had "walls" of floodlights, whose light beams converged in the sky-like arches of a Gothic cathedral. Instead of the cross, they had the swastika. Instead of God, they had God's messenger — the Fuhrer Adolf Hitler. He was the Messiah, the son of the Messiah, the Apostle to the Chosen People — the Germanic Aryan race — which had the right to rule the world. All the ingredients of such ceremonies were quasi-religious. The Nazi attitude to the Jews was also nourished by Christian and pre-Christian attitudes, which regarded the Jew as a strange and hostile creature belonging to a different world. There is no doubt that in the whole of European Christian civilization of the late nineteenth and early twentieth centuries, the Jews and the Gypsies were the outsiders. They were the only culture groups which had not acquiesced in a tradition accepted by everyone else.

The Jews were regarded by National Socialist doctrine as an alien body in this world, something like an Apostle of the Devil. After all, who else could have murdered God — as people believed that the Jews had done when they had been responsible, as one was told, for the crucifixion of Jesus? Only the Devil, a child of the Devil or the Devil's messenger could murder God. At the same time, the Jew was not regarded as the Devil himself in Christian thought. He was rather a man whose soul had been taken by the Devil's temptation, and he could be made to save himself by converting to Christianity, whether one achieved this conversion by prayer, persuasion, force or in any other way.

There was also another, pro-Jewish, Christian tradition, which was opposed to this antisemitic attitude. But Nazism was nourished by the antisemitic Christian approach, and it added to it many new elements, such as what is known as Social Darwinism, an approach which was supposed to be based on the work of the scientist Charles Darwin. In his book *The Origin of Species*, Darwin maintained that the development of species of living organisms was conditioned by their adaptation to nature and to their environment, and their compatibility with their living conditions. The Nazis distorted this theory and made it imply that species survive by fighting each other, where the strongest win. Darwin, and his contemporary Herbert Spencer, did indeed say things which could be interpreted in this fashion, but this was not the essential meaning of Darwin's theory itself.

The Nazis twisted this distorted doctrine to fit human beings and asked the question: "Which of the species of man, which of the races of mankind, are the victors and have the right to rule?" Their answer was that the strongest had such a right. The body is an expression of the soul, they maintained, and the ones who are strong and beautiful both in body and soul are the Aryan peoples.

Among the Aryan peoples, too, they distinguished between inferior and governing peoples. The Poles were Aryans, but they were regarded as Aryans of the lowest grade, and the Nazis instituted a policy of selective mass murder toward them. According to Nazi theory, the Germanic peoples are the governing groups within the Aryan race. What was the place of the Jews in

The Jews in Germany and their Fate, 1933-1937

such a doctrine?

The Jews were not Aryans at all, but they did not belong to any of the other races either. According to Hitler, the Jews are an anti-race; they are not a real race, but rather a mixture of odds and ends of other national groups, combined together by some Satanic power, and the image of the Jew is thus an image of Satan. Unlike the older Christian tradition, which regarded the Jew as a symbol of the Devil, or as someone who had been tempted by the Devil, the Nazis saw in the Jews Satan himself. Needless to say, Christian tradition left the Christian in no doubt as to how one should deal with the Devil if one met him in the street. And surely enough, in the first period of their rule the Nazis published propaganda materials (including children's books and textbooks for elementary and secondary schools) describing the Jews as Devil-like. If the Jew is a Devil, it follows that he is not human. This is to say that, while there were human and subhuman components in the Aryan race and in other races, the Jews had nothing to do with being human at all.

This approach of course, entailed some extremely serious consequences, but the Nazis did not draw these consequences from the very outset. There is no Nazi document earlier than the late 1930's which maintains that the Jews should be slaughtered. The Nazis regarded the Jews as non-human, as the Satanic force which should be driven from the midst of the Germanic peoples, and especially out of German territory, so as to stop it from disturbing them and to free the German nation from the "burden of Jewish domination."

One should add that, according to Nazi conceptions, the Jews were not merely a Satanic force, but a Satanic force aimed at dominating the whole world. This, too, is no new conception — one should make it clear that the Nazis did not produce any innovations in their antisemitism; they mostly adapted earlier conceptions. The Nazis based their view on a publication dating back to the early years of the twentieth century, *The Protocols of the Elders of Zion*, a forgery produced in Imperial Russia of all places, which claimed that the Jews — or, in fact, the Zionists (this was said explicitly) — wanted to dominate the whole world and to enslave all other

Jewish Reactions to the Holocaust

nations. The Nazis took over this legend, which was itself based on some earlier Christian theories, and made it into one of the main tenets of their doctrine. The Jews, they maintained, were planning to massacre the Germanic peoples, and especially the German nation: they should therefore be expelled from Germany before they succeeded in carrying out their plan.

The fact that, until the late 1930's at least, the Nazis did not explicitly express their wish to massacre the Jews, and the fact that during this period we have no shred of evidence to show that there existed any National Socialist plan for slaughtering the Jews — these facts should guide us in our observations of the Jewish reaction; for the Jews reacted only to what they knew or could see. They saw the rise to power in Germany of an antisemitic faction which persecuted the Jews, but there was nothing new in that. There had been antisemitic countries in the past. These persevered for a while, expelled and persecuted the Jews, and whether the Jews escaped or remained, sooner or later the government changed hands. All these were events which had occurred many times in the past. The Jews dealt with dangers which were familiar to them, whereas they did not react to dangers which they did not know and with which they were not familiar. Quite probably, they could not react to such dangers.

Some people have formulated a retroactive demand, addressed, as it were to German Jewry of the period: "Why did you not realize immediately that Hitler was about to murder you?" Such a demand is unrealistic. Hitler never spoke in this vein before 1938-9, and such things do not appear in his book, *Mein Kampf*, written in the mid-1920's. The only passage in his book which speaks in an extreme and alarming fashion of a physical threat with regard to the Jews is a passage which says that if in the First World War twelve thousand to fifteen thousand Jews had been subjected to poison gas, as was done to hundreds of thousands of German workers (and he meant those German soldiers who were injured by poison gas in the First World War), then, says Hitler, the war would not have been in vain. This is, of course, a serious, brutal and extreme expression, but it does not threaten a massacre of the Jews in the future — in the

The Jews in Germany and their Fate, 1933-1937

worst case, it hints at it. Now, after the event, we can see that Hitler was hinting at what was to come later; but in a huge book, hundreds of pages long and very difficult to read — since it is written in atrocious and boring German — this does not look like anything extraordinary compared with what antisemites of all previous generations had said. Thus, the Jews of Germany did not know what was to befall them, and they had no way of knowing. They might, perhaps, have sensed it — but that is a very different matter.

There were, indeed, Jews who read *Mein Kampf*, and this means that Nazi antisemitism was not unknown. But it was claimed that there is a difference between what a party says when it is in opposition and what it is likely to do once it has reached power — and it had already been seen, people said, that a shrill and extreme opposition moderates its policy and makes it more practical once it has achieved power. The Devil was not so terrible. And even if some unpleasant things were to occur, governments come and go, but German culture would remain for ever.

At the same time, the blow to Jewish emancipation which was to be expected from the Nazis was regarded as serious in the extreme. In the United States in this period, there were already some people who were apprehensive of what was about to come. In 1930-2 the journal of British Jewry, *The Jewish Chronicle*, published a series of articles warning the Jews of Germany of what was about to happen: the world was passing through a terrible economic crisis; millions were unemployed; there was a general tendency in political movements throughout Europe to adopt more extreme policies; and if, God forbid, Germany would turn to the extreme right wing, the Jews were most likely to forfeit all the achievements of emancipation won during the previous century.

The Joint Distribution Committee — the great American Jewish relief association known universally as the Joint — was active in Europe during these days, and in practice its activities there constituted the chief social endeavor on the part of American Jewry for assistance to world Jewry. At a meeting in New York on December 14, 1930, after the first Nazi victory in an election, when the Nazis had become the strongest party in the Reichstag —

although they were still very far from government — Dr. Bernard Kahn, who headed the Joint's activities in Europe, declared that this was a very grave development.

There was serious danger, he said, that the Nazis might achieve power, and in that case the Jews would lose all their official positions in the civic, political and administrative sectors in Germany. Very strong economic pressure would be put on the Jews, and the atmosphere would become insufferable. Kahn also maintained that if Germany were to become Nazi, antisemitism would spread from it into the rest of Europe and into the whole world. Eighteen months later, in April 1932, Dr. Kahn wrote to the president of the American Jewish Committee, which constituted the political leadership of liberal, assimilated Jewry in the United States. In his letter, he noted that one had to prepare for a most extreme situation in Germany and to draw up an emergency program for the rescue of German Jewry, since he believed that the Nazis were about to gain power.

At the same time, voices were heard within German Jewry which tried to calm people down. They maintained that although the situation was extremely grave and danger existed, one should fight, and there were good chances of victory. But there were also some German Jews who realized the danger. In the German Jewish press of those days one can find warning notes, stressing the need to unite in order to face the rising wave of Nazism.

And yet, the actual rise of the Nazis to power was to a large degree a surprise, as well as a very severe shock, to German Jewry. The way in which Hitler came to power was not strictly democratic, since he had not gained a majority in the elections. He came to power despite the fact that in the last free elections held in Germany, in November 1932, the Nazi party had lost two million votes and thirty four seats in the German parliament. Hitler came to power, not because he had won the election, but because he had lost it. To the conservative German right, which was apprehensive of the rise of the left, Hitler appeared to be a danger, but a danger that could be kept under control and restrained, and it was for this reason that he was invited to become prime minister — Kanzler — of Germany on January 30,

The Jews in Germany and their Fate, 1933-1937

1933. The event constituted a great surprise to the Jews, because just when it appeared that the Nazis were on the decline, they came to power.

Immediately, terror broke out on the streets and, as was only to be expected now, with the connivance of the police. Brown shirted members of the Nazi storm troops, the SA, took possession of the streets and assaulted the Jews. It is true that the Jews were only a small portion of those injured, since the main efforts of the Nazis were directed against their German opponents. But Jews were clearly a target, although Jews *as such* were not yet interned in concentration camps at this stage. The camps were designed for enemies of the regime, and the majority of Jews incarcerated in them — apart from a few exceptions — were detained for being members of parties hostile to the Nazis.

What was German Jewry like in the initial period of Nazi rule, in January 1933, which we shall employ as our starting-point? During this period, we are concerned with a Jewish community of about half a million people, of which a minority, probably no more than between ten and twenty percent, were Zionists. The German Zionists did not regard themselves as members of the German nation, but they felt — rightly, no doubt — that German culture was part and parcel of their heritage. Their Zionism, or Jewish nationalism, was undoubtedly influenced by the tradition of German civilization in which they had been brought up. It is true that Germany did not grant the Jews full social equality, although there is no doubt that the Jews enjoyed civic and political equality. In practice, there were some positions which the Jews could not attain, and some professions were closed to them. Social antisemitism existed without any doubt, and German nationalism was not prepared to accept the Jews as members of the German nation. In fact, the Zionists accepted this view. They maintained: "It is true that we are here and that we are German citizens. We have all the rights enjoyed by other citizens, but we have different origins." A resolution adopted at one of the Zionist conventions in Germany as early as 1912 made it the duty of every German Zionist to consider immigration to Palestine at some point in his planning of his life and career. This was no unambiguous demand for immigration to Palestine, since in 1912, just as much as in 1933, such a demand would have been impractical. But this was undoubtedly a Zionist movement, however influenced it was by German civilization.

Most of the rest of Germany's Jews — albeit not all of them — belonged to a liberal school, somewhere between Reform and Conservative in terms of American Jewry today. The Jews did emphasize their Jewish religious faith in their own way, but they regarded themselves explicitly as members of the German nation, even if their origins were different. There were among them people who called themselves a German tribe, as if they were one of the numerous tribes which contributed to the final constitution of the German nation; for one should not forget the simple fact that there had been Jews settled in Germany virtually before the arrival of the Germans themselves. The Jews came to the western parts of Germany with the Romans, at a time when that region was something of a buffer zone against the Germanic tribes who were attempting to cross the Rhine and invade the western part of that region — today part of Germany — and Gaul.

The liberal Jews regarded themselves as descendants of those ancient Jews — and for our purpose it makes no difference whether that was correct or not — and they organized themselves into an association called the Central Union of German Citizens of the Mosaic Persuasion, which they regarded as their leadership. This union, as its name makes clear, was the only expression which could be regarded as political in a Jewish community which was also organized in communal associations centered around the synagogues. During the whole period of its existence, for over thirty years at the beginning of the twentieth century, the Central Union fought bravely against antisemitism, with much strength and determination. It sought allies among the Germans, published articles and appealed to courts wherever Jews were attacked or found themselves in danger. Thus, the common image of the assimilated Jew, seeking shelter, as it were, and not daring to stand by his Judaism, is a mistaken image. This was a very proud Jewish

The Jews in Germany and their Fate, 1933-1937

community, which held on with all its might to its German nationalism, but also held on to its Jewish religion, although there were cases of conversion to Christianity.

In the nineteenth century, conversions threatened, or appeared to threaten, the existence of German Jewry; but in the early twentieth century this appeared to be no longer an outstanding issue, although these conversions did not cease altogether. There was also a considerable amount of intermarriage, but all in all, these were not the real factors behind the signs of aging and demographic decline which were beginning to appear. The main cause was a decline in the number of children, and if that situation would endure for a time, it is probable that German Jewry would have vanished in any case. (Here we have an interesting and alarming parallel to the situation in western countries in the 1980's.)

The first immediate reaction to Hitler's rise to power — and it came precisely from the assimilated groups — was: "We are members of the German nation, and Hitler will not tell us who we are. We hold on to this country with all our might — precisely we and precisely in this country. We shall not move out of here." That was a stubborn position. There was no deserting the battle, since they regarded themselves as taking part in a struggle for the most sublime values of the German nation and its culture, fortified by what they regarded as their Jewish heritage, against the Nazi threat and Hitler's regime. This is totally different from their image in our present-day public consciousness. When the Nazis launched their persecution, the first reactions of German Jewry took a number of courses: a) They tried to influence their friends — even to influence the Nazi establishment itself — to abandon their antisemitic plans, on the assumption that once the Nazis were firmly in control, antisemitic extremism would diminish of its own accord, and the situation would not be as "dreadful" as had been proclaimed; b) they tried to strengthen their Judaism, as they understood it, and bravely face the attack; c) they organized to meet the situation, and we will deal with this aspect in detail in the following chapters. There was an attempt made by the Jews of Germany to reach some uniformity, some political unity, toward the establishment of united organizations. Here one must say that the initial reaction among the Zionists was not all that much different from the reaction of the assimilated Jews. Even among the Zionists there was, at the early stages, a view (although not the only one) that perhaps the Devil embodied in the form of the Nazis was not all that terrible, and this was merely a period of transition. "We told you" — said the Zionists — "that this was to happen, since Zionist ideology has always maintained that such things were possible. You should learn your lesson now and join the Zionist movement. Let us go and build Palestine. At the same time, this brutal Nazi regime is unlikely to endure in Germany for very long, and we should persevere until then."

A fine expression of this view was given by the writer and journalist Robert Weltsch who, after Hitler's rise to power, published an article in the German Zionist journal stating, "Bear it with pride, the yellow badge." He was already speaking of a yellow badge, although the Nazis had not decreed the wearing of the badge in Germany, and eight years were to pass before it was made compulsory. But Weltsch, who had a keen intuition in such matters, was already speaking of the yellow badge. Weltsch's message was: We must strengthen our Judaism, its foundations, our Jewish knowledge, our Jewish culture, and stand upright in the face of this evil assault which is coming upon us in defiance of all the traditions on which we have been brought up (and he meant: in defiance of all the German traditions). In this article, too, we can observe how the Jews drew from the sources of German civilization; in this respect, as we have said, the reactions of the Zionists and of the assimilationists were not very far apart from each other.

The first question which arises is: To what degree was the outside world, including the Jewish world, conscious of the danger implied by the Nazi rise to power? Here one must, of course, take into account the simple fact that, at the time, in 1933, the position of the Jews in Eastern Europe was far more grave than the dangers which appeared to threaten the Jews of Germany. Polish Jewry was at the time under the authoritarian control of army officers, and, although the head of state, Marshall Jozef Pilsudski, did protect the

The Jews in Germany and their Fate, 1933-1937

Jews against the antisemitism which had by that time spread in his country, it was clear that both government and opposition did not look with favor on the Jews, whose economic and political situation was steadily deteriorating. Thus, although the danger implied by another antisemitic regime in Germany was indeed very serious, the situation of the Jews of Poland seemed to be more desperate.

From this very general survey one can draw one conclusion, which is, indeed, a very basic one: the country in which it appeared that emancipation had succeeded, the country in which the Jews were integrated within the general population, was Germany. The possibility that there, of all places, an antisemitic regime would arise, was very alarming for German Jewry, which regarded it as a terrible blow. German Jewry tried, of course, to defend itself against the danger by supporting those parties which opposed Nazism; but as we know, it was not successful.

What did the Jews of the free world do when the Nazis came to power?

American Jewry — perhaps because of the earlier partial warnings — appealed immediately to the State Department and requested that the American Embassy in Germany report on what was happening there. In early 1933, the Nazis were still in a fairly weak position. The German economy was in a state of chaos, and the Nazis could not, at that stage, afford western hostility. They therefore hastened to comfort the Americans: "These," they said, "are exceptional events. We have just had a revolution, and it is obvious that here and there some unpleasant things happen. But this will pass with time, and we will guarantee all citizens, including the Jews, full freedom of employment and economy." "Do not worry" — that was the message — "everything will be settled peacefully."

The American secretary of state, Cordell Hull, a member of the conservative wing of the Democratic Party, took exception to all the Jewish protests (perhaps because he felt a need to deal with the fact that his wife was Jewish). He comforted people: "We have received assurances from Germany, so why are you making so much noise?" The Jews were not very impressed by him. The man who was then

Jewish Reactions to the Holocaust

the head of the Zionist movement in America, Rabbi Stephen S. Wise, president of the American Jewish Congress and the central figure in the Zionist Movement, called for protests, despite the view of the assimilationist bloc in American Jewry that if anything was to be done, one should do it quietly and without public protests.

Wise, with the help of the American Jewish War Veterans and with the encouragement of the Yiddish press, which supported him, demanded action. He called for a rally in the large auditorium in Madison Square Garden in New York on March 27, 1933, to protest against the persecution of the Jews in Germany and against the prospect of discrimination against them.

At that time, the Nazis, who had just attained power in Germany, were faced with the problem of what to do on the Jewish issue. It is true that during their first six weeks in power this problem was not the one which caused them the greatest anxiety. They sought to destroy the communists, the social democrats and other opponents, and they confronted many other internal issues. But the Jewish problem was, after all, the central problem from the point of view of Nazi ideology and attitude. According to this ideology, the Jews rule the world; they are the divisive and destructive element in German civilization; they should be ejected and expelled. Nazi policy at this stage was perfectly clear and explicit: to bring about the exodus of the Jews. This was not only declared in public, but was also contained in internal debates and in documents with which we are very familiar today — the German policies were all directed to this end.

The way which appeared to the Nazis to be the most logical to accomplish this was to boycott the Jews, starting on a certain day and persevering in it until the Jews were to be utterly broken economically. The Nazis decided that April 1, 1933, would be the day on which the boycott was to begin, and it was to continue until the economic life of the Jews was ruined and the Jews had no choice but to leave Germany.

The Nazi argument was that this step had been taken in view of the Jewish reaction to the Nazi rise to power, and because the Jews were spreading horror stories throughout the world about the

The Jews in Germany and their Fate, 1933-1937

terror of the new National Socialist regime. These stories, it was alleged, were not true, and in order to take vengeance on the Jews and teach them a lesson, one had to enforce this boycott.

When the Nazi leadership was informed of the protest meeting planned for March 27 in New York, it was stricken with panic. Here an interesting, even bizarre, event occurred. After all, the Nazis believed in all seriousness and with all their hearts their own propaganda and ideology. They were convinced that the Jews were Satan, the Satanic element in history. The Jews were not human, but some sort of creatures introduced into human history by the Evil One. They were the cause of the rise of Christianity (and one should not forget that the Nazis were opposed to Christianity), they were the factor behind Bolshevism, socialism, pacifism, humanism and liberalism. Without expelling the Jews, without ejecting this element from the world, it was impossible to establish the new, strong and healthy Nazi civilization which would be bound to nature, to the earth, and to blood. Without expelling the Jews it was impossible to do all this.

Yet, the Jews ruled the world. The Nazis' great struggle was against world Jewry. And, here was a fact the Nazis could see before their eyes: Rabbi Stephen Wise was organizing a rally; world Jewry was beginning to act. But the Nazis were still weak. They had only just attained power. In the eyes of the Nazis, Wise was the head of the international Jewish organization, that organization which ruled the world and was allegedly about to topple Nazism by its pressures. The Nazis were alarmed by the creature of their own imagination. It was, after all, only a mass rally of the Jews of New York. A few thousand people would attend it and listen to speeches, and that was all. But for the Nazis, this was an outward and visible sign of the international Jewish conspiracy against healthy German civilization.

Hermann Goering, the second man in the Nazi leadership and later in the Nazi government — who was at the time prime minister of Prussia, the largest district of Germany — summoned the leaders of German Jewry to his office and warned them of the dire consequences which were to follow if they did not immediately prevent the convening of the rally in New York. The terrified Jews cabled to the United States and to Palestine: "Do not put an embargo on German merchandise, do not make things difficult for us; we are under immense pressure; do not cause trouble for us."

In Palestine, there were already the first signs of an anti-German boycott, started by Revisionist circles, and spreading to other parts of the population. The Jewish Agency and the National Council received these telegrams and were at a loss whether to comply with this request or not. In order not to cause German Jewry any difficulty, they proclaimed that they had not declared an embargo; if there was anyone who had declared an embargo, it was not the National Council. This was, indeed, true. It was not the National Council in Palestine which had called for such a counter-measure. In New York, Wise was not daunted by the telegrams. The rally took place, and it was like any other large rally of this sort. As a matter of fact, one person did speak at this rally of a possible embargo to be imposed on Nazi merchandise. Accurate reports of this rally were published. On the last day of March, a meeting of the German cabinet took place. The Conservative ministers, who were still in the cabinet, put pressure on the Nazis: "See what is happening," they said. International Jewry was organizing itself. The Nazis accepted this argument, which looked perfectly logical to them; but since they had already proclaimed an embargo against the Jews, they decided to have it for one day.

The boycott took place, and its consequences were extremely grave. It happened on Saturday, a day when some Jewish shops, those belonging to observant and traditional Jews, were closed in any case. Despite this, the Jews were severely harmed throughout Germany. The boycott was an act of humiliation and was also harmful. Slogans were painted on Jewish shops, and German clients were forbidden to enter them. The boycott also included lawyers' offices and doctors' clinics. It was severe, and constituted a moral blow against a large portion of the Jewish public.

The boycott lasted one day, and after that day the official embargo was practically over. But that is not to say that during the following years there were no local boycotts in many smaller places

The Jews in Germany and their Fate, 1933-1937

in Germany. Jews were harassed and expelled from small townships, and especially from villages, though the official boycott was over. But in the free world, including the Jewish world, Nazi ideology was misapprehended, and there was apparently no one who knew how to make use of those primitive, weak points in National Socialist ideology in order to fight, or at least to defend, to some measure, the most vulnerable part of the population in Germany, the Jews.

After the boycott, German Jewry was struck by another blow: a series of laws, promulgated between April and September 1933, which removed the Jews from all public offices in Germany: doctors from public clinics, lawyers and judges from any occupation controlled by the state, teachers from schools and universities; the trade unions were closed to the Jews, as well as the organizations of artists, newspapermen, and so on.

Numerous Jews in the United States tried to react against these measures by setting up an organization which declared a boycott of German products. This organization was founded on the initiative of one of the Jewish First World War veterans in the American army, and its influence spread eventually to include the American Jewish Council. Once again, Stephen Wise headed the organization. Wise fought for a similar embargo to be maintained by the World Zionist Movement, but his attempts were unsuccessful for reasons we shall discuss later.

From the economic point of view, this boycott was a failure. German trade was in no way injured by the embargo put on it by Jewish commercial firms or by Jewish customers, and the embargo enforcement committees, in which many non-Jews took part, did not increase its measure of success. At the same time, the embargo created an anti-Nazi public opinion in the United States, if not immediately in 1933-4, at least in the long run.

To sum up, one can say that in the 1930's the anti-German boycott had no great political or economic significance, but it had some influence on the public. If this boycott was not as effectual as it could have been inside the Jewish community itself, the reason for this is closely related to the serious controversy which arose among

Jewish Reactions to the Holocaust

the Jews concerning the transfer of Jewish capital from Germany to Palestine. We shall deal with this issue later.

If we wish to sum up what happened at the beginning of Nazi rule and how the Jews reacted to it, we should point out that what happened later, in the 1930's and the early 1940's, has overshadowed, in our own historical consciousness, what had happened at the beginning of the process. When it all started, nobody was aware of the possibility of the Holocaust and mass murder. It happened to be only a matter of another antisemitic government in Europe — and, although it happened this time in the land of the great emancipation of the Jews, one still saw in it only another antisemitic government. About 20% of the Jews of Germany were affected by the 1933 laws, but 80% carried on their usual business, albeit on a lower standard. No Jew in Germany was on the bread line, as were hundreds of thousands of Jews in Poland. At this stage, the Jewish public was not being threatened with its life. It is true that dreadful things were happening in the concentration camps, but they were not directed against Jews as such. This was the situation at the beginning of the Nazi regime.

II.

The Transfer Agreement

During the first months of the Nazi regime, a serious problem arose among the Jewish community in Palestine. It was clear to everyone that a supreme effort had to be made to absorb some of the Jews of Germany. The line taken by the Zionist leadership was to look for ways of financial investments in Palestine, and this line was adopted for a number of reasons. The Jewish community in Palestine, which at the end of 1931 consisted of 171,000 persons, grew to 180,000 by 1933. (Today, 180,000 would represent only a small part of the total population of Tel Aviv.) Such a small population was incapable of absorbing a large number of people, unless one could create a wider economic basis. This, however, was extremely difficult to achieve, since the world was in the throes of an economic crisis, and the Jewish funds in general, and the Zionist ones in particular, could not collect sufficient quantities of money. To give an example, the great American Jewish Joint Distribution Committee had collected no more than $385,225 in 1932.

It was thus clear that right then Palestine could not absorb great masses of people, but only small groups, which would prepare the ground and make it possible for larger groups to immigrate in the long run. The dismal experience of the Fourth Aliyah, the fourth wave of immigration to Palestine, a general, unplanned and non-selective immigration which ended in failure and in the emigration of a large part of its members from Palestine, was still fresh in people's memory, and they wished to avoid another failure of the same sort at any price.

The problem was, therefore, how to absorb those sectors of German Jewry who would be able to adapt themselves to the difficult living conditions in Palestine, and how to finance such a project. At the initiative of a private individual, Sam Cohen, of the Ha-Note'a Company in Palestine, the first steps were taken toward an arrangement with the Nazi authorities in 1933 for the transfer of German-Jewish capital into Palestine in a manner which would not aid Germany's foreign currency revenues.

Shortly afterwards the Jewish Agency took the matter in hand, and, through the mediation of some of its top political and economic planners, chief among them Hayyim Arlosoroff and some of his colleagues, a transfer agreement was concluded with the Nazi authorities. It is interesting that even in Germany, this agreement was known by the Hebrew name of "Ha'avarah" (transfer).

The program worked roughly as follows. A Jew had money in Germany, but could not take it out of the country, since the Nazis had forbidden the transfer of foreign currency abroad. He therefore bought merchandise with his German marks and exported the merchandise to the Middle East — not only to Palestine, but to Egypt or to any other country in which he could find customers. The customers then deposited the payment in the Anglo-Palestine Bank (today Bank Leumi le-Israel). Thus the Jew who had left Germany without a penny arrived in Palestine, and here he recovered most of his capital in Palestinian pounds sterling deposited in the bank by his customers. In this manner, no foreign currency reached German hands, but German exports were boosted.

As part of this operation, products like cement mixers and irrigation equipment reached Palestine — products which were of the utmost importance for the development of the economic infrastructure of Jewish Palestine. Thus the Jew and his capital, as well as the merchandise, reached Palestine. The immigrant invested his money in whatever he chose to invest, and whether he kept it or lost it, it increased the amount of capital available to the Palestinian economy. It is estimated that, until the end of the 1930's, about eight million pounds sterling reached Palestine in this manner. It is very difficult to estimate how many Jews actually immigrated to Palestine as a direct result of the Ha'avarah, but even this is of no great importance; for what matters is not the actual immigration of those owners of capital into Palestine, but the fact that these investments made it possible to absorb a large portion of those German Jews who arrived there.

The Jewish Agency, the Zionist Executive, the labor parties, and especially the major labor party, Mapai, defended this arrangement (which was open and public) in the Zionist congresses and in public debates, and their argument was that one was thus saving Jewish money, which made Jewish immigration to Palestine possible. After all, this was the one and only aim of Zionism at the time.

This policy was opposed by the Revisionists and other groups, who claimed that the Ha'avarah was causing damage to the Jewish boycott of German products, for one could not encourage the export of German merchandise and put an embargo on German products at one and the same time. Moreover, this was tantamount to negotiating with the Nazis, the enemies of the Jewish people. The counter-argument, used by the supporters of the Ha'avarah, was that, if Ze'ev Jabotinsky, the head of the Revisionist movement, was prepared to hold negotiations with antisemitic elements in Poland, why should one abstain from negotiating with German antisemites if the result was the rescue and immigration of Jews? When one spoke of rescue in these years, one did not mean what we mean now, the rescue of lives, but merely the rescuing of Jewish property and Jewish immigration from Germany.

It is true, of course, that there was a contradiction between the anti-Nazi boycott and the Ha'avarah. But we have reason to believe that, even without the Ha'avarah, the boycott would have failed as an economic measure because of the lack of Jewish influence on the world economy. On the other hand, the Ha'avarah agreement made a major contribution toward the construction of Jewish Palestine and the large increase in Jewish immigration during the 1930's.

Jewish Reactions to the Holocaust

The Dilemma: Illusions or Immigration?

We have already mentioned Robert Weltsch's article, "Bear it with Pride, the Yellow Badge." One of the most interesting things we observe during this period is that the Jews, and not only the Jews, mistook the Nazi movement for a return to the Middle Ages, while in fact this was a completely new and horrifying phenomenon, a development of antisemitism into something extreme, brutal and murderous. But this was not yet clear, and thus people looked for parallels in the past, in the Middle Ages, and the concepts they used were also medieval: ghettoes and the yellow badge. It is true that, some years later, the Nazis put these concepts into practice, but they filled them with an entirely different content. When Robert Weltsch spoke of the yellow badge, what he meant was mainly that the Nazis were turning the clock back toward the Middle Ages, as it were, and what the Jews were to expect was what had happened in the Middle Ages — that is, some manner of marking out the Jews. This even caused a certain feeling of relief and contributed to the illusion that the past was going to be repeated. People did not comprehend that they were facing an unprecedented development.

Nevertheless, there was a feeling of danger about, and it was clear that one had to get organized, despite the bitter controversies within German Jewry, which involved not only the assimilated and the Zionists — a phenomenon we have discussed in our first chapter — but also other groups, not all of them marginal. Thus there also existed a religious-Zionist stream of considerable importance, despite its small size, which had been fully integrated in the Zionist movement. There were also groups belonging to the other extreme, people who regarded themselves as German nationalists of the Jewish persuasion, and there even existed among the Jews a group, however small it may have been, led by Max Naumann, whose members regarded themselves as supporters of Hitler. This group consisted of about 5,000 people, and it did not long survive — but it, too, was part of the human landscape of German Jewry.

Among the assimilated Jews there also existed a group which was organized in a union of war veterans. These were German Jewish veterans, and one must not forget that some 100,000 Jews participated in the German forces during the First World War. About 12,000 Jews lost their lives in the war, and Jewish soldiers fought with strength and courage for the sake of Germany. These people believed that they had a share in the Germany they had fought for, and they were prepared to put up a struggle to support this claim.

Another sector of German Jewry was concentrated in the western parts of Germany, and especially in Frankfurt. These represented about 10%-15% of all the Jews, and these were strict observers of Jewish Law and closely attached to their Jewish religion and heritage. It was out of such circles that the initiative had come, in 1912, for the founding of the movement called Agudath Israel, an anti-Zionist ultra-orthodox movement. These orthodox Jews were mostly disciples and followers of the school of thought of Rabbi Samson Raphael Hirsch (1808-1888), who attempted to unite a strict adherence to Jewish traditional life with integration into modern life. They regarded themselves as Germans, but as orthodox Jewish Germans, adhering to the 613 commandments of Jewish Law. When the Messiah came, they believed, there would be time to speak of concentrating the Jews in the Land of Israel.

There had been attempts to unite all these bodies. The first attempt had been undertaken largely through external pressure, by American Jewry through the Joint Distribution Committee (the so-called "Joint"). This American Jewish association, which still exists today, sees its function as assisting Jews in every part of the world.

The direct intervention of American Jewry in what was happening in Germany began immediately after the Nazis gained power. The Joint was at the time the only body which directed the flow of American Jewish financial aid to Jews all over the world. Its chief concern at that stage — and we are speaking of 1933 — was with Poland, and to some extent also with Russia, where it supported agricultural Jewish colonization in the Crimea. Now a new problem had arisen — Germany. One should not forget that the leaders of American Jewry during this period were of German origin. The leaders of the American Jewish Committee, a political organization composed largely of Reform and Conservative Jews, were almost to a man of purely German-Jewish origin, whether they were first, second, third, or even fourth generation Americans. This also applied to the Joint, headed by Felix Warburg, a brother of the leading Jewish banker in Germany at the time, Max Warburg. Incidentally, the Warburg family can serve as a good example for the pooling of forces among the leadership of the Jewish *haute bourgeoisie* on both sides of the Atlantic.

The Joint asked the Jews of Germany to unite in the face of the threatening Nazi wave. And indeed, in April 1933, an attempt was made, inspired by the Joint, to unite the various groups among German Jewry. The attempt at a political union was unsuccessful, but an economic union, the Central Union for Regeneration and Construction (Zentralausschuss fuer Hilfe und Aufbau — ZA), was formed, under the leadership of Rabbi Leo Baeck, a famous Berlin rabbi of liberal traditional leanings, and under the practical leadership of a man of many achievements, a liberal Jewish leader from the south of Germany, Dr. Otto Hirsch. In September 1933, another attempt was made to create a Jewish political association, and this time it succeeded. The National Representation (*Reichsvertretung* — RV) of German Jews was founded. The liberals and the Zionists joined this association, but the orthodox still took their time. Some more extreme assimilationist groups, chief among them the group of war veterans, also joined. The assimilationists were also supported by an important and independent body — the Jewish community of Berlin. Of over half a million Jews in Germany, over 160,000 lived in Berlin, and thus the Berlin community had a great deal of influence. Its head, Heinrich Stahl, was a man of dominant personality, who laid claim to national leadership, although he did not achieve this ambition.

At the head of the two organizations, the ZA and the RV, stood Rabbi Leo Baeck and Dr. Otto Hirsch. The political and economic unions thus became united. This was brought about not by Nazi, but by purely Jewish initiative.

With the support of the Joint, the Jews of Germany began to shape new economic tools and organizations for Jewish activities. Between 30% and 36% of all the money spent in Germany during the 1930's for preserving Judaism and encouraging emigration came from the Joint. Other financial contributions came from other Jewish organizations: from ICA (the Jewish Colonial Association, the organization which had founded the Jewish colonies in Latin America, and whose branch in Palestine was PICA — the Palestine Jewish Colonization Association, the body which founded Jewish colonies in Palestine toward the end of the nineteenth century), whose center was in London; and from a Jewish organization formed in England early in 1933 by Zionist and non-Zionist bodies alike and named the Central British Relief Fund for German Jewry. Thus about 40%, or even more, of the financial resources came from abroad, from world Jewry, and constituted a most substantial measure of relief. This relief took the form of retraining Jews who had lost their jobs in special schools, by preparing them for new types of work or for agriculture, handcrafts, and the like. Jewish culture was also a major preoccupation of these organizations, with a view to keeping morale high.

Here we come to the problem of emigration, which constituted, as could only be expected, another, most vital issue. The question is, why, then, did they not escape?

During the first year of Nazi rule, 1933, there was a state of panic among German Jewry, and it is estimated that about 52,000-53,000 Jews (that is, about 10% of the whole Jewish population of Germany) left the country between the Nazi rise to power and the autumn of that year. But the Jewish communities in other countries were unprepared to absorb these Jews — not to mention the countries involved and their governments. This was a period of severe economic crisis, and the great Jewish organizations had suffered drastic cuts in their revenues. Even the Joint had only 385,000 dollars in 1932, and 1,151,000 dollars in 1933, for the rescue of suffering Jews all over the world.

About half the emigrants from Germany, about 25,000, came to France, where there was no one to absorb them. The emigrants resided in various shelters, infested with fleas and rats, and began, quite literally, to starve. As a result, many of them packed their suitcases, claiming that if one had to die of starvation, one would better die in Berlin than in Paris. Nearly 17,000 Jews returned "home" — to Germany.

Jewish emigration from Germany during that year — counting only those who did not return — amounted to 36,000-37,000 persons, about 7%-8% of German Jewry. Others, as we have already pointed out, wanted to leave, but they had nowhere to go. This was the main problem.

And yet, one still asks the question, whether the Jews of Germany really wanted to leave; and if they did, why did they not leave. One should note that among large sectors of the Jewish population of Germany there existed a powerful drive to remain where they were rather than leave. Hitler, they said, was a passing phenomenon; he had no chance of surviving in Germany. Such sentiments were clearly expressed until 1935, and a weak echo of them could be heard until as late as 1938. The Jews, especially the liberal sector, maintained that it would be an expression of timidity and weakness if they were to leave their native land on account of persecutions which could only be regarded as a passing phenomenon. The Jews, they said, should demonstrate their loyalty to their German fatherland and hold on to it with all their might.

But the truth of the matter is that throughout this period of the 1930's, although, as we have said, large sectors of German Jewry had no desire to leave, there was never for a moment a situation when there were more openings for emigration than Jews who were willing to take advantage of them. Even at the very beginning, there was already a large minority wishing to leave and escape. After 1935, most of the Jews of Germany wished to escape, and after 1938, all of them. There was nowhere to go.

The American policy was: "We have immigration quotas and an economic crisis, and we are in no position to absorb those Jews arriving from Germany." Britain was in the throes of an economic crisis, and was prepared to absorb a few thousand doctors, engineers and scholars — but the Jewish population of Germany did not consist only of excellent doctors, engineers, and various kinds of experts. Most of them were "ordinary people," mainly middle class, craftsmen and a few laborers, and all of them were attempting

The Transfer Agreement

to escape. At first, one did not require a visa to escape to France — but what was one to live on there? Many Jews — about a fifth of German Jewry — had no German citizenship, and most of these were Polish citizens. But should they return to Poland, where Jews were starving, while in Germany they had not as yet reached that condition? The gate to other places, like South America, was closing. In Palestine in 1933, there were about 180,000 Jews, and the economic basis of the Jewish community there was in no way sufficient for the absorption of large masses. In that period of a world economic crisis, the Zionist funds were straining for finances which were not forthcoming. There was a serious problem about absorbing those Jews who were willing to come. In fact, the early 1930's were a period in which Britain allowed a relatively large quota of immigrants to enter Palestine. In 1935, Jewish immigration to Palestine reached a record of 60,000, and such a number of immigrants constituted a very large proportion as against a quarter of a million local Jews to absorb them. One should note that the major part of immigration to Palestine did not come from Germany; it would be a mistake to describe the so-called "Fifth Aliyah," the wave of immigrants to Palestine between 1932 and 1941, as the German immigration. Immigration from Germany never constituted more than a little over 20% of the general Jewish immigration to Palestine during the first years of Hitler's regime. This is understandable, since the Jews of Germany were still able to subsist, and their means of economic survival had not been removed, as they had been in Poland, Lithuania and Rumania, where the economic situation was extremely grave. About one third of the Jewish population of Poland, or over one million people, was living at the breadline or below it.

Thus, when the Jewish Agency or the Zionist Executive were faced with the problem of who should be awarded certificates for immigration to Palestine, their natural and understandable inclination was to assume that the Jews of Poland, Lithuania, Rumania and other Eastern European countries were in a more dangerous situation than the Jews of Germany, despite Hitler's accession to power. And this, to be honest, was how many of the

Jewish Reactions to the Holocaust

German Jews themselves felt.

In 1938, when Ze'ev Jabotinsky publicized his initiative for the evacuation of Jews from Europe, what he had in mind was Eastern Europe, not Germany. At the time, the Jewish suffering was not under Hitler's rule; for after all, from the autumn of 1933 to the middle of 1938 no new severe restrictions were imposed on most of the Jews of Germany.

However the laws of spring 1933 had removed the Jews from the civil service, from the schools, and from any public or government employment. After April 1st, 1933 the boycott was unofficial: Jewish children were beaten on their way to school; Jews were pushed out of villages and small towns into the big cities; Jews were not accepted for employment — there was a feeling of alarm in the air, yet no important anti-Jewish laws were promulgated, except one, with which we shall deal later — the Nuremberg Laws. During this period, German Jewry could, to a greater or lesser degree, support itself economically, especially since it received aid from the Joint, from British Jewry, and to a very small extent from French Jewry, and this aid made its existence possible.

The RV did deal with emigration even before the summer of 1935, as a solution for those who had no other alternative, for the young, for those who were driven to leave by the atmosphere of terror, and for organized Zionists. The leaders assisted emigration, but they did not regard it as the only solution: the assimilationists, since they claimed that one should hold on in Germany despite the persecutions; and the Zionists, because they maintained that Palestine was incapable of absorbing a mass immigration, and those who emigrated to Palestine had to be prepared for it. At the time, the Zionists spoke of a minority emigrating, and they assumed that only as time went on would a basis be formed in Palestine for the absorption of the rest of the Jews. Meanwhile, the RV and the ZA preoccupied themselves with what was called internal reconstruction — for example, professional retraining for those Jews who had decided to emigrate, or even for those who decided to remain in Germany, but had been thrown out of work and had to search for another source of livelihood, especially in physical labor.

There were also agricultural training farms, not only those run by Zionists but also non-Zionist ones, training people for agricultural labor in areas outside Palestine.

A very serious effort was made, under the guidance of the philosopher and theologian Martin Buber, to intensify Jewish consciousness among the large majority of German Jewry, which was, as we have already noted, liberal in its views. Buber was the spiritual mentor of what was called the Culture Association (Kulturbund), and an organization promoting adult education, both of which launched a widespread campaign consisting of courses, publications, cultural circles, lectures, theatrical performances and the like, in order to provide the Jews of Germany with a more concrete impression of that heritage which had nourished their forebears and for the sake of which they were now being persecuted. This project turned out to be a success, in the midst of those days of persecution; indeed, it is difficult to discover a similar flourishing of Jewish culture, or a similar attempt to return to the Jewish sources in the idiosyncratic manner of German Jewry as that which occurred during those persecutions. The Zionists took part in this project — after all, Martin Buber himself was a Zionist. The RV also opened Jewish schools — an absolute necessity, now that Jewish children were being expelled from German schools. It also occupied itself with financial aid to those Jews who had been left without work and an income.

In 1935, a change occurred in the attitude of the RV to emigration from Germany. There is now a controversy among historians, some of whom would not concur in this estimate; but it appears that a momentous event occurred in 1935. In July of that year there was a pogrom in Berlin, and although its dimensions were relatively small, it constituted a severe emotional blow to German Jewry. In September 1935, the Nazis promulgated the Nuremberg Laws, which redefined the Jews, until then full German citizens, as German subjects. This meant that the Jews were excluded from the citizen body. They were forbidden to contract marriages with Germans; to have sexual intercourse with them, in or out of marriage; and were forbidden to employ any German woman under the age of 45. They were also forbidden to use the German flag — a very severe blow to the assimilationists, who regarded themselves as Germans — but on the other hand, they were allowed to use a Jewish flag.

In a speech in the Reichstag, the Nazi German parliament, on September 15th, 1935, Hitler declared that now, it appeared, a reasonable basis for coexistence had been created; a "tolerable" basis — to use his own expression, for coexistence with the Jewish people in Germany. This statement was a signal to the RV that, on this narrow basis, and with such a low profile, the Jews were now able to continue to live in Germany, and that these laws would not be followed by any other laws — after all, the Jews had now been defined as German subjects rather than as citizens, and that was as far as one could go. This impression was so strong, that the reaction in the Jewish press, and especially in the chief paper of the RV, was roughly on the following lines: the situation was indeed extremely bad and humiliating, but at the same time, a legal basis had been created on which, one hoped, it would be possible to reach an arrangement with the German people. From this point of view, it appears that there was a general feeling among the Jews of Germany that they had reached a certain level of stability. The Jews were not to know, of course, that on the following day Hitler would address a meeting of his party leaders, and in that meeting he would say very different things. At that meeting, he maintained that the situation was only temporary. In the long run, the Jews should be completely separated from the German people; they should be expelled, and one should find a segregated territory for them. These were very harsh words, and he repeated such statements on a number of occasions, although he always did so in internal forums. He was thus following a policy of deception, whose concealed aim was the expulsion of the Jews from Germany. But no plan for the murder of the Jews existed as yet.

The Nazis decided to hold the Olympic Games in Berlin in 1936. As part of their preparation for these Olympic Games, they returned to the various sporting unions Jewish sportsmen who had been previously expelled from them. In various parts of Germany, anti-Jewish notices were taken down. A general atmosphere of sham tolerance was created, since the Nazis suspected that if they behaved otherwise, there would be no Olympic Games in Berlin. After all, black sportsmen from the United States and delegates of various colored nations were to participate in the games. The Nazis were forced to compromise on this issue, and this created an atmosphere of relief among the Jews. It appeared that pressure on the Jews was not as hard as it had been in the recent past.

Despite all this, the RV did, as we have mentioned earlier, change its policy. The reason was that, after the pogrom in Berlin, and in spite of all that happened afterwards, it was coming around to the conclusion that, sooner or later, the Jews would have to emigrate from Germany. We, more than half a century later, must reconcile ourselves to the fact that two lines of policy — the need for emigration and the need to seek ways of remaining in Germany — existed side by side among the leaders of the RV, in spite of the glaring contradiction between these two policies. The RV believed that it was possible to spend some time on suitable preparations for emigration, since this was an issue which lay some years ahead. Toward the end of 1935, with the support of German Jewry and with the participation of British and American Jewry, a program was taking shape for evacuating out of Germany about 100,000 Jews within the next four years and resettling them in other places. The young and strong would be the first to emigrate, and they would them be joined by their families. In this manner, the Jewish population of Germany, or at least most of it, was to be eliminated by means of emigration.

The official figure for the Jewish population of Germany in 1933 was 499,000. Another, and probably more accurate, figure is that of 522,000 people, defined as Jews by religion. If we add to this those who were defined by the Nazis as Jews, the number would increase by 30,000-40,000. It appears now that in 1935 the RV was beginning to press urgently for emigration — a plan which suited the Nazi wish to see the Jews abandon Germany.

In 1936, the Nazi four year plan, which prepared Germany for the Second World War, was initiated. In his instructions for this four year plan, which were, of course, secret, Hitler maintained that unless Germany started a war within four years, international Jewry would massacre the German nation by means of Bolshevism, which was dominated by the Jews. There can be no doubt as to his literal intentions, since this was no part of some public declaration, but of a private document sent to Hermann Goering. The conclusion arising from this is clear: if the Jews were threatening to massacre the Germans, they had to be expelled as soon as possible. Thus, in 1937, preparations began for stricter policies against the Jews, with a view to driving them out of Germany in a hurry. These preparations, which were of an administrative nature, included various laws which were not yet universal, but which can be viewed as warning signals for what was to come.

In November 1937 Hitler informed the German military and political leaderships that they were to start a war in two or three years. The German ruling establishment, which was now preparing for war, regarded the Jews as Satan living among them, in accordance with Nazi doctrine; and it was clear that one could not open a war with Satan living in one's house. In 1938, a number of actions occurred against the Jews, reaching their climax in the "Kristallnacht" — of which later. But the tendency of all these activities was directed against the Jews in general; and if it were not for the assassination of a member of the German embassy in Germany embassy in Paris by a Jewish youth two days before "Kristallnacht," an event used by the Nazis as a pretext, they would have found another pretext, or they would simply have carried out their plan without any justification. What is perfectly clear is that their aim was to drive the Jews out of the general framework of German life by employing the most drastic means.

The Jews were aware of the danger. As early as the beginning of 1938, the RV began to consider another way of organizing the Jews in a new manner, as an emergency measure, for a faster and earlier emigration. It put pressure on the Jewish communities outside Germany to assist in this emigration. At the end of 1937 and the beginning of 1938, German Jewry found itself in a new position. It was becoming aware of the threat, and, although it had no accurate idea of the details, it sensed the danger. The urge to leave Germany was now stronger than ever before; organization toward emigration was assuming a new urgency; and demands were placed before the world, including the Jewish world, to assist the Jews of Germany in the face of the storm gathering on the horizon, whose results no one could predict.

It is estimated that, until the end of 1937, 129,000 Jews emigrated from Germany — that is, about 25,000 a year. This was, on the whole, an orderly and organized emigration, and many of the emigrants reached the United States, which was, despite everything, the chief haven for immigrants. In 1933-4, 4,392 people emigrated to the United States, perhaps 90% of them Jews; in 1934-5, the number was 5,201. In 1935-6, there were 6,346, and in 1936-7 10,895 (that is, a jump, in a few years, from 4,000 to 11,000); and in 1937-8, 17,199. The German quota for immigration into the United States was 27,000. After 1936, the number of German immigrants to the United States rose, but still remained within the quota, which the American authorities were not prepared to change. We know that antisemitism reached a climax in the United States in the 1930's. About half the American population in the late 1930's expressed antisemitic views, and about 10%-15% of these people were willing to employ Nazi methods against the Jews of the United States. In such circumstances, it was clear to the Jews and to their supporters that if any proposal for changing the quota was to be raised, all the quotas, and Jewish immigration in general, might be reexamined. The Jews, therefore, made no sustained demand for increasing the quotas. We shall return to this in the next chapter.

The rest of the emigration from Germany was divided between immigrants to Palestine, to the countries of South America, to Poland, and to other European countries.

JEWISH IMMIGRATION FROM AREAS OF NAZI RULE

	1933	1934	1935	1936	1937	1938	1939	1940	1941
From:									
Germany	37,000	23,000	21,000	25,000	23,000	35,369	68,000	16,000	13,000
Austria						62,958	54,451	6,500	6,000
Czechoslovakia						15,000	20,000	?	?
Danzig						3,900	1,600	?	?
Total:									431,409

IMMIGRATION TO PALESTINE (LEGAL)

	1933	1934	1935	1936	1937	1938
From:						
Germany	6,803	8,497	7,447	7,896	3,280	4,223
Austria	328	928	1376	581	214	2,964
Percentage of general immigration	22.3	21.4	14.5	26.8	28.1	40.5

EMIGRATION OF JEWS FROM GERMANY AND AUSTRIA BY DESTINATION (estimates)

1. Countries not conquered by the Nazis

United States	85,000
Latin America	85,000
Palestine	60,000 (including so-called illegal immigration)
Shanghai	18,000
Britain	60,000
Switzerland	12,000
Total	320,000

2. Countries later conquered by the Nazis

Belgium	15,000
France	30,000
Holland	27,000
Other countries	38,000
Total	110,000

III.

The Evian Conference and its Consequences

The attitude of the United States government to the issue of Jewish immigration was based on an endorsement by the administration of the principle of strict quotas. There were a number of reasons for this: the unwillingness of large sectors of the American public, including the trade unions, to absorb new immigrants at a time of mass unemployment (17 million unemployed in 1933) caused by the major economic crisis; opposition on the part of the right-wing organizations to any immigration, and to the immigration of Jews (and Chinese and Japanese) in particular; and a wave of antisemitism in the United States in the 1930's, which was itself to a large extent the result of the crisis. Officials of the State Department responsible for maintaining the quota law did not treat the Jews with sympathy, and tended to adopt the stricter interpretation of any regulation concerning immigration. The president was, indeed, liberal-minded, but he was first and foremost a politician who wanted to be reelected, and the issue of immigration was not crucial enough to make him risk his position in the face of the rising wave of citizens demanding the restriction of immigration into the United States.

In September 1933, the Dutch government, at the initiative of the Jewish community of Holland, addressed a request to the League of Nations and to the United States, which was not a member of the League, to form an institution to deal with the

Jewish Reactions to the Holocaust

Jewish emigrants from Germany. As the proposed new body was not expected to belong to the League of Nations, the Americans agreed to have it founded, and even proposed as its chairman — after internal deliberations in the State Department — James Macdonald, who was later to be the United States' first ambassador to Israel. This man, a practicing Christian who was very close to Jewish circles in the United States and economically dependent on the Warburg family, whose members were leaders of the Joint, was appointed chairman of the League of Nations Committee for the Aid of Refugees (Jewish and Other) from Germany. The words "Jewish and Other" were added in parentheses, since the people involved were not prepared to admit that this was, first and foremost, a Jewish problem. It is true, however, that between 10% and 20% of those who escaped from Germany were non-Jewish Germans who fled Hitler's regime. They, of course, found it easier to enter other countries; the real problem was that of the Jewish refugees.

During his two years as chairman of the committee, Macdonald did his very best to obtain places of absorption for Jews leaving Germany, especially in the countries of South America, but to some extent also in European countries like Britain and in his own country, the United States. His attempts were unsuccessful. The Latin American countries were in no way interested in immigration, both on account of the antisemitism which existed there, and because — and this was the main reason — the Jews involved lacked the qualifications appropriate to the economic and social needs of these countries. A Jew who reached Argentina on a luxury boat, as a first-class passenger, with his pockets full of dollars, was allowed to land; but there were not many Jews with private means which would guarantee asylum for themselves and their families. In this matter, too, Macdonald was unable to break through the barriers. What was worse, he could not persuade the Germans to facilitate the transfer of capital from Germany. Since these were two aspects of the same thing, there was no possibility of absorbing these Jews unless they brought their money with them. It was thus clear that a transfer arrangement was necessary for other places beside

The Evian Conference and its Consequences

Palestine. And indeed, some time later, in 1936-37, the Joint arranged for something like that transfer arrangement with other countries as well. But this arrangement did not work properly and never attained the dimensions of the transfer to Palestine, mainly for technical reasons.

Macdonald's problem was that, while Germany was not allowing its Jews to leave under reasonable conditions, the countries destined to absorb them were not prepared to do so under the conditions offered by the Germans to emigrants. By the end of 1935, Macdonald despaired of the whole affair, and offered his resignation. His letter of resignation was composed by Norman Bentwich, who was later to be the senior Jewish official in the British administration of Palestine, a brilliant lawyer, who was active throughout the 1930's in the absorption of Jewish refugees in Britain. This letter of resignation was printed in the most important papers of the west: the London Times, the New York Times and the Washington Post. In it, Macdonald warned the world that while the problem could still be solved at the time, there was no knowing whether it could be in the future. He argued that with the claim that this was an internal German problem, and said that that was an illusion. He put the blame for the lack of treatment of this problem on various countries, implicitly including his own, and called for "fresh collective action." The Germans should be asked "for a modification of policies which constitute a source of unrest and perplexity in the world." After Macdonald's resignation, a British general, Sir Neil Malcolm, was appointed as chairman of the committee. From 1936 on, he did not convene the committee at all. We shall meet with this committee later on, but in a different incarnation.

The years 1935-36, as we have seen, witnessed a Jewish initiative of mass emigration. The plan, to have 100,000 young people emigrate within four years, and to have them joined later by their families, was unrealistic, partly because the United States and Britain were not prepared, at that stage, to do anything practical for the absorption of such immigration.

As a result, toward the end of 1935 the leaders of the Joint and

Jewish Reactions to the Holocaust

the American Jewish Committee addressed an appeal to President Roosevelt. They asked him to open the gates of the United States to these Jews, at least as an administrative measure, and to relieve the pressure without impairing the immigration quotas. And indeed, from the beginning of 1936 there was a change in American policy. From 1936 to 1938-9, there was a steady rise in the number of Jewish immigrants entering the United States, until, in fiscal 1939, the whole quota of immigration to the United States, which was not all that large, was filled (32,759 people arrived, while the quota was 27,000).

We are, of course, entitled to raise the question: What did the Jews of the western countries do? Did they put no pressure on their governments? On this issue, we should see things in their true proportions. Contrary to what most people believe today, during those years world Jewry had no real political influence, either on the government of the United States or on the British government. The Jews were under pressure in Nazi Germany and in Poland, where they had good reason for being apprehensive of their regimes. The British, on the other hand, began to realize that the Jews had no influence in America, and this diminished the Jews' influence in Britain as well. While the Jews were mobilized by what was happening in Nazi Germany and by the antisemitic regime in Poland, they had no real power anywhere. The Jewish population of Palestine was as yet small and lacked any influence. This does not mean that no attempts were made at rescue operations. As we have seen, the Joint and the American Jewish Committee succeeded, through a quiet appeal to the president, to wield some influence here and there. But no massive economic influence existed, since the world was in the midst of a crisis and the Jews had no significant economic influence in the United States or in Britain. The actual state of affairs was very different from the popular picture we have of these years, and it is of some importance to make this point clear.

In 1938, the United States government initiated a conference, which convened in July of that year in Evian. This conference was to carry on the work done by Macdonald, which had now been discontinued, and to offer new solutions, for in the meantime the

The Evian Conference and its Consequences

problem had become more acute. The Nazis continued to put pressure on the Jews, and in 1938, with their conquest of Austria, the problem of 200,000 Jews living in that country was added to that of the Jews of Germany. As the Evian Conference convened, it had to deal with nearly half a million Jews still left in Germany and Austria, and the one item on the agenda was to find a solution to their problem.

The United States convened the Evian Conference since Roosevelt had come to the conclusion that, for internal political reasons, it was in his interest to make a gesture to those liberals who were pressing for a solution of the Jewish refugee problem. But at the Evian Conference itself, Roosevelt's representative declared that the solution was not to be at the expense of the United States; quotas were not to be increased, and no money was to be allocated. Thus, if Roosevelt was attacked from the Right, he could always say: "What are you complaining about? I convened the conference in order to find a different solution, not at the expense of the United States. As for us, we shall remain within the quota permitted by Congress" (which was, indeed, filled during that year, 1938-9).

Thirty two delegates from various countries gathered in Evian, and each of them explained in turn why his country could not receive the Jews. The Australian delegate, for example, said: "Since we have no racial problem, we have no intention of importing one" — meaning, of course, the Jewish problem. The delegates of Peru, Ecuador, Bolivia, Brazil and other countries said that they were quite capable of admitting them — but only agricultural laborers and miners. They knew very well that the Jews did not belong to these categories of workers. Thus, the result of this conference was entirely negative. The Jews, on their part, appeared before this committee speaking in dozens of different voices, and they did not even manage to offer it one single memorandum endorsed by all. Each of the Jewish bodies was allotted five minutes to explain its position. The World Jewish Congress, which suggested that the various countries should open their gates to the Jews; the Jewish Agency; the representative of the Jewish population in Palestine; and numerous other bodies and organizations, were each allotted the same five minutes. This was a shameful demonstration of impotence, since all the proposals were identical; open the gates of all countries, including Palestine, to the Jews, and you will solve the problem of the Jews pressured by the Nazis.

Poland and Rumania attempted to jump on the bandwagon. If the Americans were proposing to transfer the Jews of Germany and Austria to other countries, "Why," they said, "not also evacuate our own Jews from Poland and Rumania?" The United States and Britain panicked, and refused to discuss emigration from these countries. They emphasized that they intended to deal only with the problem of the Nazi regime and the Jews suffering under it.

In Evian an event there also occurred which reads like a proper suspense story, and the mystery surrounding it has not yet been solved. The whole affair was made public in Hans Habe's book, *The Mission*, This is the story of an Austrian Jewish surgeon (holding a title of nobility), dispatched by the S.S. to the Evian Conference with an offer to sell the Jews to the west. But the delegates of the western countries, as Habe writes in his book, refused to take the man seriously. In its main outlines, this story is real enough. There was indeed such a surgeon, his name was von Neumann, and he was dispatched by the S.S. Who exactly sent him, and what exactly he said, we do not know. In interviews with the main participants of the conference who were still alive many years later, they could only say that the man appeared in Evian and offered, in the name of the German authorities, a sale of the Jews, or Jewish emigration in exchange for money or its equivalent in goods. The details were extremely hazy. We have no minutes recording this affair, but all those interviewed remembered that it happened, and that the man returned to Austria. It is probable that this can be connected with events with which we will deal in some of our next chapters, when other offers of payment were made in exchange for rescuing Jews.

Our main question, of course, is what the results were of the Evian Conference. The only decision adopted by the conference was to form an Inter-governmental Committee for Refugees. As its chairman, the committee eventually appointed an American lawyer, a Democrat and a supporter of Roosevelt, George Rublee. The task

The Evian Conference and its Consequences

of the committee (whose venue was in London) was to form contacts with the German government and to attempt to persuade it to permit the emigration of Jews together with their property. To begin with, the Germans would have nothing to do with Rublee; but as time went on he established contacts with Germany's "economic wizard," Hjalmar Schacht. Schacht, who was not a member of the Nazi Party, but had in the past been a member of the Nazi cabinet as an extreme right-wing economic expert with Nazi sympathies, was now head of the National Bank of Germany.

Schacht returned, in fact, to the Jewish proposition of 1935-36, to have 100,000 young Jews leave Germany over a certain period, to be joined later by their relatives. He linked this to an economic program which implied a confiscation of all the Jewish capital in Germany, using part of it for the purchase of goods which the immigrants would then take with them to their countries of destination. In addition, the Jews of the other countries were to collect immense sums of money (the figure of one hundred million dollars was mentioned), so that the Jews leaving Germany would be able to be absorbed in a reasonable fashion and in turn absorb those who followed them from Germany and Austria. As to the elderly Jews who were to remain in Germany, the German government was willing to undertake that they would come to no harm, and that they would subsist on the interest from that part of the confiscated capital which was to remain in Germany. This program was somewhat reminiscent of the Ha'avarah arrangement. Schacht made this offer since it was likely to boost German exports, as well as "rid" Germany of its Jews. From Rublee's point of view, this was precisely the solution he had been expected to offer: to "export" the Jews from Germany. The real problem was: Where would these 100,000 emigrants go? Rublee assumed that one could do without a single center to absorb all these Jews by using the existing possibilities of immigration to the United States and Palestine. The conditions for immigration were limited, but since one was planning for a long period, this appeared to be one way of solving the problem. The other problem was how to form an international Jewish body capable of collecting a hundred million dollars.

Jewish Reactions to the Holocaust

Another problem was whether Schacht had Hitler's full backing, and whether the Germans were really prepared to solve the problem of the Jews of Germany and Austria by "exporting" them to the west. On January 2, 1939, Schacht received Hitler's endorsement for this plan. We may ask in this context whether the Germans were really and truly willing to release the Jews, even in exchange for capital. The answer appears to be that they were. The "exporting" of Jews did not constitute any contradiction to Nazi ideology. We now possess two documents of the utmost interest, one addressed to the head of S.S. Security, Reinhard Heydrich, and dated January 24, 1939, and the other, of January 25, issued by the German foreign office. From these two documents it transpires that the Nazis opened an Office for Jewish Emigration in Berlin. The task of that office was to drive the Jews out by any means, not excluding force. But if the Schacht-Rublee programme was to materialize, the Jews could be expelled in this manner. The German foreign office believed that if the Jews were to be expelled to other countries, this would increase antisemitism in those countries, and as a result, sympathy would grow toward Germany. Besides, this would also weaken those countries, since it was well known that the Jews were a corrupting factor. Thus there was no contradiction between the Schacht-Rublee plan and Nazi ideology.

Why, then, did this plan never materialize? The main answer is simply that there was no time. The war which broke out was planned by Hitler to be "lightening quick," at the end of which he would be able carry on implementing Nazi policies, including those concerning the Jews. As we know, this did not happen, and the war took longer. Another problem was that of finding destinations for the emigrants, and here Rublee proved to be too much of an optimist. Besides, the Jews themselves found it hard to swallow the propositions which could make them: a) offer their own assistance to the export of merchandise from Germany; b) form that very "international Jewish government" of Hitler's fantasies in order to raise the necessary capital for carrying out this plan. True, this body was to be formed for the purpose of saving the Jews of Germany — but the Jews still recoiled from the idea.

The Evian Conference and its Consequences

Thus, during those spring months of 1939, a heated controversy took place in the Jewish world as to whether one should accept this plan or reject it. Roosevelt intervened personally, and under pressure from him and at a meeting with the American Jewish leaders, a "Coordinating Foundation" was established in June 1939 in order to raise the necessary capital. But once war broke out this body ceased to operate.

In Britain, too, there was a change of policy toward the German Jews, connected with the events of *Kristallnacht* and their results. *Kristallnacht* created a rising wave of sympathy for the Jews in British public opinion. The British government felt the need to take some action, and since this was the time when it had closed Palestine to Jewish immigration, it decided to open the gates of England to Jewish immigration from Germany. During that year, about 45,000 German Jews reached Britain; and, for a country like Britain, in the midst of an economic crisis, this was a heavy burden. Among those arriving were close to 10,000 Jewish children who came without their parents and were absorbed with the assistance of the British government, first in camps erected especially for them, and later among fostering families. These children, it is true, did not have an easy time; but there is no doubt that the British government, and British public opinion as the time, saved their lives.

IV.

Kristallnacht *and After*

We have already seen that toward the end of 1937 the Nazis were preparing for the speedy exclusion of the Jews from the economic life of Germany, by means of a series of laws whose effect was to hasten their expulsion from Germany.

At the beginning of 1938, the Nazis deprived the Jewish communal organizations of the right to act as legal persons, and in June 1938 they began a wave of arrests of Jews on various offenses like parking tickets and the like. The attitude to Jews in general was becoming harsher. One should bear in mind that, until this period, no Jews had been sent to the concentration camps merely for being Jews. There were, of course, Jews who had been sent to these camps as opponents of the regime, but as a rule the concentration camps had not been populated by Jews until 1938.

In 1938, preparations began in the concentration camps for absorbing masses of Jews, who were to be sent to these camps in order to create an atmosphere of terror among the Jews of Germany and Austria and make them leave. It was in these circumstances that on November 7, 1938 a Jewish youth named Herschel Grunszpan shot to death a member of the German Embassy in Paris, Vom Rath, whom he mistook for the German ambassador. The man was, in fact, only a third secretary at the embassy, and as chance would have it, an opponent of the Nazis. Grunszpan's aim was to assassinate the German ambassador as an act of revenge for the expulsion from Germany of his parents, Jews holding Polish citizenship. This

Kristallnacht and After

expulsion had been carried out a few days earlier, on October 28, when the Nazis drove out to the Polish border and beyond it, with great brutality, about 18,000 Jews of Polish citizenship. Among those expelled were Jews born in Germany, whose parents had emigrated from Poland, but who did not possess German nationality.

The Nazis exploited this act of revenge by the Jewish youth to do what they had been planning to do all along. Two days after the event, on the night between November 9 and 10, an event took place which has come down in history as *Kristallnacht* (Crystal Night), named for the smashing of Jewish shop windows which broke into crystal-like shards. This action was carried out by crowds of members of the Nazi Party, especially SA brownshirts and youths, who had been incited to do so. One should add that the large majority of German citizens did not regard *Kristallnacht* with excessive sympathy.

But the citizens took no action in defence of the Jews. With some measure of indifference, and in fear of Nazi terror, the citizens of Germany looked on as their Jewish friends were being beaten in the streets, their shops plundered, and the male Jews sent to the concentration camps. It is estimated that about 30-35,000 men were interned in concentration camps on this occasion. The explicit purpose of this operation was to hasten Jewish emigration from Germany. Most of the Jews who were interned in the camps and did not die there (and many did) were soon expelled from Germany, since their terrified families did all in their power to obtain for them visas or any other means, legal or illegal, for leaving the country. And indeed, during these years, 1938-1939, Jewish emigration from Germany assumed very serious dimensions.

During these years, the number of Jews leaving Germany (and we do not include Austria) reached over 103,000. If we remember that, at the beginning of the Nazi regime in Germany, there were a little over 500,000 Jews in the country, we can see that this was a considerable proportion of the total. One should also remember that in March 1938 Austria was annexed to Germany, and another 200,000 Jews were added to the Jewish population. During these

Jewish Reactions to the Holocaust

two years, 1938-1939, about 117,000 Jews of the 200,000 left Austria — that is, 60% of the Jewish population left in a panic. In contrast to Germany, where a proper leadership of the local Jewish community existed, the leadership in Austria was terrified, oppressed and meek, and it was incapable of standing up to Nazi pressure. The Austrian leadership was, in fact, that of the Jewish community in Vienna, since the small Jewish communities outside Vienna were very soon liquidated. We can discern here the great difference between the Jewish reaction in Austria and in Germany — a difference in the quality of Jewish leadership rather than in the reaction of the Jewish public.

As early as the beginning of 1938, when Nazi attitudes to the Jews became more extreme, the demand for organizational change was aired among the leaders of German Jewry, since the Jewish communities had already lost their legal status. It is clear that the Gestapo's attitude was becoming harsher, and this created the pressing need to reorganize under an emergency leadership. The leaders were not changed, but the Jews proposed more centralization, with greater powers to the center. They proposed such a reorganization to the Gestapo, but after *Kristallnacht* the matter assumed a very different shape, since during that night the Jewish leadership, both in Germany and in Austria, had been decimated. It is true that some sectors of the RV, especially those concerned with emigration, were not hit by the operation, but many of those active in the offices of the RV were interned, and the need for reorganization was now quite obvious.

To this was now added Nazi pressure. The Nazis wanted the Jewish community to reorganize itself in a way which suited their own aims. In July 1939 the Nazis accepted the statutes of what was now called "The Reich Union of the Jews of Germany (Reichsvereinigung — RVE)," as against the earlier RV. The Union was headed by the same leaders.

This leadership, like its predecessor, was on the whole independent and proud, and it faced Nazi pressures — albeit without the power to react with strength or in an open argument — in an impressive manner. This may be somewhat different from the

Kristallnacht and After

image of this Jewish leadership current among Jews, especially among the younger generation, and one should state here as emphatically as possible that this is a false image. We will bring a few examples.

After the outbreak of the war in September 1939, the Nazis initiated further measures against the Jews of Germany. In 1940, they expelled to Poland the Jews of Stettin (Szczecin), which was then a German city and is now part of Poland. The leaders of the RVE protested against this measure to the Gestapo. They knew very well what was involved in such a protest: arrests and persecutions of the leaders themselves. But they did it because they believed that such an event must not be passed over in silence.

Later, in October 1940, the Jews were expelled from some of the cities of western Germany, such as Mannheim and Karlsruhe, where considerable Jewish communities existed. A total of 7,654 people were expelled to France. The RVE protested. Its leaders came to the offices of the Gestapo and said that they were not prepared to see Jews expelled. Again, they knew exactly what to expect: some of them were arrested and sent off to concentration camps for this protest. But although they knew what to expect, they protested.

The leaders of the RVE dealt chiefly with the emigration of Jews from Germany. They also made desperate efforts to strengthen Jewish morale in the face of Nazi pressure. All these facts imply that most of these leaders behaved in an honorable manner, although they were entirely incapable of reacting in a proper fashion and were utterly devoid of power. The manner in which they faced their Nazi oppressors should elicit our respect.

We will bring one more example. One of the most prominent leaders among this group of the German Jewish leadership, a man called Julius L. Seeligsohn, was in England when war broke out. He declared that, as a responsible leader of the Jews of Germany, he would not shirk his responsibility, but was returning to Germany. He did just that, and returned to the country. Another man, Paul Meyerheim, was instructed by the Nazis at the beginning of 1941 to go abroad and take part in negotiations for further emigration of Jews. He returned to Germany, although he knew exactly where he was returning. These are examples of personal valor which we will do well to remember.

The actual reaction of the Jews of Germany, from 1935 on, and in a far more pronounced form from 1938 on, was immense pressure for emigration. Indeed, the Jews exploited any subterfuge, not always to the liking of free Jewry in America or in Palestine. One example was the Chinese city of Shanghai, almost the only place in the whole world at that time which one could enter without a visa. Since 1931 there had been a war between China and Japan, where the latter attempted to conquer China, beginning with Manchuria and then moving southward. In 1937, the Japanese launched a massive invasion of China and conquered the huge maritime city of Shanghai, causing the local Chinese population heavy losses and terrible suffering. The harbor area of Shanghai was not subject to either the Chinese or the Japanese, but was under an international rule administered by foreign consuls. This was the international area of Shanghai, bordering on another area which belonged to the French. When the Japanese conquered Shanghai, they of course, became a very important factor, but the whole area remained international. This was, as we have said, one of the few places in the world (we shall come across another such place later) which could be entered without a visa. Not many people wished to come to Shanghai and settle there, since there was nothing for destitute Europeans to do in this city. Millions of Chinese who lived in Shanghai were unemployed, living in misery and hunger or at an extremely low economic level. But where there was no choice, even Shanghai would do. The Jews discovered that one could reach Shanghai by boat or train and could obtain entrance permits for a certain sum of money.

Owing to a disagreement among the various consuls concerning reforms in the regulations, the regulation requiring no visa for entering Shanghai also remained unchanged. From 1938, a stream of Jews began to arrive in Shanghai. Not every one of them had the money available for a train ticket from Berlin via Moscow to Vladivostok and hence by boat to Shanghai, or by train to Vladivostok and from there to Shanghai. But one could also reach

Kristallnacht and After

Shanghai by ships all the way from Europe, and there were people who did this. Some came to Shanghai by ships which travelled around the world from Italy.

The families of many of the Jews who had been put in concentration camps after *Kristallnacht* mobilized all their money to buy liberty of their fathers, husbands or sons. The whole family would then leave by boat or train and reach Shanghai. By the end of 1939, some 18,000 Jews had reached that city. But what were they to do there? No work was available for these people in Shanghai, at least not in the early stages. The Joint and some local benefactors — for there was in Shanghai a Sephardic community of some distinction, as well as a Russian-Ashkenazi one — collected funds and supported them. As time went on, some of these people began to support themselves as tailors, owners of entertainment clubs, engineers, and, occasionally, as businessmen, but their situation was extremely difficult. The climate, the language, the alien environment and the abject poverty of the non-European residents — all these created difficult problems for the new immigrants. To the Jews who arrived in Shanghai from Germany, the choice appeared to be between death of starvation in Shanghai and a similar death in Germany. As yet, no one had even dreamt of a holocaust. The problem was a concrete one. Anyone who left for Shanghai was mad. It was an exodus to a distant country, where there was no food and no subsistence except charity, while in Germany one had, at least, home and family. Why, then, escape to such a place? Those who escaped to Shanghai did it because of the concentration camps, because of a vague feeling that something harsh was about to take place, and one had to escape, no matter where. Besides, one could reach other places from Shanghai.

This group of Jews who remained in Shanghai at the end, formed an extremely interesting community. In February 1943, the Japanese created in Shanghai, under German instructions, a ghetto. But this was a Japanese ghetto. The Japanese, who were unfamiliar with Jews, did not know what to make of such a ghetto. Thus, they were hostile toward the Jews, but nothing more serious happened. The Jews who died in Shanghai, among those who did not succumb to starvation or epidemics, were mainly casualties of American air raids during the last phase of the war. The Jews were finally freed by the American army and most of them reached the United States and Canada, while a small percentage arrived in Palestine.

We will now bring another example, this time from Vienna. There, pressure was put on the Jews to leave for Yugoslavia, but the Yugoslav government was against such immigration. The Yugoslav Jewish community tried to come to the rescue, but the Joint did not view with favor the attempt of Jews to immigrate to Yugoslavia without visas and with no means of subsistence. But the Viennese community pushed them into Yugoslavia, simply because there was no alternative, and the Jews went.

We should mention here another internal Jewish project, Youth Aliyah. Youth Aliyah was founded before the Nazi rise to power by a wonderful woman who, until her recent death, lived in Jerusalem, Recha Freier. It was she who began to organize Youth Aliyah (immigration to Palestine), as early as 1932, before the Nazis came to power. She felt that, with the threat already hanging over the Jews of Germany, the children should be saved. It was, of course, not easy to persuade parents to part with their children, and then to convince the great Jewish organizations to bring these children to Palestine in the conditions prevailing in the early 1930's, with a lack of funds, the hard work and the difficult climate in Palestine.

The first group of Youth Aliyah children only reached Palestine in 1934. They were sent to Kibbutz Ein Harod, and then to various other places: to kibbutzim, private farms, children's institutions and religious institutions. This immigration, although it was small in dimensions, was of very high quality and importance. In Palestine, Henrietta Szold assumed responsibility for the administration of Youth Aliyah, the allocation of the children to various places, financing, and the like. Recha Freier remained in Germany until 1940, when she left with the last organized group of Youth Aliyah and reached Yugoslavia illegally. From Yugoslavia, she later arrived in Palestine.

Youth Aliyah was part and parcel of the immigration of German Jews to Palestine. We will mention here one story, which belongs to a later period, but is connected with the Youth Aliyah. We refer here to a group known as the Nonantola (or Villa Emma) group. This group was organized by Recha Freier in Zagreb, Yugoslavia. It consisted mainly of girls from Austria, who were later joined by children from other places. A young youth leader in the Hashomer Hatza'ir youth movement, Joseph Indig — today Yosef Itai — was in charge of this group, and after the Nazis entered Yugoslavia in April 1941, he escaped with the children to the Italian occupied zone in Yugoslavia. He spent a year with the children there, financing their subsistence out of thin air and educating them, under strict discipline — a Hebrew education and training in physical labor — to prepare them for their immigration to Palestine. In 1942, when conditions in the Italian zone became harder, Indig succeeded in establishing contacts with the Italian village of Nonantola in the mountains of central Italy. He smuggled the children to that village, with the assistance of the Italian army, and there, with the help of two Italian priests and the cooperation of the whole village, he managed to keep the children one more year. In September 1943, when the Germans conquered North Italy as well, he smuggled the children to Switzerland with the help of his Italian friends, and from there, at the end of this long odyssey, he brought them to Palestine safe and sound. Most of them are still in Israel today. This story deserves to be better known than it is. It may also be worth mentioning that the village of Nonantola still keeps in touch with its truly glorious past action of saving a group of children to this very day.

All the facts we have surveyed here add up to a story of an intense desire to emigrate anywhere, and of various initiatives, some of them taken by the Jewish leadership of Germany, and others of the sort described above, to immigrate to Palestine.

V.

Aliyah B and Emigration from Germany at the Beginning of the War

"Aliyah B" (the illegal immigration to Palestine), which was one of the main ways of escaping during this period, fits naturally into this picture. In the years 1938-1939, about 11,000 Jews from Germany and Austria reached Palestine. This is not a large number, but it is not to be despised in the prevailing conditions. After all, the British authorities had closed the gates of Palestine, and were using methods, both of a diplomatic and of a physical nature (like the coast guard and British men of war along the coasts of Palestine) to stop the attempts of Aliyah B to break into the country.

Who organized Aliyah B into Palestine? There were three forces: the Aliyah B Center (*Mossad le-Aliyah B*) of the Haganah (which was established early in 1939) and the immigration activists of the Kibbutz Me'uhad, the largest of the federations of kibbutzim at the time, and of the Histadrut (the Jewish Labor Federation); the Irgun Zvai Leumi and its branches in the diaspora; and private organizers, some of them attached to various political parties and others working independently. The chief force during this period was the IZL. Of 17,420 Jews brought into Palestine before the outbreak of the war, 9,640 were brought by the IZL and private organizers, and 7,780 by the Aliyah B Center. Those transports that originated in Germany were carried out in concert with the Gestapo. One should bear in mind that at the time the Gestapo wished to drive the Jews out of Germany, while the various Jewish bodies were trying to rescue the

Aliyah B and Emigration from Germany

Jews. In this manner, cooperation was reached between the murderer, who was not yet to know that he was to become a murderer, and the victim, who was already beginning to sense a threat to his life.

First priority was given to the rescue of Jews who were already in concentration camps, and who could be released from them on producing evidence of their inclusion in a list of candidates for Aliyah B. The Nazis assisted them in leaving Germany itself, and sometimes even enabled the organizers to rent boats which would carry them along the Danube to the Black Sea. From there, the organizers of Aliyah B from the three groups we have mentioned hired or purchased boats to take them to Palestine.

Some of the Jewish immigrants during this period came from Germany and Austria, but others came from Eastern Europe. This was based on the consideration with which we have already met, that the economic situation in pre-war Eastern Europe was such as to necessitate the inclusion of Jews from those countries in those maritime transports, since their situation in their countries of residence was intolerable.

There is another place which should be mentioned here, the city of Danzig. This city, which is today the Polish harbor town of Gdansk, was then a free city, which was not officially under either German or Polish rule. In practice, though, the Free City of Danzig had been ruled, since 1935, by a Nazi council, and great pressure was put on the Jews to leave. It was also clear that any violent clash in the future would be followed by an immediate occupation by the Nazi army, since Danzig was surrounded by Nazi territory, with the exception of a narrow corridor of Poland which stood between it and German territory. It was clear that the Poles were in no position to protect Danzig. The result of this situation was that the Jewish community of Danzig prepared for an organized emigration. That is not to say that there had not also been many private citizens who had emigrated on their own initiative, either to Poland before the outbreak of the war, or to the United States and other places. But in this case it was the local Jewish community which took the major initiative, and organized a number of transports, that is, groups of

Jewish Reactions to the Holocaust

Jews to be sent to Palestine through Aliyah B. And indeed the large majority of this community was rescued. This was a special case, since not every community had the opportunity to act in this manner. The Jews of Danzig were given the opportunity, and they made the best of it.

In the first phases of the war, Nazi pressure was still aimed at the expulsion and emigration of the Jews, and this created a somewhat paradoxical situation. During these years — the end of 1939, the beginning of 1940, and even the early months of 1941 — the endeavors of the Gestapo itself to drive the Jews out of Germany ultimately contributed to their rescue. Thus, the same force which was shortly to organize the murder of the Jews first aided in their rescue by driving them out at the earliest opportunity. The notorious Adolf Eichmann, who was living in Vienna at the time and was in charge of the brutal expulsion of the Jews — including their immigration to Palestine on unsanitary, primitive boats — made the greatest contribution to this.

At the end of 1939 and the beginning of 1940, more strenuous attempts at increasing Aliyah B into Palestine were undertaken by the three organizing forces mentioned above: the IZL and its European branches, the Mossad, and private individuals. These efforts now met with extremely vigorous opposition by the British administration, which suspected — as simple military logic would dictate — that German agents might infiltrate into these transports of immigrants, and thus reach the Middle East. This idea, of course, never occurred to the Nazis, since it would have been inconceivable to them to plant "pure" German agents into groups of "inhuman" Jews.

The British apprehension of Aliyah B contributed its share to British policy in the Middle East in general. Britain's weak position in that area strengthened its pro-Arab policy, and the last thing it wanted was the infiltration of more Jews into Palestine. From its point of view, these Jews were illegal immigrants; although from a Jewish and European point of view this was already a rescue operation — not yet, indeed, rescue from certain death, since even then no one could predict the Holocaust, but one could speak of

Aliyah B and Emigration from Germany

rescue from persecution and from the danger of death. This aim of rescuing the Jews from Europe also contained a very important element of increasing the strength of the Jewish community in Palestine for the coming struggle for its political future. More decisive than the view that the Jews had to be saved from extinction — for, after all, this was not yet an issue during this period — was the consideration that one should reinvigorate the Jewish population of Palestine.

In February 1940, the IZL and its branches succeeded in bringing to Palestine a large ship — the Sakariyeh — from Rumania with over 2,000 people. Such endeavors continued later, but without much success. There were great difficulties in obtaining boats and providing them with the technical arrangements. In fact, after the Sakariyeh affair, the initiative for Aliyah B passed into the hands of the Gestapo in Vienna. The Gestapo put a man named Berthold Storfer, a Jew who was eventually sent to Auschwitz and died there, in charge of Aliyah B. Storfer was a businessman of great will power, and he regarded himself as the man who was to rescue as many Jews as possible and ship them to Palestine.

At the end of 1939, the Mossad brought a sizeable transport of Jews to the small town of Kladovo, on the Danube, in Yugoslavia. There, the group remained stuck, as the activists were incapable of bringing it to Palestine for lack of financing and a suitable ship. Reacting to this, Storfer said that when the Palestinian Jews attempted to organize matters, they did not succeed; whereas he, at the European end, could accomplish things.

The Kladovo convoy was, indeed, stuck there. It never reached Palestine, and its 1,200 members were later murdered by the Nazis. Only a small group of Jews, mainly children, who managed to escape in time and with legal permits, was saved. At the same time, at the end of 1940, Storfer's organization succeeded in bringing to Palestine three large passenger ships — the famous Atlantic, Pacific and Milos — with nearly 3,600 immigrants. The Jews who were on two of these ships were caught by the British, brought to Haifa and transferred to a ship named the Patria, in order to expel them to the island of Mauritius. The Haganah exploded the Patria, which sank

Jewish Reactions to the Holocaust

in Haifa harbor on November 25, 1940, and more than 200 people drowned. The people from the third ship, the Atlantic, were later shipped to Mauritius. After this disaster, the British allowed those who had been rescued from the Patria to remain in Palestine, and they were later released. But what matters is that these three boats did, indeed, rescue Jews — and these were boats organized by Storfer.

The last of this wave of immigrants reached Palestine in the Mossad ship Darien, which had originally been destined to bring the Kladovo convoy. When this proved to be impossible, it brought 789 Jews into Palestine, the last to arrive in this fashion, in March 1941. Most of these Jews came from areas directly ruled by the Nazis, but some of them were Rumanian and Bulgarian Jews who joined the convoy. The general picture to emerge from all this is that attempts to bring Jews to Palestine were still feasible in the early stages of the war. The question now arises whether no opportunities were wasted, whether internal conflicts on the one hand, and the difficulty — which was objective enough — in finding suitable boats, did not prevent people from exploiting the possibilities which still existed at this period as far as the Nazis were concerned. From the beginning of the war until March 1941, 10,600 Jews reached Palestine through Aliyah B, and another 1,770 immigrants were expelled to Mauritius. About 400 drowned in the Patria disaster and in another disaster, when the S.S. Salvador sank in the Sea of Marmara near Istanbul. Five hundred other Jews were on board another boat, the Pencho, which was shipwrecked in the Aegean. Its passengers eventually were eventually taken to an Italian prison camp and spent the war there.

One should bear in mind that the stream of emigration was not directed only toward Palestine. The Jewish leadership in Germany supported the emigration of Jews to any possible place, and there existed an illegal immigration not only to Palestine, but also to South America. During 1938-1939, while various boats were wandering in the Mediterranean heading for Palestine, there were other boats and ships with Jews on board, sailing toward the shores of Central and South America. The most famous affair in this

Aliyah B and Emigration from Germany

context is the story of the Saint Louis, which reached the harbor of Havana, Cuba in July 1939, with passengers holding half-forged Cuban entry visas. The Cubans did not allow the boat to anchor or the Jews to disembark. The Jews were returned to Europe, and it was only through the last minute intervention of the Joint that they were allowed to disembark before reaching Germany. But there were other boats which did return to Germany, since there was no one willing to accept the Jews. In the South American countries, it was chiefly the Joint which succeeded — often at the very last moment and by means of extensive bribery — to convince the local authorities to let the Jews disembark and be absorbed by the local Jewish communities.

One of the countries toward which the Jews headed (this, too, through the efforts of the Joint), was the Dominican Republic, the only country which had declared at the Evian Conference that it was willing to take Jews. But this willingness was, in fact, an act of deception. The dictator of the Dominican Republic, General Trujillo, had asked the State Department whether it would view with favor a declaration on his part that he was prepared to accept Jews into his country. The State Department gave him a positive answer; any such gesture would be welcome. The Dominican ruler did, indeed, make this gesture, but at the same time also informed the State Department that he had no serious intention of letting 100,000 Jews into his country, as he had proposed. The truth of the matter was, he now said, that if the Jews could bring capital and assist in developing the agriculture in his country (and this is an admission of the success of Jewish agricultural settlement in Palestine), he would be glad to let in a very small and limited number of Jews.

The Joint, a non-Zionist organization, had had previous experience in the settlement of Jews in the Crimea, in the Soviet Union, under the Communist regime. It decided to accept the new offer. Representatives of the Joint purchased land in the Dominican Republic near a small town called Sosua, for the purpose of establishing Jewish agricultural settlements there. They mobilized for this purpose Jews from Germany and other countries, and

Jewish Reactions to the Holocaust

believed that this would be a rescue operation resulting in the settlement of Jews in the Dominican Republic and in the creation of an autonomous Jewish body in that country.

What the Joint was totally unaware of was that the Dominicans had no intention whatsoever of taking in such a mass immigration. The attempt met with failure. Throughout the war years, no more than 1,000 Jews immigrated to the Dominican Republic. 159 settled in Sosua itself, and another 285 moved to a neighboring town, but not for the purpose of agricultural settlement. As far as we know, today there is only one Jewish farmer in the Dominican Republic, and he — as might be expected — employs Dominican laborers for running his farm. The people who came to the Dominican Republic ostensibly in order to settle, regarded it only as a first stage in their immigration to the United States. They had no intention of remaining in a country with such a harsh climate. Most of them were German Jews, steeped in German culture, and this could hardly go together with milking cows and with hard agricultural labor which was devoid of any ideological basis and of any moral, political or other such motivation. Thus, on the purely personal level, a German Jewish lawyer would naturally prefer to become, in the long run, an American German Jewish lawyer — and this, indeed, is what most of them became. The whole affair absorbed huge sums of money, and was a terrible waste of capital which could have been invested, during those years, in rescuing Jews from the Nazi purgatory. Instead of this, they were poured into the Dominican Republic. So much for that affair.

All these endeavors indicate that the main tendency during those years, 1938-1941, was toward emigration. It may sound surprising, but until October 1941 Jews still emigrated from Germany, Austria and Czechoslovakia. The Nazis were still willing to encourage such an emigration, and the main obstacle was the attitude of the other countries of the world, which were unwilling to absorb the Jews.

At the same time, as we have already noted, the leadership of the Jews in Germany made endeavors to strengthen the community itself. It did this by establishing farms for agricultural training,

Aliyah B and Emigration from Germany

where Jewish and vocational education was provided; attempts were made to prepare young Jews for the future by means of retraining, and large-scale cultural activities took place. All this was done to strengthen the morale of the Jews and to prevent their collapse under the ever-increasing assaults.

When the war broke out, the Jews of Germany were conscripted into forced labor. In fact, this forced labor did something to save the Jews of Germany for another brief period, since they were paid for it, albeit only a small pittance. But even in such strenuous circumstances — and with the help of the Joint from abroad — one could still subsist. Here we meet with another paradoxical phenomenon: the forced labor, which put a heavy burden on the Jews, also made it possible for them to go on existing.

VI.

Jewish Leadership in Poland and German Policy, 1939-1940

On September 1, 1939, the Nazis invaded Poland, and the Second World War broke out. The Germans conquered the whole of Poland in a lightening campaign, within about four weeks. The last week of this campaign was wholly spent on the siege of Warsaw, the only city which remained in the hands of the Polish army. On September 17th — that is, in the middle of this campaign — the Soviet army entered Poland from the east, and about one third of pre-1939 Poland was conquered by the Soviet Union. Of 3.3 million Jews living in Poland before the Holocaust, about two thirds — a million and nine hundred thousand people, perhaps a little less — remained under German occupation. The rest, about a million and four hundred thousand, were now under Soviet rule.

Even at this stage, the Nazis still did not know that they were to massacre European Jewry. This point should be repeatedly stressed. One tends now to accuse the Jews of that period, as if they were to know that the Nazis were about to murder them. But even the Nazis themselves were not yet aware of this.

Himmler, who was to become the murderer of European Jewry, sent a memorandum to Hitler on May 25, 1940, in which he spelled out what was to be done about the Poles, the Ukrainians, the Jews, and other such groups in the conquered area of Poland. They were not, wrote Himmler, to be given any education, and should be employed as slaves. The Jews, as Himmler explained to Hitler,

Jewish Leadership in Poland and German Policy, 1939-1940

should be deported to Africa, and his reason for this was that the Bolshevik solution, namely liquidation, was not a solution which National Socialism could endorse. Hitler replied that this was the right and proper attitude.

Murder was implicit in Nazi ideology, but it had not yet been raised or expressed in any practical program, though the motif of murder had been raised by Hitler in a public speech, delivered to the German Nazi Reichstag on January 30, 1939. In that speech, Hitler threatened to murder the Jewish race if a war were to break out. But this was not followed by any program, and the only practical program in existence was that of the expulsion of the Jews. One should bear this in mind if one is to understand the Jewish and non-Jewish reactions in the free world. What did they know? They knew that the Germans were conquering Poland and murdering Poles — and the truth is that, in the first stages, from September 1939 until the middle of 1940, it was mostly Poles who were murdered in Poland. The Nazis massacred the Polish intelligentsia, the Polish leadership, and the Polish clergy in western Poland. Many Jews were also murdered — as, for example, in Wloclawek — and there were pogroms against Jews in Czestochowa and other places in Poland. These constituted serious attacks on the Jews, but there was as yet no organized mass murder.

These facts become confused at times, even in the memory of Holocaust survivors. Some of them remember incidents of murder and repression; and there were, indeed, many incidents of murder and repression — but some of the survivors confuse this with what was to happen later. At this stage, the Nazi operational or spearhead divisions, who were to massacre the Jews of the Soviet Union eighteen months later, were already active in Poland, but their main targets were Poles.

On September 21, while the battle was still going on, the head of the security and of the political police of the S.S., Reinhard Heydrich, issued an order, which has become one of the fundamental documents for the whole history of the Holocaust. In this document, Heydrich gave the order to establish inside the ghettoes (and it was apparently obvious that one had to establish such ghettoes, since the document contains no such explicit instruction) committees of elders, as he called them at the time. Later on, they were mostly named the "Judenrat," or Jewish Council. The task of the Judenrat was to pass on to the Jews instructions received from the Germans, death being the penalty for disobedience.

These instructions were addressed mainly to the S.S. spearhead units ("Einsatzgruppen"), which were the most radicalized armed force of the Nazi Party. The task of these spearhead units was to concentrate all the Jews of the countryside into the major cities, and to expel all the Jews from the western areas of Poland, which had been annexed by Germany, into the center of Poland. The Germans had by now divided Poland into two parts, one of which was annexed to Germany, and the other, the "Generalgouvernement" (GG) remained separate under a German governor. It was into the GG that the Jews of western Poland were to be expelled, and everything was to be made ready for the "Final Aim," which was mentioned in this document without any comment. There have been some historians after the Holocaust who interpreted this term, "Final Aim," as the plan for the massacre of the Jews, known to us as the "Final Solution" or the Holocaust.

That is not the case. Even here there was no intention of massacring the Jews, but of expelling them. The aim of this document was to concentrate the Jews in order to facilitate their expulsion, in the first instance (October 1939-April 1940) to the southwestern part of Poland, in the region of the small town of Nisko in the Lublin area, and hence, perhaps, to the Soviet zone. Later on, when this program fell through because of opposition on the part of various German authorities who were against such a large concentration of Jews in an area under German rule, a new, alternative plan was formed. The Jews were to be expelled from the whole of Europe to the French island of Madagascar. It was expected that once peace was established by Germany, Madagascar would fall under German rule, and the expulsion of the Jews to that island would be possible. The figure of four million Jews was mentioned. They were to be held in a concentration camp or in a

Jewish Leadership in Poland and German Policy, 1939-1940

huge ghetto in Madagascar, and were to serve as hostages for the "good behavior" of the Jews of America.

Heydrich's instructions were therefore to prepare everything for the expulsion of the Jews, and meanwhile, no doubt, to extract from them everything possible, like property and labor, as well as to decrease their number by putting them into ghettoes and letting "natural" death and epidemics do their work.

The question arises: What was the Jewish reaction, on its various constituents, to the establishment of such Judenraete or committees of elders? One has to understand that in the eyes of the Jews, who had, of course, no inkling of Heydrich's document of September 21, 1939, the whole affair assumed a very different complexion. Here were the Germans, entering the cities and towns and demanding of the Jews — or, to be precise, of the prominent Jews, as Heydrich's document has it — to constitute councils of Jews. What was a council of Jews? The Germans referred to it as a Council of Jews or a Council of Elders, but in Jewish eyes they appeared to be nothing other than a community council, since someone or other had to represent them before the new conquerors. In the eyes of some of the Jews of Poland, despite all they had read in the newspapers, the Germans appeared, at first, to be the very same Germans who, during the 1914-1918 war, had protected the Jews from the Czar's regime in Russia. The Germans appeared to the Jews to be an extremely civilized and polite nation, and even if the country was now ruled by antisemites, things could not get too bad. Thus the initial reaction of the Jewish leadership in the various localities was in no way negative. Hence the local Judenraete in Poland were generally not committees appointed by the Germans and chosen among certain circles amongst the Jewish population which were, perhaps, not popular among that population. On the contrary, the Judenrat was usually the old community council; and the Germans, who were hardly familiar with local circumstances, raised no objection to this.

We can follow this phenomenon in every single locality, but we shall take Warsaw as an example, not only because it was the city with the largest Jewish population in Poland, but also because we possess extensive materials which make a thorough examination possible. On September 6, 1939, while the Polish struggle against the Germans was still being vigorously maintained, something like an instruction was issued by the Polish radio, saying that the Polish government was abandoning Warsaw. This was a great shock, since people still believed that Poland was going to win the war against Germany — and here was a call to all men, Polish and Jewish, all male residents, to go east, where the Polish army was to reorganize in order to continue its campaign against the Germans. The result was sheer panic.

Large numbers of Jews were now on the move east, toward those eastern regions which were to be conquered by the Soviet army as it advanced into Poland on September 17. Among those escaping were most of the national leaders of the Jews in Poland at the time — men like Moshe Sneh, leader of the General Zionists, and Zerah Warhaftig, leader of the religious Zionists. The leaders of the Bund — the largest socialist anti-Zionist party, supported by one third of the Jews of Poland — men like Viktor Alter and Henryk Erlich, also escaped east along with the rest of the refugees. Even those leaders who stayed on in Warsaw, like the leader of Agudath Israel, Rabbi Isaac Meir Levin, or Abraham (Apollinari) Hartglass, one of the leaders of the General Zionists, remained there only for a very brief period, and at the beginning of 1940 they too fled.

Thus, when we speak of the national leadership of the Jews in Poland as against local leaders, one must admit that most of the leaders took to flight. This is not meant, of course, as an accusation. These people were under great pressure and the temptation to leave was strong, since they were well-known, and it was reasonable to assume that once the Germans came, they would first strike at the acknowledged national leadership. One can therefore only note the fact that they escaped.

Some of the leaders of the Jewish youth movements also fled, but returned to Poland after its conquest by the Nazis. Members of the leadership of the Zionist-socialist youth movements of Hashomer Hatza'ir and Dror escaped east, and most of them managed to reach Lithuania, which was still independent at the time. Once they

Jewish Leadership in Poland and German Policy, 1939-1940

reassembled in Lithuania, they said to themselves: "What have we done? We have left the youth entrusted to our guidance and training under Nazi occupation and escaped to east Poland or Lithuania." In full consciousness of what they were doing, they reached a consensus. The leadership of the Jewish youth movements divided into three groups. Some of them possessed entry permits into Palestine. These were mainly the veteran leaders, 22-23 years old and older, who had already gone through all stages of training for immigration. Some of this group of leaders were to go to Palestine, while others were to stay in Lithuania, since there was a large concentration of refugees in the country at the time. The remaining leaders returned to Poland. This included Mordechai Anielewicz, later the commander of the Warsaw Ghetto, and Yitzhak Zuckermann, who was to be his deputy and later the head of the pioneer Zionist movements in Poland, as well as some other leaders. They returned from Lithuania, or from the parts of Poland occupied by the Soviets, into the Nazi occupation zone. The only Jewish organizations whose leadership was reconstituted were thus the leftist Zionist youth movements, some of whose leaders returned to Nazi occupied territory.

The leadership of the older Jewish population in Poland was now virtually in the hands of local people. These were various types of community leaders, and they were now faced with Nazi pressure to establish the Judenraete. In Warsaw, for example, there was Adam Czerniakow, an engineer, a member of the community council and the deputy head of the community, whose former head had fled east. Czerniakow was a local leader, and he had been in charge of the national Polish Union of Jewish Craftsmen. He was close to Jewish Agency circles, and was somewhere between a Zionist and an assimilationist. He preferred to speak Polish rather than Yiddish, but at the same time was involved in Jewish life and extremely faithful to the Jewish cause. While the battle for Warsaw was still going on, he asked the Polish mayor to appoint him as the head of the Warsaw social aid organization. The last Polish mayor of Warsaw appointed him to that post only a few days before the city was conquered, on September 23. When the Germans came, they

Jewish Reactions to the Holocaust

found what was in effect a local Jewish council already there, and they accepted it officially. This, in fact, became the Judenrat. Later on, Czerniakow was asked to appoint additional members to this Judenrat, but the Judenrat was not originally created by the Germans but by the Poles, and it was a sequel to the Jewish community council of Warsaw.

Similar things happened in many other localities in Poland. In some places, something like an emergency coalition, comprising the members of various Jewish parties, was established. In Lublin, for example, a Judenrat was established, and a municipal "wall to wall" coalition was formed, headed by a Zionist named Dr. Mark Alten, a representative of one of the sectors of Zionism. All the Zionists, as well as Agudath Israel and the Bund, also joined with him for the formation of this coalition. This was a Judenrat which was virtually as representative of the community as the community council had been before the Holocaust.

There were, however, places, where things did not happen in this fashion. There were places where a certain person, whether he had been previously active in community affairs or not, was appointed by the Nazis as head of the Judenrat.

One should bear in mind that, despite Heydrich's instructions, the famous efficiency of the Nazis had its limitations. It was in working order later on, when the operation for the murder of the Jews was under way; but when one goes into details, one discovers that even this was not always true. One should note here that inside the German governmental machine, certain satrapies, or semi-independent feudal areas, were created. These areas were under the control of different masters, each of whom held his own territory, and these masters quarreled among themselves. Up to a certain limit, although not beyond it, one could play one of them against the other. On the issue of the Jews, an unambiguous decision was eventually reached. But meanwhile, there was some margin left for action — and when one was concerned with what was to happen in a month or in two months, with the rescue of a few more people, or with achieving some small points here or there, this was of some importance.

Jewish Leadership in Poland and German Policy, 1939-1940

One should note in this context that the first Judenrat in Poland was established on October 6, 1939, in the town of Piotrkow, while the last ghetto in Poland, which was conquered in 1939, was established in 1943. This was a ghetto in a southwestern area of Poland named Zaglembia, where a Judenrat, in the town of Sosnowiec and in other towns was, indeed, established quite early, but where ghettoes were formed only in 1943. Between these two extreme dates, the process of ghetto building was carried on. This implies that, in the majority of places, ghettoes did not exist for a certain period, while serious steps and orders had been taken, aimed against the Jews. A ghetto, of course, multiplied the threat.

Another point one should make here is that the economic steps taken against the Jews were immediate and severe in the extreme, and they drove the Jews out of the Polish economy virtually at one fell swoop. Instructions were issued for the confiscation of Jewish property; Jews were forbidden to travel by train, or to travel freely in any manner; and Jewish money deposited in the banks was not to be used. Within a brief period — about three or four months — the Jews were left with nothing but small-scale trade here and there, chiefly peddling; manufacture in the few Jewish workshops which still existed in some places — and forced labor. Theoretically, at least, the Jews had no way of subsisting at all.

One should add that the food rations officially allocated to Jews were such that, had the Jews had to survive on them alone, the Jewish population of Poland would have dwindled away in time; and that these rations grew smaller and smaller at an ever-increasing pace. In Warsaw, for example, they were about 220 calories a day — that is, about 10%-15% of the required quantity. Calculations, however, show that after the Warsaw Ghetto was established, the Jews consumed about 1,700 calories a day each. If we ask where these additional calories came from, it is clear that they had nothing to do with German rationing. It was obvious from the start that, if the Jews were to subsist, they simply could not follow German instructions literally.

Immediately after the Nazi occupation, the expulsions hinted at by Heydrich in the document we have discussed above began to be carried out. The Jews were to be expelled from all small places, and from western Poland which had been annexed by Germany. In that annexed area, there remained two very large concentrations of Jews; the industrial city of Lodz, which contained the second largest Jewish population in Poland, and the area of Zaglembia, that is Sosnowiec, Bendin and their neighboring towns. Except for these areas, the Jews were expelled from western Poland. But they were not only expelled from there, but also from some parts of central Poland, the Generalgouvernement, which were under the governor general, Hans Frank. Altogether, about 380,000 Jews were expelled from their places of residence in the early stages, and were concentrated in the larger cities, chiefly in Warsaw. Later, in 1940-1941, another expulsion from smaller places to larger ghettoes followed, and comprised about 150,000 Jews. It follows that a very large portion, perhaps as much as one third, of those 1.9 million Jews who were under German occupation from the beginning of the war until the German attack on the Soviet Union in 1941, were expelled from their homes and turned into refugees. When one had virtually no source of subsistence and was also faced with a refugee problem, the question arose of who would maintain the refugees. This, indeed, was the most major and pressing problem facing the Judenraete in the various localities.

Another pressing issue was that of forced labor. People were now being kidnapped in the streets and taken to various places of work where the Germans required forced labor, which was in fact tantamount to slave labor. Rarely were the people paid for this labor; however, of all German organizations, it was the army which sometimes paid for this work. The Jews were recruited, either to places of work near their places of residence, or into labor camps erected especially for this purpose, mainly to fortify the new German-Soviet border, which passed through the midst of Poland. In the beginning, some were still allowed to return from these camps, which were not permanent establishments nor concentration camps, but merely provisional camps for forced labor. The sanitary and nutritional conditions in those camps were such that the mortality rate was very high.

Jewish Leadership in Poland and German Policy, 1939-1940

Because of the concentration of masses of people in circumstances of unbearable crowding, lack of food, and no adequate living conditions, plagues began to spread. By April 1940, more than 400 Jews in Warsaw were already suffering from typhoid, and the plague was not restricted to Warsaw, but spread in other places as well. This began even before the establishment of ghettoes, and circumstances went from bad to worse once they had been erected; a situation which had been hard to suffer became insufferable. These were the circumstances in which that Jewish leadership, the Judenrat, had to operate.

To exemplify this state of affairs, we shall take a rather extreme case, a leadership severely and harshly chastised by historians in the period after the Holocaust as one which did not do its duty to Jewish history and to the Jewish public, namely the leadership of the Lodz Ghetto. Shortly after the Nazi conquest, an old man of about seventy with previous connections with the Zionist movement, a former industrialist who had been in charge of a Jewish orphanage in Lodz before the war, named Mordechai Haim Rumkowski, was appointed as head of the ghetto. There was virtually no Judenrat in this ghetto, and Rumkowski, although he had the assistance of some sort of council, had the final word.

The ghetto in Lodz was formed in great haste, and by March-April 1940 the Nazis began to seal it off. In May, it was already hermetically sealed. This was the only ghetto in Eastern Europe which was absolutely sealed off. In other places one could, in some form or other, get out, smuggle, make outside contacts — but not in Lodz. The ghetto was established in the poorest quarter of town, and in the rest of the city, an accelerated process of replacing the Poles by Germans was taking place. The ghetto was surrounded by the most watchful German guards, and one could no more escape from it than from a concentration camp. This, of course, precluded any possibility of establishing contacts with the underground later to arise in other places, and it also prevented smuggling, so that in the Lodz Ghetto one had to subsist on rations handed out by the Germans.

But what happened in the ghetto in Lodz was that even the rations brought into it by the Germans were not bought by the population, since they had no means of paying for them. That is, those starvation rations supplied by the Germans were often not utilized because of the terrible poverty and hunger inside the ghetto. It was a vicious circle. Hunger made people incapable of coming to work, or made them weak and ill, and as a result, they could not receive the starvation salaries paid for their labor and were unable to buy their food.

Thus, the situation in the Lodz Ghetto was severe from the very beginning, It was, in fact, established as a slave labor camp, and Rumkowski's only target was to maintain the ghetto by means of this forced labor. His ideology was as follows: If we are to be slaves of the Germans, it is clear that they will not harm us, for after all, the master is unlikely to kill his own slaves. The only way of keeping the ghetto going is by supplying all the services required by the Germans and offering all the property and all the labor one can squeeze out of the people.

Rumkowski had his opponents inside the ghetto, and there was even an underground there. But one should bear in mind the effect of starvation on people. The ability to stand up and fight, both physically and psychologically, dwindled away under these conditions of extreme hunger. Rumkowski also had his own assistants in the ghetto, both police and individuals of criminal tendencies, who suppressed any sign of opposition. Wherever the slightest marks of opposition appeared — attempts at a strike and the like, they were forcefully and brutally suppressed.

Were people in the free world aware of this terrible suffering in the closed ghettoes? In fact, it was known to people, and the facts were published even in Palestine. The New York Times, Life — the high-circulation American picture magazine — and its British counterpart, Picture Post, all reported these facts. The United States was still neutral, and American journalists were still around in Europe. Nobody knew as yet about any massacre, since there was no mass murder until 1941.

VII.

Rescue Attempts

We have already seen that the passengers of the Atlantic were expelled from Palestine in a rather brutal fashion in December 1940, and spent all the years of the war on the island of Mauritius. British policy was totally uncompromising. In the early stages of the war, Britain's position in the Middle East was extremely weak, and this strengthened its opposition to anything which might endanger the policies of the May 1939 White Paper, policies which limited Jewish entry to Palestine within five years to 75,000 people, and which promised in effect an Arab-controlled Palestine within ten years. Hence every action which was likely to bring into Palestine Jewish immigrants, especially those who were regarded by the British as illegal immigrants, was to be rejected in principle.

It is obvious that at that time the Jewish Agency for Palestine saw things in a different light, although its leaders were prepared to reach some agreement with the British. In 1940, Chaim Weizmann, President of the Jewish Agency, and Moshe Sharett, head of its political department, informed the British authorities that if they were to allow the immigration of Jews, not only into Palestine but into any other part of the British Empire, the Jewish Agency would bring them there. They regarded this issue as a matter of rescuing Jews, not necessarily in order to bring them to Palestine. At the same time, they expressed the strongest opposition to any expulsion from Palestine of immigrants who had already arrived. The Jewish Agency was prepared to bring the immigrants to Palestine in boats belonging to the Aliyah B Institute; and if the British captured these boats on the high sea, they would have no objection if the Jews were to be shipped elsewhere, as long as they were rescued.

The British were not prepared even for this. They regarded the whole issue of Aliyah B as a Zionist act of collusion with the Gestapo — since, after all, the Gestapo supported the emigration of Jews from Europe — a plot which was intended to undermine British policy in the Middle East. Besides, the British were absolutely certain that there were German agents among the immigrants. The British could not realize that the last idea which would occur to the Nazis was to use Jews as S.S. agents. As we have already noted, this, for the Nazis, would be an act of defilement.

The policy of the men on the spot, the activists of the Mossad, often contradicted the official policy of the Jewish Agency. After their great success at the beginning of 1940, the activities of the Revisionists in Rumania came to a standstill. The Mossad also slowed down its operations, but it renewed its activities toward the end of 1940, sending a delegation to Constantinople which was to organize the dispatch of another boat, the Darien, which we have already mentioned. This gave rise to a stormy controversy in Palestine, both among the leaders of the Jewish underground and among the leaders of the Jewish community there. What was to be the purpose of this boat? There were some who aimed at cooperation with the British, at helping them in their war effort, as a means to break through the restrictions and increase the number of immigrants. If the British were to agree to an increased number of immigrants, or at least of Jews rescued from Europe, such a change would, of course, be far more effective in saving Jews than another small boat bringing another few hundred refugees.

Against them stood the men of the Mossad, among them Yehudah Braginski, Zeev Schind and Shemariahu Zameret, who said that one should exploit any opening, large or small, for the concrete rescue of people, and that this had the first priority, before any grand program whose chances of success were far from certain. They regarded the Darien as a bird in hand. Against the view of the leaders of the Haganah and the leaders of the Jewish community,

Rescue Attempts

the Yishuv, they brought this boat, destined for the rescue of the Jews from Kladovo, to the coast to Rumania. After the Jews of Kladovo had failed to reach Rumania, they boarded refugees who were on the spot and ready for immigration, filled the quota of immigrants with people waiting for them in Bulgaria, and brought the boat to Palestine with nearly 800 people on board. This was virtually the last boat brought by Mossad until the final stages of the war.

RESCUE ATTEMPTS OUT OF LITHUANIA

At the beginning of the war, at the end of 1939 and the beginning of 1940, about 14,000 Jewish refugees from Poland, including more than 2,000 yeshivah students and their teachers and over 2,000 members of youth movements, especially of the left-wing Zionist movements, reached neutral Lithuania. The members of Betar, the Revisionist youth movement, had been directed to go to Vilno (Vilnius) before the outbreak of the war, and were already there. The left-wing Zionist pioneer movements reached Lithuania, complete with their leaderships. Yitzhak Zuckermann, Mordechai Anielewicz and Yosef Kaplan — people who later became famous in the ghetto uprisings — had all reached Vilno, which was then neutral, crossing the border under the most harsh of conditions.

Those leaders of Zionist movements in Poland who had escaped earlier to the Soviet-occupied eastern part of Poland felt there was danger in remaining where they were, and they thus made their way to Vilno. These included such men as Moshe Sneh, then leader of the General Zionists in Poland, and later head of the high command of the Haganah in Palestine, and Zerah Warhaftig, later the representative in the Knesset of the National Religious Party. Also there were Abraham Bielopolski, leader of the Right Poalei Zion, and some of the leaders of the anti-Zionist Bund. One could say that a large part of the national leadership of Polish Jewry was now concentrated in Vilno.

The problem facing them was how to get out. A small group managed to leave, with the assistance and the initiative of a man now named Zvi Barak, who was then head of the Palestine Office in

Jewish Reactions to the Holocaust

Kovno, Lithuania. He organized around himself a group of those people, and they did their utmost for the immigration of Jews into Palestine. Thus, a few hundred of them who were in possession of entry permits left Lithuania for Sweden, some of them by air from Latvia, through the services of the same airline which had earlier included among its pilots one of the leaders of the Nazis, Hermann Goering. In 1940, these Jews were flown through Sweden to Holland and France, and from there they made their tortuous way to Palestine.

But in June 1940 the Soviets occupied Lithuania, and the gates of emigration were locked. Most of these Jews had Polish passports, and they had nowhere to go. The Soviet belt was tightening around these refugees, and they faced expulsion to Siberia. How was one to escape? It appears that a certain yeshivah student came to the office of the Dutch consul in Riga, Latvia, and asked him if there was any place to which one could escape. The consul replied that there was one place where one needed no entry visa — it is true, one would not be allowed in, but an entry visa was not required. This place was Curacao in the West Indies. The young man asked for a written document. The consul had no objection, and stamped his passport with a rubber stamp which said that there was no need for an entry visa into Curacao — which was the plain truth. Following this incident, many Jews came and received such stamps or pieces of paper.

Here, then, was a place one could not enter, but which required no entry visa. But how was one to reach Curacao? Through the Soviet Union, of course: but the Russians were not issuing any transit visas. Later on, it transpired that one could obtain a transit visa, provided the destination was Japan. The visa to Japan could also only be used as a transit visa, since the Japanese were obviously not willing to take in Jewish refugees as permanent residents. They searched for a Japanese consul, and, strangely enough, a Japanese consul was found in Kovno. His name was Sempo Sugihara. There was also a German employee in the Japanese consulate, a local German resident, and the consul's task was to spy on behalf of the Japanese government. The Jews addressed themselves to Sempo

Rescue Attempts

Sugihara, explained their situation to him and asks for visas to aid in their rescue. The consul cabled Tokyo, asking whether he was authorized to issue transit visas, since the passports had a stamp in them confirming that no entry visa was required for Curacao. The answer was delayed, presumably since the Japanese Foreign Office in Tokyo had more urgent preoccupations. Such was the situation in early August 1940, and everyone knew that by the end of the month Mr. Sugihara was to close his consulate and leave Kovno, as he was ordered to do by the Soviets.

It was clear to the Japanese consul that issuing these visas meant rescuing these people. He began to issue transit visas without waiting for instructions from his superiors. Meanwhile, on August 20, he received an urgent message from Tokyo, forbidding him to issue visas. But Sempo Sugihara continued to issue them, and it appears that he issued no fewer than 3,000. With these visas, 2,400 Jews reached Japan. After the war, Sempo Sugihara was put on trial by the democratic Japanese government, and was required to pay the penalty for refusing to obey the orders of the wartime Japanese authorities. He was dismissed from the diplomatic service. Today, there is a tree in his name on the Avenue of Righteous Gentiles in Yad Vashem in Jerusalem. It seems that he deserves 2,400 trees, since that is the number of people saved by this single individual, who knew nothing whatsoever about Jews. He saw before him suffering human beings, and he decided to sacrifice his career for their sake.

An additional 1,100 Jews were also saved and arrived in Palestine. These included Dr. Israel Scheib-Eldad, Nathan Mor, future leaders of the Stern Group (LHY), some of the leaders of the youth movements, and some private individuals, Some of them had entry permits into Palestine — that is, promises that immigration visas had been issued. The British consul in Kovno, Thomas Preston, whose attitude to Zionism was hostile, was supposed to issue their permits. Until the very last moment — he was to leave Kovno on September 4, 1940 — he delayed and postponed the issuing of the permits. At the last moment he announced that he was willing to issue the permits but had no paper, secretary or typewriter. Zvi

Jewish Reactions to the Holocaust

Barak and his friends brought him the materials, and they began to print the permits which bore the consul's signature. He soon left, but many Jews wanted to be rescued. Permits were forged, but one could hardly do this on a large scale, since detection of the forgery would annul all the permits. Despite this, about 400 additional permits were forged, complete with "British" stamps and signatures. But whereas on the genuine British stamp one had a lion and a unicorn, as on British passports, on the stamps forged in Kovno there appeared two cats! With the help of these "cats", 400 Jews were rescued, and they came by boat from Odessa to Constantinople. In Constantinople, the British authorities detected the forgery. Some of these people had to suffer in a Turkish transit camp, but eventually they reached Palestine.

Altogether — whether by means of Jewish self-help or with the assistance of the Japanese consul and his German assistant — 3,500 Jews were rescued; 2,400 of them reached Japan and 1,100 reached Palestine — this out of 14,000 Jewish refugees in Lithuania, quite apart from 250,000 indigenous Lithuanian Jews, out of millions of Jews in Eastern Europe. In practice, there was no way out; but by means of combined ingenuity, Jewish and non-Jewish, a few managed to escape. The vast majority remained.

The Palestinian contribution to this issue was support from afar. Palestinian Jews were not positioned in Lithuania or in Moscow, and there was nothing they could do on the spot. They dispatched cables and wrote letters, and they knocked on the doors of the Foreign Office in London, asking for help through the British ambassador in Moscow. They demanded of the immigration department of the British Administration in Palestine the issuing of immigration permits — and this was the sum total of the possibilities open to them. Initiative could not come from Palestine, but from the other end.

That was the Lithuanian story. Another story, almost parallel to the story of Sempo Sugihara, occurred in Bordeaux, France. In June 1940 the Germans occupied France, and numerous Jewish refugees assembled in the harbor city of Bordeaux, since there existed in it, both before and after the surrender, the French government in

Rescue Attempts

transit. Bordeaux became tantamount to the capital once Paris had fallen. It was there that the representatives of the American Joint in France, who had previously been stationed in Paris, came, as did about 30,000 Jews.

The United States was very far away, and it did not issue entry visas. No one knew where to escape. Those who could, jumped on the British ships evacuating British troops from France in June 1940, and some Jews were successful. The large majority, however, remained there with nowhere to go.

These Jews felt that they had to leave in a hurry, since the Germans were approaching. The nearest place was Spain, but the Spaniards would only issue transit visas to those who possessed entry visas to Portugal, and the Portuguese would only issue transit visas to those who had an entry visa to a further destination. The Lithuanian story repeated itself in Bordeaux. In Bordeaux there was a Portuguese consul general, Aristide de Susa Mendes. He had very clear instructions from Lisbon: he was to issue no visas at all, least of all to Jews, since Portugal would be unable to rid itself of them. Portugal was locked and sealed.

What happened now is not entirely clear, but we have the testimony of a Belgian rabbi of Polish origin, who was himself a refugee in Bordeaux. He mentions in his testimony that he spent a night in the house of the consul, de Susa Mendes. His family included five children, and they had nowhere to sleep. He came to the Portuguese consulate and asked for a visa. The answer was negative. He then said to the consul: If you cannot give me a visa, let me at least sleep on your floor with my family. De Susa Mendes agreed. During the night, the testimony continued, they talked. We are not absolutely certain that the story is accurate, but it makes sense. It is a fact that de Susa Mendes was a descendant of Marranos, although he was a believing and practicing Catholic. From his brother, who was the Portuguese ambassador in Warsaw, he had learned about the Jewish problem. By the morning, he had come to the conclusion that if one Catholic could inflict all that injustice on the Jews (and he meant Hitler, who was officially a Catholic), it was permissible for another Catholic to sacrifice himself for the sake of the Jews.

He threw open the gates of the Portuguese consulate general in Bordeaux and began to sign visas. He had ten children, and the older ones sat with him and his wife and stamped Portuguese visas in the passports of Jews who were seeking an escape route from France. This is an incredible story, but it happens to be true. We do not know quite how many thousand visas he stamped, but it is clear that the number was extremely large. Some days later, the consul received urgent telegrams from Portugal, in which he was required to explain his action, which was contrary to all regulations. In another day or two, a representative of the Portuguese Foreign Office who outranked de Susa Mendes arrived in Bordeaux. It appears that the people in Lisbon had come to the conclusion that he had gone out of his mind, and he was ordered to return to Lisbon immediately.

On his way to Portugal, he passed through the small town of Hendaye, near the Pyrenean border, where there was a Portuguese deputy consul. For several hours, Mendes sat in that consulate and put more stamps in passports before crossing the border. When he arrived at the Spanish border, he came across a large crowd of refugees. The Spaniards did not understand what was going on, since all these refugees had Portuguese transit visas, and this looked suspicious to them. De Susa Mendes came to the rescue once again. He presented himself as the Portuguese consul general in Bordeaux who had issued these visas, and demanded that the refugees be allowed to cross.

Thanks to the intervention of de Susa Mendes, whole convoys crossed the border. It is difficult today to reconstruct the exact figures and dates. Mendes returned to Lisbon, was dismissed from the diplomatic service, and worked for a period in the small Jewish community in Lisbon. No one recognized him or looked after him, and he died in abject poverty. His daughter, who later emigrated to the United States, sent a letter to the Israeli government, in which she related the whole story. At first, she was not believed, and was asked to produce witnesses. But a large number of witnesses came forward, and the story was authenticated in all its details. There is

Rescue Attempts

now a tree in the Avenue of the Righteous Gentiles bearing the name of Aristide de Susa Mendes. It appears that he, too, deserves a whole forest.

If we take an overall view of this issue, it is very disturbing. The two largest operations for the rescuing of Jews, both in quantity and in impressive quality, were those conducted in Lithuania and in Bordeaux. Among the two, the larger one, as far as the number of people rescued is concerned, was the one carried out by a single individual, Aristide de Susa Mendes. He did it for religious and humanitarian reasons, as a Catholic who wanted to save human beings and was prepared to sacrifice himself in the process. Had there been many like him in the international political leadership circles of the time, among those people who wielded far greater influence than that of the insignificant consul general, it is likely that many more people might have been rescued. Jews have been nurtured on a civilization which maintains that he who has saved one soul is like unto him who has saved a whole world. Here there were so many worlds which could have been saved. It cannot, of course, be claimed that all the Jews who perished in the Holocaust could have been rescued, but numerous individuals could have been saved; very few of them were saved, and Aristide de Susa Mendes, single-handed, saved a few thousand of them.

No aid in these two affairs by the western governments was to be seen. The initiative was taken *in spite of* the western and neutral governments involved. It was the initiative of individual persons, and no more than that.

VIII.

The Sanctification of Life

We have already spoken of some aspects of the problems facing the Judenraete, the Jewish Councils in Eastern Europe between 1939 and 1942. We now have to clarify another point, which may help us understand the historical development in this connection. In many places in Eastern Europe there existed, beside the Judenraete, parallel organizations so to speak, or parallel leaderships. Thus, the Judenrat was not the only body of leadership in every place. This is of some importance when we come to examine not only the reactions of the leadership to Nazi persecution, but also the reactions of the Jewish public. Before the Nazis began to massacre the Jews, the Jews believed that they would be able to go through the period of the war and of Nazi domination by establishing institutes and organizations which would maintain Jewish life in the ghettoes, and thus help them to "outlive" ("iberlebn" in Yiddish) the Nazis, an expression used by the people during that period.

Instead of the concept of the Sanctification of the Name of God, which was current during the Middle Ages, when the oppressor was after the Jew's soul and the Jew responded by saying: "You can take away my body, but not my soul," a new phenomenon was now in evidence, the German demand for the Jew's body. The Germans paid no attention to what the Jew believed in: whether he was faithful to the Jewish religion or did not believe in it was of no importance in their eyes. The Nazis included in their anti-Jewish measures even people whose grandparents had become Christians.

The Sanctification of Life

The problem for the Jews now was how to outlive the German physically. Instead of the concept of the Sanctification of the Name of God, a new concept was coined, reputedly by Rabbi Yitzhak Nissenbaum of Warsaw — that of the Sanctification of Life. This meant that one should do everything to preserve Jewish life — a life with Jewish content — since this was what the enemy was seeking to take away. Here followed a whole series of reactions, not all of them organized, and at least some of them spontaneous, on the part of the Jewish public.

The example of Warsaw is the best one in this context, since there were some periods where over 400,000 Jews — that is, more than 20% of the Jewish population of Occupied Poland before the German invasion of the Soviet Union — lived in Warsaw. This was the largest ghetto in Europe. As early as 1939, during the German air raids on Warsaw, committees were already established in Jewish houses. One should note that a typical Jewish house in Warsaw was not a single residential home, but four apartment blocks around an inner courtyard, which in some cases contained a few hundred families. Such a house council began with mutual aid, with assistance to those who were worst hit by the air raids. When the German measures against the Jews were announced after the conquest of Poland, and later, with the establishment of the ghettoes, these councils became the centers of active unarmed resistance. They dealt with aid and with education, since the Nazis prohibited the education of Jewish children in Warsaw in the school years of 1939-40 and 1940-41. The Germans allowed junior school education, within very restricted limitations, to continue from September 1941 until the final massacre of the Jews in Warsaw in 1942.

During those days, the house committees supplied some of these needs by maintaining children's corners, and they employed counselors — young people or adults — from the four buildings around the courtyard, to keep the children busy during the day. The committees occupied themselves not only with aid to individuals and families, but also with culture — a matter of central importance. There was nothing like a lecture, a musical evening, or any other cultural activity, in a cold apartment, on a cup of tea — in fact, there was no tea, only hot water with a little saccharine — to warm the heart of the Jews, in both senses of this expression. This strenuous concentration on cultural affairs was explicitly and quite consciously directed at keeping up the morale — for, if the Nazis were to break people's morale, they would succeed in breaking their souls, and their bodies as well. The stand taken on this issue by the house committees was of immense value in this huge ghetto.

There were occasions when the Nazis took steps which were not only murderous in themselves, but were aimed at increasing people's suffering. Take for example, the issue of pest control. The fumigation of homes against lice, insects and rats sounds a most humanitarian idea. But the Nazis dispatched to the ghetto for that purpose doctors — mostly Polish, but some of them Jewish — who would enter the apartments and take all the sheets and blankets, so that people had nothing with which to cover themselves, and would send them away for fumigation. These items came out of fumigation so worn out and torn, that one could hardly use them. Then the people themselves were taken; they were made to stand in places appointed for delousing humans, were stripped naked, and had their clothes fumigated. All that time, they had to stand naked in the bitter cold of a Polish winter. Then the people were taken to be deloused in hot water, and when they came out they had no means of drying themselves. Instead, they were forced to wear their clothes which had just been fumigated, and were of course still wet. In this state they were brought back to their homes. The consequences were inevitable: plague became widespread and the mortality rate increased.

The house committees tried to offer help on this as well, in order to avoid suffering or to minimize it. They attempted to do this by supplying alternative clothing, bribing the fumigators, and many other *ad hoc* measures. It was not organized by anyone, but grew naturally out of the feelings of the public itself. There were, of course, house committees which proved to be an absolute failure, which were divided among themselves, inefficient, and achieved nothing. But out of over one thousand house committees which

The Sanctification of Life

existed in Warsaw during the ghetto period, the large majority did alleviate suffering and were an expression of initiative and of standing up to the enemy. This expression which we use today, "standing up to the enemy," describing as it does the opposition offered by unarmed Jews during that period, was not unique to the house committees. There had been in pre-war Poland key organizations which looked after children, health, the development of vocational training, and similar activities. After the Nazi conquest, such groups were, of course, disbanded or abolished. But they rose again, or continued with their activities underground, using different names, or sometimes under the same old names. In Warsaw, a union was formed, which was virtually the central body of the house committees and dealt with social work. This organization was called Zetos, the initials of its Polish name. Zetos was headed by a public committee which conducted and supervised its activities and represented the underground Jewish political parties. Thus, social work in the Warsaw Ghetto, which started at the earliest stages and continued throughout the existence of the ghetto, was run largely by the Jewish political underground.

At the head of the Zetos in Warsaw stood a very remarkable man, a historian and Joint activist, Dr. Emmanuel Ringelblum, who organized all these activities with the explicit aim of outliving the Germans and of strengthening people's bodies and minds with all the facilities available to him. Among other projects, Ringelblum established, under the aegis of Zetos, an institution named Oneg Shabbat (Festive Meetings on the Sabbath), ostensibly consisting of cultural get-togethers of the intellectual elite of the ghetto. But the real purpose of these Oneg Shabbat meetings was entirely different: the documentation of everything the Nazis did in the ghetto and in the whole of occupied Poland, and not only in Warsaw. Members of Oneg Shabbat poured into their archives materials which chronicled the events of the time, and employed teams of scholars who turned these materials into working documents. One of these documents, a piece of medical research carried out by doctors in the Warsaw Ghetto concerning the effects of hunger on the human body, is still considered a major research paper in this field to this

Jewish Reactions to the Holocaust

very day. It was published in Warsaw after the war.

There were also sociological, economic, cultural, historical, and educational research projects, reports by journalists, and the like. All these documents were lodged in the archives, and eventually were put into three large milk cans which were buried under the ghetto. Two of these milk cans were discovered after the war, and what we have narrated here is largely based on the materials found in these two thirds of the Oneg Shabbat archive unearthed so far. The third can has not yet been found. It is likely that it is still buried somewhere underneath the area which was once the Warsaw Ghetto.

This activity was organized to a large extent by the Joint, which in Poland had a very different character from that of the American Joint. The Joint in the United States was at that time an organization for aiding Jews, run on behalf of the Jews of America by rich, assimilated Jews whose loyalty to the State Department and to American policy was unimpeachable, and who would do nothing contrary to American law, as interpreted by the State Department.

In Warsaw, on the other hand, there was a different group of people, who had indeed been appointed by the American Joint before the war, but once they became isolated after the German conquest, were virtually independent. This group consisted mainly of people with leftist leanings and the large majority of them were Zionists. Ringelblum belonged to the Left Poalei Zion, a Zionist-Marxist group, and others were members of the Bund, or of other left-wing Zionist groups. These people regarded as their task doing their utmost to rescue the Jewish population economically and socially. At first, before the United States entered the war in December 1941, they received valuable help from the American Joint. It was illegal to transfer money; but in a very complex roundabout way, with the connivance of the Germans, money, which in fact belonged to the Joint, was transferred into Poland through the Jews of Germany, Austria and Czechoslovakia. This was only part of the financing. More money was provided by the Polish aid organization, with which the Joint was on very good terms; and, although this, too, was only a small part of the needs

The Sanctification of Life

and a very modest contribution, it still helped. Much money came from Jews in Poland itself. The Joint addressed the Jews of Poland with the following argument: "Your money is worthless now anyway, and you stand to lose everything; give us your money now, and we will return it to you in dollars after the war." And people did donate money. One should not have a rosy, unrealistic picture of this affair. All that the Joint collected, for example, in 1940, was about 14 million zloty, which at the time amounted to $150,000-200,000. The sums were very small in relation to the minimal needs, and they were collected with tremendous effort; but there can be no doubt that these meager finances saved many lives throughout Poland, and especially in Warsaw.

Yet the Joint was unsuccessful in saving the refugees. In Warsaw alone, out of a population of about 400,000-500,000 Jews in the ghetto, about 150,000 — that is, one third or more of the whole ghetto population — were refugees. Very soon these refugees were unfit for labor, since hunger had drained away their physical strength, and they were unable to go out to work. In addition, there was a scarcity of work, and when work was available, it was given to the residents of Warsaw, who were familiar with the circumstances and lived in houses. The refugees did not live in houses. They were put in old cinemas, schoolrooms which were now unused, synagogues and the basements of houses, all without any heating and with broken windows, through which the cold of the Polish winter, 20-25 degrees below zero Centigrade, penetrated.

The refugees had no clothes or food. Then, plagues broke out in the Warsaw Ghetto — and they began even before the ghetto was established; however, the worst period was in the ghetto, in 1941, when about 43,000 people perished: that is, about 10% or more of the population of the ghetto died in one year. One is not even certain that this is the accurate figure — it may have been higher. Most of those who died were refugees.

The soup offered in the charity kitchens organized in the ghetto by the Joint was simply insufficient. The few calories added to their diet by the Joint soup mainly helped those people who still had a chance to live. To the refugees, or to most of them, this was of no help. The Joint failed completely in saving the lives of the refugees; but there is no doubt that it helped the others.

Something similar happened with the children. Here, the initiative came from the Judenrat, and from organizations connected both to the Judenrat and to the underground, such as the organization for the rescue of children named Centos, whose head at the time was Dr. Adolf Bermann. This organization saved some of the children through the children's homes it established and through its attempts at educating orphans, who were running free in the streets without anyone to look after them. But there were still thousands of children roaming through the streets of the ghetto with no one to help them or to offer them succor. There simply was no money, no food, no housing and no clothing.

Jewish perseverance was very intensive and, one could say, extremely courageous. People worked far beyond their physical strength in order to save what could still be saved. If we point out that they did not succeed in saving many people, that is no criticism. We simply point out the fact that an attempt was made, but that it was incapable of succeeding.

Similar things could be said about the problem of health. There was a woman in the Warsaw Ghetto, Ljuba Bilecka, the wife of one of the leaders of the Bund, the anti-Zionist socialist movement in Poland, who continued to organize a school in the ghetto for nurses. These nurses sacrificed their own lives when they treated the victims of the typhoid plague. They went everywhere together with the doctors, and many of them became infected; but although some died of typhoid, the others continued to treat the patients. The nurses' school continued to exist until the end of the ghetto and the expulsion from Warsaw. It was even successful in saving people during the expulsion itself, when nurses appeared in their white uniforms, and here and there, in a number of cases, this made an impression on the Germans.

Other aspects of life in the ghettoes should be mentioned in this context of standing up to the enemy — for example, religious life. The Nazis prohibited any official form of religious life in any fashion whatsoever in the first two years of the occupation. But in

The Sanctification of Life

the Warsaw Ghetto alone, Ringelblum counted at least 600 minyanim (small congregations for prayer purposes). One aspect of the endeavors to keep up morale and to maintain moral values, both Jewish and universal, was intense religious activity, whose aim was the same — maintaining the spirit, since a powerful spirit would keep the body alive.

The continuation of religious life is described in many of the documents, as is education. There was no formal education, and children walked the streets while there was nothing one could do about them. There were some children who were lucky enough to have a slice of bread to eat. Beside those children included in the children's corners organized by the house committees, there were some who were organized into what were called *kompletts* - not in the sense of "whole" or "complete," but in the sense of "group." These *kompletts* were joined by former teachers who no longer had schools to teach in, and they gathered the children into private houses and taught them, camouflaging their activity in various ways. These teachers were usually paid with slices of bread. That was how teaching was organized - not centrally planned, but arising spontaneously. Sometimes, this education was organized by house councils, sometimes by groups of parents, and sometimes by groups of the children themselves. Here and there, former teachers from the same school came together and arranged for an organized network of such classes, which operated in the mornings, afternoons or evenings. The aim was to teach the children in order to give them some employment and to prepare them for the future.

The Zionist youth movements, especially the pioneer left-wing ones, occupied themselves with education in a more organized manner. Thus, for example, there was an underground school run by the Dror movement, which prepared young men and women for the Polish matriculation examinations. No pens, of course, were available. One wrote with pencils, and the questions were based on pre-war model examinations. But teaching went on in the most studious manner, in basements and other hiding places. The pupils studied and passed their examinations.

These endeavors at education were signs of great optimism.

Jewish Reactions to the Holocaust

People believed that they were to survive, and that, in the future, they would have something to show for what they had done during this terrible war period. Until quite late, people could not believe that they were not to survive, and the great concentration of effort in education is evidence of this.

Perhaps the most outstanding and impressive example of unarmed resistance occurred in an entirely unorganized area: economic life. Beside the official workshops run by the Judenrat in concert with the Germans, many "black" workshops arose inside the ghetto. People organized themselves underground, obtained the machinery and began to produce brushes, clothes, metalware and products made of recycled garbage. The gatekeepers of the ghetto were bribed, and they allowed Polish trucks to enter the ghetto, supply the raw materials and take out the finished products. This economic organization, though, did not include the refugees. Large sectors of the ghetto were hungry. But this was still an impressive attempt to stand up to Nazi pressure.

Later on, there was the need to exchange products of the ghetto for outside products, and the main problem was how to get food into the ghetto. Everything was controlled, there were gates, and the Germans did not allow anything to enter. The answer was smuggling. Smuggling created a semi-aristocracy of professional smugglers, who were corrupt, but was vital for saving the ghetto from starvation. One way of smuggling food into the ghetto was by using children, who squeezed through the cracks in the ghetto wall beyond it, into the Polish city. There, they exchanged anything they had in hand - products they brought or stole, or the little money they could take out of the ghetto. Many of these children fell victim to bullets of Nazi guards. But this resistance of the Jewish child, this powerful will to live and to save the family from hunger with one's own body, by smuggling food on one's own person, was a unique phenomenon. If one discusses Holocaust monuments, it would be proper to raise one of those monuments to the Child Smuggler. Such a monument, it seems to me, would give the clearest and finest expression to the whole issue of Jewish unarmed resistance. which we have surveyed in some detail in this chapter. It is also, perhaps,

The Sanctification of Life

the only manner in which we can honor the memory of these children today.

IX.

The Decision to Murder the Jews — First Reactions

After its conquest by the Nazis in June 1940, France became the only country in Western Europe ruled by the Nazis to which the Allies had access, for its southern part was not occupied by German troops. The new French government, which cooperated with the Germans, had its seat in that southern section of France, and was called the Vichy Government, named after the city of its residence. At its head stood the aging Marshal Henri Philippe Petain. The Jews were immediately made into second and third-class citizens, but the French government tried, at least at the beginning, to distinguish between a merely hostile attitude to veteran French Jews and real persecution of those Jews who were in France as refugees, or who were born in France of immigrant parents. The latter was interpreted to apply mainly to people who had been granted French nationality after 1927. In the first stages, about 15,000-18,000 foreign Jews, mostly refugees from Germany and Austria, were interned in the French concentration camps which had been erected for enemies of the regime. Beside these Jews, these camps also contained numerous Republican Spaniards, non-Jewish Germans, enemies of the Nazi regime, and the like. Among these interned Jews was also a large group, numbering about 7,700 people, which had been expelled from western Germany to France in October 1940. These people were subject to terrible suffering in the French concentration camps, where not a single Nazi guard was in

The Decision to Murder the Jews — First Reactions

evidence.

The problem was how to assist these Jews — and one must remember that the American embassy in Vichy France was still open, and there were full diplomatic relations between the two countries. The difficulty lay in finding local forces which could come to the rescue with the aid of external Jewish forces. Here, the Joint made some real contributions. It assisted Jewish and non-Jewish groups which came together in the town of Nimes, a small town in the south of France. This committee was named after it — the Nimes Committee. The committee decided to offer help to the inmates of those camps. At the head of the committee stood a Baltic princess, who was, of all things, a member of the Quakers, that Christian sect which did so much to help the Jews during that period. But the most picturesque figure on this committee was Father Alexandre Glasberg, the abbot of one of the French monasteries. Glasberg was a Ukrainian Jew who had converted to Christianity. He acted as a representative of the French Cardinal Pierre Gerlier of Lyons, and together with a Jesuit priest named Pierre Chaillet, dedicated himself to assisting the Jews. One should note that these two, at least, did not act in order to be rewarded by Jewish conversions to Christianity, and that they dealt mainly with children. For a year and a half, until 1942, the Nimes Committee succeeded in extracting Jewish children from of the camps, and anyone who came out was saved from eventual deportation. Once the deportations to Poland and to the death camps began, the prisoners in these camps were like birds in cages, and they could be taken to be transported any time. Only those who had been taken out of these camps before 1942 escaped that fate. This rescue operation was, of course, the result of aid proffered by the French population. The churches, both Catholic and Protestant; various organizations, Jewish and non-Jewish, including some in the United States; and French-Jewish aid organizations — all made their contributions to this operation. What we have here is a rescue operation which was conducted, still with no knowledge that people were being delivered from death. In the eyes of the rescuers, this was an operation for saving Jews from persecution.

Jewish Reactions to the Holocaust

One should point out again that during that period, 1940-41, there was still no information concerning large-scale mortality and mass murder, since these things were not yet happening. The United States still maintained diplomatic relations with Germany, and during the whole of this period not a single American protest was launched against what was already happening: the ghettoes in Eastern Europe, hunger, plague and the persecution in the west and in the whole of Europe. This absence of any reaction shows that the Americans did not understand or appreciate that they were being faced with a phenomenon which was to bring about disaster, not only to the Jews, but sooner or later to the whole of non-Nazi mankind.

On the contrary, in June 1941 the United States tightened the limitations on immigration to such an extent that even those who had some relatives under Nazi rule could not enter the United States, and the gates were almost hermetically sealed. During that very period, the Nazis were still permitting the emigration of Jews from Western and Central Europe, and there was nothing to prevent the rescue of these Jews from the most stringent persecution except for the American policy, which closed the gates of emigration while they were still open in Europe. The main reason for this was connected with security: a perception, similar to that of the British in the Aliyah B affair, of Nazi agents who might infiltrate into America. One should add to this fact that in 1939-1940, antisemitism in the United States in general and in the State Department in particular was on the ascendant. There were also some conservative forces who were apprehensive of the Nazis, and antisemites (and these two are not necessarily identical), who sealed off America almost completely. The only avenue left was the obtaining of visas, mostly forged, to South and Central America. And indeed, until October 1941, Jews continued to leave Germany, Austria and other countries in the west for Spain and Portugal, and these were the last Jews who managed to leave Europe and arrive in the western hemisphere.

When did the Nazis decide on the total liquidation of the Jews? This is, of course, a central question, and although it is only part of

The Decision to Murder the Jews — First Reactions

the background of our own subject, since we are dealing with Jewish reactions and world attitudes, we can hardly ignore it. Otherwise, we would not be able to understand the motives of those who worked for the rescue of the Jews, as well as of those who refused to have anything to do with this cause.

We can say with certainty that until October 1940 — that is, until a fairly late stage of the war — the Nazis did not know that they were about to murder the Jews of Europe. We know this from the fact that they had other plans for the Jews, as we have already explained. When the decision of the Nazis to invade the Soviet Union finally materialized — a process which began in September 1940 and ended in November of the same year — it was a decision to launch an ideological war: the war against the Soviet Union was no economic war. The Soviets were ready to give the Germans whatever they demanded, as long as they did not attack them. It was a war which the Nazis launched in order to suppress and liquidate what they regarded as the last great obstacles in the way of their domination of Europe — "Jewish Bolshevism." From the Nazi point of view, this was a regime run by the Jews and forming part of the international Jewish conspiracy. The Nazis sincerely believed in this nonsense, and their attack on the Soviet Union was thus an ideological war, aimed in the last resort at the Jews.

It is thus clear that, at this point, the veil was removed and all inhibitions disappeared. The murder of the Jews, which had been implicit in Nazi ideology since the party had been formed, but had had no outside expression and had not penetrated into people's consciousness (except, perhaps, Hitler's, but not anyone else's), and had not appeared in any practical program — this murder of the Jews now reached the stage of consciousness and hence passed to the operational stage.

Another reason for the decision to carry out mass murder was that the Nazis believed that the Soviet Union contained another five million Jews. It was clear that one could not expel so many millions of people to an island near the coast of Africa. What is more, Madagascar was not in German hands. The British had not surrendered, and the British navy still ruled the seas, so that the

Jewish Reactions to the Holocaust

Germans could not carry out the Madagascar program. Another reason for the Nazi decision to murder the Jews was that the Americans had not protested against what had been done to the Jews until that time. There was thus no obstruction offered by the public opinion of a neutral superpower. Mass murder, which had been implicit in Nazi ideology, could thus now reach the stage of planning and operation.

In May 1941, orders were issued to the spearhead units (the "Einsatzgruppen" — EG) of the S.S., which were now being prepared to invade Russia together with the German armed forces, to kill Jews found in the Soviet areas which were now to be conquered, Gypsies, and anyone who had been an official of the Soviet regime. It now appears that the original instructions had been somewhat vague and general. From August 1941, the EG's adopted the universal policies of murdering Jews. Most historians believe that the original instruction was at least approved by Hitler, probably in March 1941. This is of great importance, since, if the Nazis themselves did not know until the beginning of 1941 that they were about to murder the Jews of Europe, one could hardly expect the Jews and the free world to have been aware of this. Once the decision concerning mass murder had been taken, it began to be carried out, at first, from June 1941, in the areas of the Soviet Union. By the summer, Hitler appears to have given an oral order to murder all the Jews in Nazi-controlled areas. From the autumn of 1941, preparations were made for extending the mass murder from the Soviet areas to the rest of Europe. At the beginning of December 1941, the death camp in Chelmno, a small town in western Poland, was set in operation. The Jewish victims themselves, of course, knew nothing of this process, and when the first fragmentary news began to seep through, they were a total surprise to the victims themselves and the western world.

The first authoritative piece of information — at least at the official level — reached the external Jewish world on January 6, 1942 — that is, seven months after the operation had begun, and when at least one million Jews had already lost their lives. This was an announcement by the Soviet prime minister of the time,

The Decision to Murder the Jews — First Reactions

Vyacheslav Molotov, published in the Soviet newspaper *Pravda*. It dealt with the murder of Soviet citizens, but for the first time Jews were specifically mentioned. For the first and last time. Later on, they did not point out that Jews were included, even when they talked of areas where the greater part of the population was Jewish.

There had been no precedent to the Holocaust. We know now that the total murder of a people is possible, but people who were alive in 1941-42 had no such knowledge. In their eyes, the news which was beginning to arrive constituted mere war propaganda, and even if it contained some core of truth, the way things were expressed was surely exaggerated. The Soviets, moreover, said nothing of total murder, but only spoke of atrocities. No one imagined that the Soviets had not only not exaggerated, but had given this information much less weight than it deserved. The Jewish world could not believe in mass murder and was unwilling to believe in it, since this would imply that its very existence was being threatened. After all, one was speaking now of the lion's share of the Jewish world at that time, of the nine million Jews who were living in Europe; and if the Nazis had decided to murder the Jews, these were the ones most likely to be affected. This terrible feeling was strongest among those people who received this information. They refused to believe these reports, because they ought not to have been true. This psychological rejection had its roots, not in timidity or in a revulsion from negative or bad news, but because it had such a powerful impact that it might make it impossible to carry on with one's routine life.

This applied even more to the non-Jewish world. Here, one should understand one central point. In 1941-42, the Jewish people in the free world, including Palestine, had no means of assistance and rescue. There was a war on, and the only way to achieve action was to persuade the great powers, whose strength was immense, while Jewish political strength was almost non-existent. Before the entry of the United States into the war, and after it entered the war in December 1941, the Jews had no way of influencing its policy makers. However little this may fit in with out own historical consciousness of the circumstances today, we have to accept this as

Jewish Reactions to the Holocaust

a basic fact. The Jewish public in the United States, and even more so in Britain, had no influence whatsoever. This is now well known to us from our readings of the internal American and British documents of the period.

To the great powers, the Jews were a factor which had no choice but to support them. After all, would the Jews support Hitler? There was only one very small Jewish body which attempted to reach an agreement with the Nazis — the Lehi (LHY — the "Stern Group") underground in Palestine. Its leader, Abraham Stern, believed that by reaching an agreement with the Germans, rebelling against the British, occupying Jewish Palestine and establishing a Lehi dictatorship with the collusion of the Germans to follow, he could bring the Jews of Europe into Palestine. Lehi was then a minuscule group of people, some 100-120 in early 1941, devoid of any influence. The proposal did reach the Germans, in January 1941, but it was not discussed and simply filed away, and the Jewish public at large knew nothing about it. Apart from this little group, there was no one in the whole free Jewish world who put his trust in the prospect of a covenant with Germany for any possible purpose. The British and the Americans were well aware of this. Objectively, the Jews were already committed to the Allied cause, and they were therefore devoid of any real influence.

At the beginning of 1942, the Nazi murder machine began to spread into other countries beside Poland and the Soviet Union. In January 1942, a convention met at Wannsee, a street in one of the suburbs of Berlin, and many people have believed that this is where decision was taken concerning the "Final Solution," the mass murder of the Jews. But we have already pointed out that this had been determined about three quarters of a year earlier and had been in operation since June 1941. At Wannsee, a meeting of the senior officials of the central German ministries took place, and its aim was to lay the foundations of the administrative operation involved in extending the mass murder from the actions by military groups in the Soviet Union to the whole of Europe, an operation requiring trains and extensive administration. The various ministries were required to cooperate. This cooperation of the chief ministries and

The Decision to Murder the Jews — First Reactions

government offices implies that the whole of German high officialdom knew of the mass murder and cooperated in it. The operation itself began before Wannsee and continued after it, chiefly in the towns and cities of Poland, beginning with Lublin and extending to other places.

The Jewish public in Poland reacted to the first reports which reached it concerning this mass murder by sending out signals abroad through the Polish underground. In May 1942, a detailed report by the Bund reached the Polish Government in Exile in London. This report said that the Nazis had decided upon the mass murder of Polish Jewry (it did not speak of European Jewry), and it stated that 700,000 people had already been murdered. The message was passed on to the two Jewish delegates in the Polish National Council in London, Szmuel Siegelbaum, the representative of the Bund, and Isaac Schwarzbard, the representative of the Zionists. These two passed on this information to the BBC, and it was broadcast to the whole world. Thus it reached the United States, Hungary, Poland and all other places.

Those who heard or read the news believed, in most cases, that it was a splendid piece of wartime propaganda, but was, of course, greatly exaggerated. The British minister of propaganda cooperated in a press conference convened by the Polish Government in Exile, which believed in the truth of this report. The Poles unceasingly appealed to the western governments and demanded that they believe that there was no exaggeration in the report. But the British propaganda minister remarked later, in an internal memorandum to the Foreign Office, that this had been an important act of propaganda. The news was also published in the press, including the Jewish press in the United States and in Palestine, with the same headlines. Everything which had been passed on from Poland was fully reported, and no one silenced the publication of the information. But was it possible to believe such things? They could hardly be true. One did not do such things nowadays. Here, in the gap between the report and its psychological acceptance, lies the major point.

Jewish Reactions to the Holocaust

It is important to note that the Polish Government in Exile made immense efforts to spread the news. In October 1942, a messenger of the Polish underground, Jan Karski, a Catholic (today professor emeritus of political science in Washington), arrived in the west. Karski claimed that he had spent a day in the death camp of Belzec with a Gestapo man he had bribed. He had also visited the Warsaw Ghetto. He presented his information to the British foreign secretary, Anthony Eden; to President Roosevelt and to many others. There is no way one could claim that the Polish Government in Exile and Jan Karski tried to conceal the smallest detail. On the contrary, they succeeded eventually in convincing the west that here, indeed, cold-blooded murder was being carried out. But their cry, like that of the Bund representatives before them, fell, if not on entirely deaf ears — it was, indeed, publicized — at least on human minds whose capacity, in 1942, to believe such things was limited. This was the root of the difficulty in initiating real action.

The time gap was also decisive. By their swift action in carrying out the mass murder, the Germans were far more efficient that the slow machinery of the human mind, which takes its time between receiving information and absorbing it as real knowledge. By the time all this reached the incipient stages of consciousness and operation, the Jews who should have been rescued were no longer among the living. As Stephen S. Wise, the leader of the Zionist movement in the United States, put it: "You tell us that the Jews will be saved by victory in this war; but by that time you win the war, there will be nobody left to be saved."

One has to admit that we have no precise information as to how many Jews were murdered by the four EG's of the S.S. in the Soviet Union. They were assisted by units of the regular German forces, by ordinary police battalions, by special mobile S.S. forces subject to Himmler's personal command, and by local forces — Ukrainians, Belorussians and Balts — which were either set up by the Germans or arose spontaneously, without any plan, and had their share in the murders. We estimate — with the proviso that we may be mistaken here — that from June 1941 until the end of 1942, between 1.4 and 1.5 million Jews were murdered in these Soviet territories.

The Decision to Murder the Jews — First Reactions

This fact is horrifying precisely because we possess no exact figures. The implications is that we are speaking here of a margin of error of tens of thousands, or hundreds of thousands, of people. There is now no way of ascertaining the exact numbers of those killed. Heading the EG's stood four commanding officers, three of them with doctorates or a university education. The actual task of murdering the Jews was entrusted to the National Socialist intelligentsia. One should note that these EG's were not comprised purely of members of the Gestapo: they included ordinary policemen, army clerks, other people who were not fit for battle and were given easier tasks, and members of the S.S.

Another point should be made here. The usual form which these murders took was a surprise attack on a town or city. The people were dragged out in a mass, usually without any possibility for rescue on the part of the local Jewish leadership. The Germans came and took everyone who was known to be a Jew, or called on people to present themselves; and, since these people did not know what the purpose of this roll call was, they came. No one imagined that the purpose was mass murder, so they came. The Jews usually believed that the aim was to transfer them to another place, as was the usual practice with the non-Jewish residents, many of whom were taken away to do forced labor. The Jews were murdered, either with machine guns or by gas poisoning in specially constructed lorries.

This method of using gas and lorries was, in fact, a sequel to what had taken place in Germany itself still earlier. Since the beginning of the war in September 1939, the Nazis had practiced what they called "mercy killings." These "mercy killings" were nothing but the planned murder of Germans by the Nazis. People who suffered from hereditary diseases, the mentally ill, and sometimes criminals who were considered beyond rehabilitation, were transported to special institutes and were murdered there by gassing. The program also included Jews, but the Jews were usually murdered because they fell into one of those categories. The large majority of these people were Germans. In this fashion, between 70,000 and 100,000 people were murdered before the churches, both Protestant and Catholic, woke up to this affair and began to protest. It is interesting that these protests by the churches did help, and in August 1941 — that is, exactly in the period with which we have been dealing, soon after the invasion of the Soviet Union — these mercy killings were stopped, at least officially (they went on sporadically throughout the war and even later). The Nazi teams which had performed these killings served as the nucleus of the teams now in charge of murdering the Jews. Their methods — mercy killing by means of poison gas — were the same methods and the same techniques used for murdering the Jews of Eastern Europe.

We must now deal with the extension of the area of mass murder, when, toward the end of 1941, the Nazis began their preparations for the murder of the Jews by large scale methods. From August 1941, we have the evidence of Rudolf Hoess, the commander of the concentration camp at Auschwitz, a camp which had hitherto been used for the internment of Polish prisoners. Hoess said that he was ordered to prepare his camp for the mass murder of Jews. We have testimony referring to September 1942, concerning the first, experimental murder by gas at Auschwitz, not of Jews, but of Soviet prisoners. Afterwards, the buildings were made ready, and apparently the murder of the Jews continued until early in 1942. In March-April 1942, mass killings by gas began at Auschwitz. The gas used was a derivative of prussic acid, whose commercial name was Zyklon B. In other death camps, other gases were used.

Mass murder in permanent installations began at Chelmno in the west of Poland, in the area annexed to Germany by the Nazis. There, in December 8, 1941, the murder began of Jews living in that area. The victims were loaded on lorries with hermetically sealed passenger compartments, and the gases emitted by the motor were channelled into the passenger compartments. Six extermination camps were then erected: Auschwitz, Chelmno, Belzec, Treblinka, Sobibor, and Majdanek near Lublin. At the latter four camps, permanent buildings were used, and the gas was pumped into concrete cells. We have used the word "extermination" only in this particular context, dealing as it does with the extermination camps, as they were called by the murderers themselves. But one should

The Decision to Murder the Jews — First Reactions

note that this term, "extermination," was a Nazi concept. In normal language, one speaks of exterminating germs or parasites, but when one speaks of people, the proper word is murder. We should therefore avoid using the term "extermination" altogether to describe what happened in the Holocaust, and use the proper term, the murder of Jews.

From the Wannsee Conference of January 1942 onwards, murder was no longer the work of S.S. men alone, but extended to include all echelons of German bureaucracy. This is, perhaps, the place to raise another issue connected with this affair, which is still subject to controversy and should be clarified. Who else was involved in the murder of Jews? We have already mentioned the S.S., assisted by army units — this despite the allegations of the commanders of the army after the war that the army was entirely innocent of this affair. Others who cooperated in this murder, as we have mentioned, were the staffs of various government offices in Germany. The man officially responsible for the whole policy was Hitler's deputy, Hermann Goering, who was in charge of both the Nazi air force and all the economic affairs of Germany. He was the man who issued the official instruction to Heydrich, as early as July 1941, to have everything prepared for the "Final Solution" of the Jewish problem in Europe. It is reasonable to assume — although this was denied by Goering after the war — that he received all the detailed reports, since officially the order of command was Hitler, Göring, and then Himmler or Heydrich. In practice, things were decided between Hitler, Himmler and Heydrich; but Göring was anxious to have a hand in this affair, which was so important and central to the Reich's policies.

From the beginning of 1942, the mass murder was extended to all parts of Europe, and the Jews were faced with something which had never before happened in history and for which they were unprepared. In order to understand the Jewish reaction, we must bear in mind that in the whole affair of the Holocaust, we come up against the problem of people's psychological inability to accept the reports for what they were and to internalize them. The mere fact of receiving the information was hardly sufficient, since this was so utterly incredible, so entirely remote from any human experience before this period. We, living as we do in the generation after the Holocaust and knowing for certain that it did take place, find it difficult to comprehend the lack of reaction and the absolute shock on the part of people who heard of it for the first time.

Let us take an example. We are now in possession of the testimonies of people ho worked as laborers in the gas chambers of Auschwitz, dealt with the corpses, and in a miraculous way managed to survive. These people tell us how the Jews arrived at the gas chambers. It seems that, by 1942-43, the inmates should have known about the mass murder, since news about it had already infiltrated into the outside world. But those who have survived tell us that the people were utterly surprised and in a state of absolute shock: they simply did not believe their eyes. If this is true of people who were eye witnesses to the Holocaust, what can we expect of those who only heard of it?

The immense speed of the performance of these mass murders and the slowness of the reaction to it are two sides of the same coin. The slow reaction originated in that gap between information and awareness, between receiving the information and internalizing it. Even in Poland itself, it was difficult for the Jews to believe what they were told. The first to give credence to the news were members of the Jewish youth movements.

The first reaction which aimed at using armed resistance came from the Zionist youth movements in Vilno, the capital of Lithuania, which was now in that Soviet territory captured by the Germans soon after their invasion of the Soviet Union. Even there, it took some time — almost until the end of 1941 — before the first news about the murder of Jews, which had already taken place in Vilno itself from July 1941 on, reached the inner city. At that time, some women who had escaped from the firing trenches reached Vilno. Among them was a woman who escaped toward the end of 1941 and was hospitalized in the ghetto. This woman told the news to the head of the ghetto, but she drew no reaction from him. Meanwhile, the news also reached Abba Kovner, the central figure in Hashomer Hatza'ir in Vilno, who was then in hiding in a Polish

The Decision to Murder the Jews — First Reactions

nunnery near the city. Kovner arrived in the ghetto from his hiding place, assembled the members of the youth movements, and told them, based merely on the information he had received regarding Vilno, that the Jews of Europe were being subjected to wholesale murder, and that this, he believed, was part of a general program. This was, admittedly, only an intuition, a guess, but he was convinced of the truth of his analysis. His conclusion was that one had to prepare for rebellion. One had to offer armed resistance, since there was no other way. This personal intervention of one individual, who had no evidence of documents or testimonies, but merely sensed, on the meager evidence, that here he was faced with an overall plan, was the first breakthrough in the direction of armed resistance.

This, of course, was not enough, and Kovner needed a public which would trust him and accept his message. The message was given on the night of December 31, 1941, at a meeting of members of the youth movements in the ghetto. After many doubts and perplexities, people accepted his view. The fact that this view was accepted by young people, and young Zionists at that, is of considerable interest.

The immediate conclusion was that one should set up an underground organization which, despite the terrible obstacles, would attempt to gather arms and prepare for armed resistance inside the Vilno Ghetto.

X.

The Western World and News of the Holocaust

Considering the little credence given to the first report, in May-June 1942, of a planned massacre of the Jews of Poland, one can hardly be astonished at the fate of the second report. This was the famous telegram sent by Dr. Gerhart Riegner, Secretary of the World Jewish Congress in Geneva. On August 1, 1942, Dr. Riegner received information from a Swiss Jewish journalist named Segalowicz, who had received it from a Swiss industrialist, who had heard it, in turn, from a German industrialist with access — so he claimed — to the German economic and military leadership. The information was that, in the autumn of 1942, the Germans were planning a general massacre of the Jews of Europe by means of a certain poison gas. From this source, it appeared that no massacre of the Jews of Europe had taken place before that date, although we know now that it had begun a year and two months earlier. But Riegner's information stated that the massacre was planned by Hitler for a future date. Riegner's cable containing these items also said that Riegner himself was not certain about the information he had received, and implied that he wished it to be verified. The telegram was despatched on August 8 — that is, a week after Riegner had received his information. It appears that here we are up against the same phenomenon. Was the murder of a whole people possible? Such a thing had to be checked.

This affair of the Riegner cable gave rise to a whole detective

The Western World and News of the Holocaust

industry. For years, scholars and historians tried to track down the name of the German who volunteered this information. Throughout this time his name was not discovered, as Dr. Riegner refused to disclose it. Only recently, after three different historians pieced together the identity of the man, did Dr. Riegner confirm that he was Dr. Eduard Schulte, the head of the Giesche Mining company, one of the leading German mining firms. Schulte, though, was of no particular importance. He had merely heard the news and felt it his duty to warn the Jews that something of the sort was about to happen. His information was not even precisely true, since the massacre had begun over a year earlier and was no longer a matter of planning for the future.

When Riegner sent his telegram to the United States and Britain, he asked in it that the Jewish leaders be informed. The British did pass the information to the head of the British office of the World Jewish Congress, Sydney Silverman, MP, but the Americans refused to pass on the telegram to Stephen Wise, as Riegner had asked them to do. When Wise discovered the contents of the telegram from Silverman in England, he hurried to the State Department. But there he was told: Look at the telegram itself. Riegner himself believed that the matter requires investigating. We do not want to create panic as long as we do not know that this is the truth. We have been asked to check the facts, and this is just what we are doing. Until we have our facts clarified, we ask you not to publicize this telegram.

Wise did not publicize the telegram, and he did not even mention Riegner's name. But he made speeches and published articles in which he spoke of the threat to the lives of the Jews in Europe, without mentioning the telegram itself. His words reached Germany, and in November 1942 Himmler sent a letter to the head of the Gestapo: "Rabbi Wise is stating in public in the United States that we are massacring the Jews. One has to put a stop to the spread of this news."

In Palestine, too, people did not believe that such a mass murder was possible. The information which arrived there before August 1942 was published, but with reservation. The information was not concealed, and no one hushed it up, intentionally or unintentionally. At the same time, these reports were often published with qualifications, or in such a manner as to make it clear to the reader that he was faced with a piece of news which had not been verified or proven to be correct. In Palestine, too, the same psychological obstacles which we have witnessed elsewhere were operating.

Eventually, this piece of information broke through the bounds of credibility, and both the great powers and the Jews accepted it as the simple truth. The chief factor in this change of mind was Karski, whom we have already mentioned, and who had an immense influence on the Poles and the British and did his best to demonstrate the truth of these reports. Furthermore, the deputy director of the International Red Cross at the time, Professor Carl Burckhardt of Switzerland, met the American consul in Geneva in early November 1942 and confirmed these reports. There was a third source of information on the massacres going on, but it was influential only in Palestine. We refer here to sixty nine people, mainly women and children, mostly Palestinians or married to Palestinians, who reached Palestine as part of the exchange of citizens. In exchange for these individuals, Germans from Palestine were transferred to Germany. The Jews arrived in Palestine on November 19, 1942. A few days later, horrifying news, printed inside a black frame, appeared in all the papers of Palestine: *A Wholesale Massacre of the Jewish People in Europe*. The reaction of the Jewish community of Palestine to this mass murder is subject to controversy even today. It appears that the reaction veered between two extremes; and, whereas earlier on people had refused to believe the story altogether, now everyone was shrouded in black despair. The leadership of the Yishuv (the Palestine Jewish community) came to be reluctant to believe that a single Jew would still be alive in Europe by the end of the war. This found expression in many of the speeches made in the rescue committee of the Jewish Agency, then headed by Yitzhak Gruenbaum. Gruenbaum himself said on one occasion that whatever one was doing, was only done in order to have a clear conscience and know that something had been done,

The Western World and News of the Holocaust

but he did not believe that anything could help any longer.

The objective difficulties were that the Jewish community in Palestine had no influence on the policy-making forces in Britain and the United States. The way to Europe was closed by the sea, the war and the armies, and the only way to reach Europe was by means of the British army. The British army did not go out of its way to make it possible for the Jews to help their brethren in Europe. As early as January 1943 — that is, as soon as the new information arrived — the Jewish Agency tried to persuade the British to send parachutists into Europe. The British turned a large-scale plan, involving the dispatch of large numbers of paratroops to arouse the Jews of Europe to resistance, into a minuscule operation of sending a small group of Jews to Cairo to train as parachutists. Even this plan was not put into operation until autumn 1943, when the first of these Jews were indeed parachuted into Europe — but not to areas under Nazi rule where Jews were still to be found, but to an area held by Tito's partisans and to Rumania. A larger group was parachuted in 1944, when the majority of Jews were no longer alive, and the parachutists' mission was of no avail.

One can see the pendulum swinging between despair and a powerful desire to go out and try to rescue whoever could be rescued. This can be seen especially among the members of the military underground movements, especially the Palmach (the shock troops of the Haganah) and the IZL. These tried to find ways to aid in the rescue, but without any results, since there was simply no way. This underlines the political impotence of the Palestine Jewish community, and of the Jewish people of that period as whole. Hence the chief reaction was despair.

Following the receipt of this information, and once the truth of the massacre had been accepted, the Allied powers — especially Britain and the United States — declared that the Jews were, indeed, being murdered and that the criminals would be punished.

Such a declaration was read out in the British parliament on December 17, 1942, and all the powers and countries fighting against Germany endorsed it. At the proposal of one of its members, the whole British parliament stood up — for the first and only time in its history — in honor of the Jewish victims. But once the members had stood up in silence for one minute, they sat down again. It was one thing to honor the Jewish victims, but it was quite another matter to do something to rescue those who were still not victims.

On this issue, there was a difference between Britain and the United States. In Britain, public opinion began to press for the rescue of the Jews. Pressure groups were formed in parliament. The Catholic Cardinal Arthur Hinsley and the Anglican Archbishop of Canterbury appeared at the Foreign Office to be a serious danger, since they were pressing for concrete action for the rescue of Jews. A group of members was organized in the House of Lords and in the lower house, chiefly under the leadership of Eleanor Rathbone, who was then MP for Oxford. She organized a group for the defence of victims of the Nazis, and put pressure on the government to come up with concrete actions. The press joined this campaign, and letters from all over Britain began to swamp the newspapers, the Foreign Office and the Home Office — letters from priests, trade unions and private citizens, the overall tone of which was: We are willing to absorb in our house a Jewish child, or any person who is persecuted by the Nazi regime, whether Jewish or not.

The British government "bravely" weathered the pressures put on it to save the Jews, and staunchly refused to act. It refused to enter into negotiations with the Germans concerning the rescue of Jews; it was not prepared to release ships for that purpose; it was not prepared to break its embargo regulations and send food and products to the European ghettoes — in brief, it refused to do anything but make empty gestures.

Britain appealed to the United States and demanded some token action, because of public pressure on the government. In the United States, the situation was different. Public opinion was divided. There were some organizations which attempted to create favorable public opinion, but this had not yet reached the stage of strong and persistent pressure on the American government; since it was not subject to the same pressures as the British government, it was not willing to go out of its way and take action. But as the months

The Western World and News of the Holocaust

passed, by January-March 1943, pressure was growing in American public opinion as well. It was then agreed to convene a secret conference, in a place where journalists were unlikely to arrive, and thus the Bermuda Conference began. This Anglo-American Conference was convened to deal with refugees of the Nazis. It spoke explicitly of refugees — that is, people who had already left the areas of Nazi domination — not of those who were still threatened with massacre in Nazi Europe itself.

By sheer accident, this conference was convened on the same day when the Warsaw Ghetto uprising began, April 19, 1943. The delegates of the two governments reached a truly idyllic unanimity: There was nothing which could be done; no negotiations could be entered into — and the conclusions of the conference should not be published. There were no conclusions, but the conclusions which had not been reached should not be published. The one thing agreed on was the re-establishment of the Inter-Governmental Committee for Refugees which had been set up in Evian, as we have already related. It was also decided to establish a refugee camp in North Africa, in Fedalla and then in Philippeville, for Jewish refugees who had already reached Spain and who were to be evacuated, in order to assist Spain in absorbing additional refugees who were likely to cross the Pyrenean border. This decision was presented as extremely important. At the end, after a long controversy between Britain and America, the Americans did set up this refugee camp. Altogether, a few hundred Jewish refugees were transferred into it from Spain. This was the very little mouse to which the great mountain of the Bermuda Conference gave birth.

The terrible thing about the Bermuda Conference was not the decision itself, but the mere fact that this was an attempt to fool public opinion in the two great powers and to hint to the people of both states that something significant had been decided, but on account of the war and the need for secrecy, it was not to be disclosed to the public. The conference took place in April 1943, and during this year news was arriving that the massacre was taking larger dimensions. The information which arrived now was reliable and accepted even by the western governments. Together with them

Jewish Reactions to the Holocaust

one hears of new plans for rescue, some of them more fantastic than others. One of them was based on information arriving from Rumania, according to which the Rumanian Commissar for Jewish Affairs had met the local representatives of the Zionist movement in December 1942, and offered to "sell" them 70,000 Jews for an incredible sum of money. He proposed to transport these Jews from that part of the Soviet Union now occupied by Rumania, through Odessa and Constantinople to Palestine, or to any other place determined by the western powers. This report reached the west and was published in the *New York Times* in February 1943. What the *New York Times* and the Jews did not know was, that as soon as the Rumanian antisemitic Commissar for Jewish Affairs, Radu Lecca, had spoken with the Jews, the German embassy in Bucharest intervened and immediately nullified the whole affair, preventing any further negotiations on this plan. A few days after it had been proposed, this plan was no longer real — but this, of course, was not known in the west.

The information was also received in the office of the World Jewish Congress in America, and Nahum Goldmann and others put pressure on the State Department to do something — at least, to send some money to Switzerland, in order to assist in the rescue of Jews from Rumania. The Jewish Agency for Palestine also attempted to persuade Britain to take this plan seriously. But the Allies had formulated a strict doctrine, according to which no dollars were to be paid to the Nazis for the Jews, whether as a bribe or as ransom. This doctrine became so firmly embedded in the Allies' policies that when the World Jewish Congress suggested that a rescue fund of ten million dollars be established, the Americans managed to delay this affair for many months, and eventually to turn this large-scale program of financial aid to a pathetic grant of 25,000 dollars, which were passed to Dr. Riegner in Geneva to use as he found fit. This was nine or ten months after the proposal had been made in December 1943.

Throughout 1943, the American State Department did everything it could to prevent any real assistance to the Jews. It even came to the point where the State Department sent instructions to

The Western World and News of the Holocaust

the United States minister in Switzerland, Leland Harrison, not to transmit to the United States any more messages from Riegner. The department simply did not want to know or to hear of it. Meanwhile, an interesting change took place in American public opinion. Various organizations, including the official Zionist movement, and especially a delegation of the IZL which was operating in the United States, published the facts in the press and through churches and public bodies. The news about the fate of the Jews in Europe began to accumulate, and a slow but certain change in American public opinion began taking shape.

A small group of officials in the department of the treasury, none of them Jewish, including John Pehle, Josiah E. DuBois, Jr., and Raymond Paul — whose names are worthy of mention in this context — reached the conclusion, in the middle of 1943, that the State Department was supporting the mass murder of the Jews of Europe by its silence and lack of initiative, while any initiative might lead to the saving of lives. These officials caught the State Department, as it were, with its pants down. In the autumn of 1943, they unearthed the telegram sent to Harrison in Switzerland at the beginning of that year, telling him not to pass on any information. They pieced together the incriminating evidence they had laid their hands on, and composed a memorandum to President Roosevelt. The title of that memorandum was "Report on the Acquiescence of this Government in the Murder of Jews." They came with this memorandum to their superior, the (Jewish) Finance Minister Henry Morgenthau, Jr., and convinced him that the information they possessed was correct and that something had to be done. The memorandum was given another title and was presented to the president in early January 1944. From the American point of view, this was a complete reversal, due to the initiative of three non-Jews who were in positions of power and could wield influence — unlike the Jewish organizations which were begging from door to door with no success.

On January 22, 1944, Roosevelt ordered the setting up of the War Refugee Board (WRB). This body, to which we shall have occasion to return, was undoubtedly something new in American policy. Its mandate was not only to assist the refugees, but also those who were still under Nazi rule. Through this committee, instructions went out to all American institutions, military as well as civilian, to do all to save human life: to supply ships and financial assistance — and there was even a hint at negotiating with the enemy. The United States was consciously breaking all its internal laws in order to assist. Too little, too late — but at least it was done. In practice, of course, the WRB was severely limited by inter-agency rivalry and bureaucratic obstacles.

It appears that here we have something new. The three people who did most of the work were not moved by political interests, since they had none. They were moved by humanitarian feelings. They stood to lose a great deal by this action, but the humanitarian cause prevailed and it became a political decision, in the midst of a war, and contrary to all the war regulations of the United States.

XI.

The Warsaw Ghetto Uprising

In this chapter, we will deal with the preparation for the uprising in the Warsaw Ghetto. But before we do so, it is important to point out that the accepted version of the Holocaust and of Jewish resistance is interpreted by many young Israelis as if there were there were two separate events: the massacre of six million Jews on the one hand, and the Warsaw Ghetto uprising on the other hand — that is, six million were massacred and only seven hundred and fifty fought. That is quite wrong. Uprising and resistance assumed far wider dimensions, although it would be true to say that the uprising and rebellion in a place like the Warsaw Ghetto, in which there had been about 400,000 Jews before the transports to the death camps began, was a very central and important action. Warsaw housed the centers of most of the movements which took part in the resistance. The organization which was eventually set up tried to influence the behavior of Jews not only in the capital, but also in other places in Poland. From that point of view, the Warsaw Ghetto uprising is, indeed, a major event.

News of the mass murder reached the Warsaw Ghetto at the beginning of 1942, in two ways: through women and men who went out from and to the eastern areas as messengers from the youth movements in autumn 1941 and reported on the wholesale murder of Jews in those areas (one of these messengers, Frumka Plotnicka, of the Dror youth movement, brought the major part of this information to Warsaw); and through the testimony of Jacob

Jewish Reactions to the Holocaust

Grojanowski, "the Shoemaker of Chelmno," who escaped from that death camp in late January or early February 1942 and related what his eyes had seen. The youth movements — Dror and Hashomer Hatza'ir — believed that the only assistance they could obtain would be that of the Soviet army. They therefore tried to make contact with the Jewish communists, since they hoped to get Soviet aid through their mediation.

At the very same time, in March 1942, the Polish Communist Party was being reorganized, and, following the line taken at the time by the communists, demanded an immediate rebellion in Poland in order to help the Red Army. One should bear in mind that the decisive majority of the Polish population was anti-communist, and its support was given to the government-led underground with right-wing leanings, an underground which included some socialist and liberal elements which were not antisemitic, but which tended generally to antisemitism.

It was therefore natural that the first outward contact established by the Jewish youth movements was with the communists, who were also represented in the ghetto. In March 1942, a movement called the Anti-Fascist Bloc was set up, headed by the Jewish communists. The Anti-Fascist Bloc was organized underground in small groups and started to train — but it had nothing to train with, since there were no arms in the ghetto. The communist movement outside the ghetto was apparently too weak at the time to be able to supply the ghetto with arms. Just as the bloc began to organize, an order was issued against it by the Germans — one assumes that someone had denounced it — and the bloc was destroyed by Nazi action. A number of communist activists who had been involved in the bloc were arrested and executed. Officially, this movement continued to exist, but in practice, it had been liquidated. This was a very crucial development, since at that very time the Zionist movements were in the throes of a crisis as to the approach to adopt. Their initial attitude up to early 1942 had been that they were educating the young for the possibility that they might outlast the Germans. They should thus be strengthened toward that future, so that they would not lose all their ideals during this war. The

The Warsaw Ghetto Uprising

movements had been preparing the young for self-fulfillment in Palestine — but it now became clear that immigration to Palestine was not to be, since all were doomed to die. The transition was so sharp and horrifying, that one had to adapt oneself quickly to alternative activities and to a new vision of oneself and one's future.

The painful reversal which took place during those months finds expression in the press of the multifarious Jewish underground in the Warsaw Ghetto (published in Hebrew translation by Yad Vashem). One can see in it the transition from an attitude which implied no interest whatsoever in what was happening to the Jews in Poland, since their destination was Palestine and the Jews should rise and go with them; to a new approach, in the light of which these organizations were beginning, for lack of an alternative, to regard themselves as the leadership of local Jewry. The lack of an alternative was due to the fact that the veteran leadership — the Judenraete and the various parties, including the Zionist parties underground — did not regard the time as suitable for an uprising and for armed resistance. An example was the anti-Zionist socialist Bund, whose line was that it would rise up against the Germans, but only once the sign had been given by the Polish Socialist Party. The Polish Socialist Party of course gave no sign, and the Bund maintained that it would not cooperate with the Zionists.

On July 22, 1942, the Germans began to transport the Jews of Warsaw to the death camps of Treblinka. On the second day of these transports, the head of the Judenrat, Adam Czerniakow, took his own life, since he guessed where the Jews were being taken and what fate awaited them. The ghetto remained without a leader. The heads of all parties, from Agudath Israel to the Zionist left and the youth movements gathered together in hiding and discussed the situation. A proposal for resistance was brought up. Most of those present, especially the leaders of Agudath Israel, the General Zionists and the Bund — all, in fact, except for the minuscule left-wing Zionist party, Left Poalei Zion — were of the opinion that the time was not yet ripe for an uprising since there were no arms, and all were doomed to die if they were to offer any resistance. An illusion was being created even among the best people present that

Jewish Reactions to the Holocaust

the Nazis would only take away some of the inmates of the ghetto — and, in any case, it was in no way clear where they were being taken, so why assume that it was to their deaths? The majority of the people were likely to remain, but if there were to be an uprising, everyone would be killed. Rabbi Zusia Friedmann of Agudath Israel said, in profound religious faith: Look, you all rely on the Allies, whereas I rely on a Supreme Power who will come and save the Jews from death. The Zionist youth delegates to this meeting came out of it totally disillusioned regarding their elders. The members of the youth movements decided to set up a fighting underground organization, and a few days after this meeting, at the end of July, the Jewish Fighting Organization (Known by its Polish acronym as ZOB) was established in the ghetto, consisting of members of Hashomer Hatza'ir, Dror, Gordonia and Akiva (a General Zionist youth movement in Poland). The Bund had not as yet joined in.

The youth movements set up an underground — but, as we have said, they had no arms. At the head of the underground stood Yosef Kaplan and Shmuel Braslaw of Hashomer Hatza'ir and Yitzhak Zuckerman (Cukierman) and Mordechai Tennenbaum of Dror. With a tremendous amount of effort, they collected one sack of armaments — five pistols, some hand grenades and incendiaries. They sought, in the first place, to have the traitors inside the ghetto removed. These were people who cooperated with the Germans in rounding up people for transports, and there were two assassination attempts against heads of the Jewish police who did cooperate. Posters were hung on walls: "Do not go to your death." The arms collected were, as we have seen, few and pathetic. During this period of transports, it became increasingly difficult to get out of the ghetto and to smuggle arms into it. A man caught by the Germans gave them the identity of Yosef Kaplan and his place of hiding. A Gestapo car drove in, and Yosef Kaplan was arrested while working at the workshop in which he was registered. The members of the underground tried to remove the arms, and a young woman member went out with them hidden in a vegetable basket. By sheer accident, she was caught by a German patrol, and the arms were discovered. Kaplan's deputy, Shmuel Braslaw, came out into the

The Warsaw Ghetto Uprising

street, was caught by a patrol, pulled a knife on the Germans, and was killed on the spot. On that one day, September 3, 1942, the two chief commanders of the underground were killed and its arms seized. During the course of the big transports from Warsaw, about 265,000 Jews were taken away and another 10,380 died or were killed in the ghetto, 11,580 were sent to forced labor camps, and about 8,000 managed to escape to the "Aryan" (non-Jewish) part of Warsaw.

Thus there was no uprising and there were no arms, and the underground was left without leaders. Some of the surviving members of this underground, who gathered together a few days later, on September 13, 1942, entertained serious thoughts of suicide, or of going into the street and attacking the Germans with no arms. Their leaders, Zvia Lubetkin, one of the heroines of Jewish fighting in Europe, her husband Yitzhak Zuckerman, and Aryeh Wilner, persuaded the youth to carry on — or, in fact, to start afresh.

The youth did reorganize, and in October the Jewish Fighting Organization was set up again. It was joined by the communists, the Bund, and representatives of various Zionist parties. A semi-political body was established and entrusted with negotiations with the Polish underground in order to obtain arms, and messengers were sent to the non-Jewish side of Warsaw to muster arms. The organization's major action was to take charge of the ghetto. The Judenrat had plainly lost all authority and was no longer active; the Jewish police no longer had any power, and toward the end of 1942, arms were beginning to arrive after all. The Joint, as we have mentioned in the previous chapters, aided in raising money, and the underground's authority in the ghetto became stronger. The Jews left in the ghetto — and there is a controversy as to their numbers: it appears that it now stood at 60,000, but some would put it lower than that — fortified themselves in underground bunkers. This implies that they now accepted the line taken by the underground, that transport meant death, and there was no alternative to fighting. With no arms in the hands of the Jewish population, they dug themselves in and were determined not to turn themselves over

Jewish Reactions to the Holocaust

to the Germans. Thus, we are not speaking only of a few hundred young men and women with arms in their hands planning to revolt — the revolt was of the entire ghetto. It is true that only a few hundred young men and women carried arms: 14 rifles, 2-3 light machine guns, a few sub-machine guns, about 500 pistols and hand grenades — and it was with these arms that they fought the German army.

There was a second group in the ghetto: the Jewish Military Organization (ZZW — its Polish acronym). This group had been founded by the Betar movement. The group suffered a major blow when it sent a large number of its members to a village far from Warsaw for training, and the members were caught and executed. The number of those left in Warsaw was very small. There are various and contradictory testimonies, as most of the organization's members were killed, and not a single officer survived the war. The group had two leaders: Pawel Frankel and Moritz Appfelbaum. The head of the political leadership was David Wdowinski, a member of the Revisionist Party in Poland. This organization had ties with two Polish groups, which, while organized within the official right-wing underground, belonged to its liberal wing, and their people were willing to aid the Jews. One of the groups, headed by a Polish major named Henryk Iwanski (whose wife was Jewish), tendered aid of great value to the organization. A considerable portion of the arms mentioned above reached the ghetto through these Poles and ZZW. There was a time in which ZZW was part of the ZOB. Afterwards, though, it split off, because its members were not prepared to accept Mordechai Anielewicz as their commander. In addition, they wished to be accepted in the ZOB as a group, whereas the ZOB insisted that they join up as individuals.

In the end, a compromise was reached, and literally on the eve of the revolt the members of ZZW accepted Mordechai Anielewicz as their commander, so that the two groups fought together. The first attempt at revolt occurred in January 1943, when the Nazis entered the ghetto and attempted to take out 8,000 people. The underground believed that these people were being taken to their

The Warsaw Ghetto Uprising

deaths. Today, we know that at that time the Germans planned to take the people for forced labor, but of course the underground could not know this. In truth, the Germans took out their quota of people (between 6,000 to 6,500), and left the ghetto after doing so, but the underground believed that it was its fighting which had brought about a German retreat from the ghetto. That was incorrect, but what matters is that the underground, as well as the Poles, were convinced that it was the fight put up by a Jewish underground which had stopped the transport out of the ghetto. That did much to strengthen the spirit of resistance among the Jews in the ghetto.

During this action of January 1943, two methods of fighting were employed. One was that of Mordechai Anielewicz, the head of the ZOB. He and some members of Hashomer Hatza'ir marched together with a group of Jews who were being led to the transport trains, and in the midst of this march they fell on the Germans. The only one who survived of this group was Anielewicz himself, who was dragged by someone into the entrance of one of the houses. The Nazis, once they got over their shock, opened fire and killed all the other fighters. The other method was that of the Dror group, a group of fighters which, when it saw the Germans approaching the house it was hiding in, allowed them to enter it, and then fell on them inside the building. This action succeeded, and the Germans retreated. This method was then adopted, and it was also employed in the great uprising.

The fact that the Nazis left the Jews all those months for preparations, rather than entering the ghetto immediately in January 1943 and destroying it — that was what made the uprising possible. When the Nazis decided to liquidate the ghetto, they already knew that there was an underground, since they had already come up against it; and they also knew, from their informers inside the ghetto, that this was not an insignificant organization. Despite this, they were probably convinced that the Jewish uprising would come to a speedy end. Since they were accustomed to carrying out all their large massacres during the Jewish festivals (and they were perfectly familiar with the Jewish calendar, which they followed in

Jewish Reactions to the Holocaust

these actions), they entered the ghetto on Passover eve, 5703, April 19, 1943, with tanks, since they had prepared for a semi-military operation. They met with the strongest resistance, and had to retreat with heavy casualties, including one tank destroyed. They renewed their offensive on the following days, and at first they did not dare enter the ghetto at night. The real, open fighting lasted only about ten days.

In the course of this fighting, there was one day when Iwanski's group entered the ghetto, and eighteen Poles fought for a day beside the fighters of the Revisionist group. They could not bear the burden more than a day, and retreated through the sewers. During these days, open resistance on the ground came to a standstill, since it was utterly impossible to stand up against the force of thousands of S.S. men, policemen and soldiers, who entered the ghetto with heavy equipment. The fighting turned into guerilla warfare, carried out at night. The Nazis set fire to the buildings of the ghetto, to avoid clashes with fighters who were escaping from place to place.

Many fighters remained in underground bunkers and basements while the buildings above caved in on them; when the terrible heat of the fire penetrated into the basements, they were forced to come out, since they could not bear the heat. There were some who jumped into the street from their hiding places in the upper stories. Most people were unwilling to hand themselves over to the Germans, even in the most extreme situations. The Germans therefore had to move from one building to the other and to evacuate the people by force. The ghetto was already on fire, and the Nazis were trying to discover the bunkers. Day after day, week after week, they moved from one place to another, discovered the bunkers and drove their inmates out.

In early May the Germans discovered the central bunker of the high command, where Mordechai Anielewicz and his command staff were staying, and poured poison gas into it. This was the only place during the whole of the Second World War (except for the death camps) in which the Nazis employed poison gas. The men took their own lives in order to avoid death by the poison gas. Only a small group, which discovered at the very last moment a hitherto

The Warsaw Ghetto Uprising

unknown escape route out of the bunker, was saved. These people had not planned to save themselves but to fight to the end, and that is what they did.

The battle lasted for weeks. At the end of May 1943 — that is, after six weeks of fighting — the commander in charge of the Nazi operation declared that the Warsaw Ghetto had given up fighting and that he had called off the operation. But fighting continued in the ruins of the ghetto. We have testimonies which speak of shooting in the ghetto area even as late as October, and very reliable evidence for such occurrences in September. In any case, it is clear that the fighting went on for many weeks. We do not even know who did the fighting, whether it was the remnants of the fighting organizations, or private persons who remained in hiding in the bunkers and obtained arms to defend themselves, to attack the police, or to attempt to reach the non-Jewish area of Warsaw.

This was a great uprising, not only because it was the revolt of the few against the many — there were altogether about 750 armed people against thousands of soldiers of the German army, behind whom stood the huge army which had conquered the whole of Europe — but also because the war fought by these people was conducted for the sake of vengeance on the mass murderers, for the defence of Jewish national honor, and for the future. This was an important factor in the whole battle: to let the Jewish people know that Jews had been there, that Jews knew and that Jews fought. This thought accompanied the fighters until the last stages of the uprising.

Some of the last fighters managed to come out through the sewers. This was not their original plan, but in the course of the fighting they discovered that there was this way out of the ghetto, and there were sewerage workers about who showed them the way. Some drowned in the sewers and others were caught by the Nazis while attempting to come out of the sewers, but there were some who were saved, and tried to carry on their fighting in the forests outside Warsaw. But Warsaw was not surrounded by large forests, and they returned into the city — to the non-Jewish part — and stayed there until the end of the war, trying to organize uprisings and any other forms of armed resistance, based on the model of the Warsaw Ghetto, among Jews in other communities in Poland.

What we have here was a resistance movement which succeeded in rallying the Jews of the ghetto to support it — so much so, that besides the organized 750 fighters, there were hundreds of others, of whose identity and number we have no information, who armed themselves with pistols and with various primitive weapons, and fought the Germans on their own accord and with the means at their disposal. Thus, it was the uprising of a whole ghetto, not just of a group of fighters, however important the organized part of the uprising was.

The Warsaw Ghetto uprising has become a symbol. It was the first and an unprecedented organized rebellion in an urban area against the Nazis in Europe. It was, in fact, one of the very few rebellions during this whole period which took place in a built-up urban area. For the Jewish people, it serves as a symbol of heroism; but not only of heroism, but of unification and continuity. What is of great interest is that for many people of moral conscience throughout the world, the Warsaw Ghetto serves as the same symbol. It is no accident that the day of the uprising, the 27th of Nissan, which is marked in Israel as Holocaust and Heroism Day, is also celebrated as such by 400 Christian communities in the United States, which hold this very day every year as a memorial day to the Warsaw Ghetto and the Holocaust of the Jews in Europe. And that is only one example.

XII.

Jewish Fighting

In the last chapter, we spoke of the Warsaw Ghetto. We should perhaps, add two points here, which are also applicable to other uprisings. The attitude of the Polish underground to the Warsaw rebels was ambiguous in the extreme. We refer to the official underground, the right-wing A.K. (Armia Krajowa — the Home Army), which took its instructions from the Polish Government in Exile in London. It had very large stores of arms in Warsaw, yet the arms it supplied to the Jews in the ghetto uprisings were ridiculously meager in quantity. In Warsaw, of the thousands of rifles and hundreds of machine guns it possessed, the Jews were given a few dozen pistols, and in other places even less than that. The general attitude was negative, either because the Polish underground regarded the Jews as communists, or because it simply could not believe that the Jews were likely to fight. The Poles themselves did not plan to revolt until the final stages of the war, when a revolt would have some chance of success. The Jewish revolt, of course, had no chance of success from the start.

Antisemitism, which was widespread among large sections of the Polish underground, was a factor in producing a public opinion opposing any cooperation with the Jews. That is not to say that, inside the official underground, there were no units which cooperated with the Jews; but on the whole one can say that the A.K. underground gave no assistance to the Jewish underground, and that parts of it were even actively hostile to the Jews. That is not true

Jewish Reactions to the Holocaust

of the communists, who at least tried to supply arms.

Both undergrounds — the one under communist leadership which was named A.L. (Armia Ludowa — the People's Army), and was very weak at that stage, and A.K. — engaged in some diversionary operations during the Warsaw Ghetto uprising. The right-wing underground performed this by means of some groups which did not identify with the general antisemitic line, while the leftist underground acted in its own fashion, with Jewish commanders involved in its actions. But the activities of both sides were few and far between, and they were practically of no use to the Jews fighting inside the ghetto.

The arms in the hands of the rebels, both in Warsaw and other places, had been bought from the Poles or stolen from German warehouses. On rare occasions, it was possible to attack a German soldier and rob him of his weapon, or to buy arms from soldiers in the armies of Germany's allies — Hungary, Italy, and the like — who passed through Poland and might be prepared to sell their weapons.

There were differences between the uprisings in various places. In some, there were armed undergrounds which tried to organize for the uprising, some of which reached the stage of fighting while others did not. There were also those who eventually left the cities and tried to reach the forests and fight as partisans within them. Many who tried to organize for fighting were caught and murdered.

The undergrounds were not unique to the Warsaw Ghetto: they rose up in dozens of places — in the central and western areas of Poland alone, there were at least seventeen ghettoes where armed undergrounds existed — and they all tried to obtain arms, some more successfully than others. One should mention briefly the Jewish resistance organized in the industrial town of Czestochowa, which took almost the same form as that of the Warsaw Ghetto. A branch of the Jewish Fighting Organization was set up, with the youth movements at its nucleus. The youth of Czestochowa managed to collect arms, perhaps even a little more than those collected in Warsaw, since some of them worked in the German arms factories and managed to smuggle out arms from them.

There were probably some informers, and the Germans surprised

Jewish Fighting

the fighters in June 1943, while they were still unprepared. They attacked their chief arms storehouse, killed the people who were on the spot during the attack, and took the weapons. The fighting, which was very brief, did not work according to the original plan, and proved to be a failure. Following this failure, the remnants of the fighters left the ghetto while still fighting the Germans, and tried to find a forest from which they could continue their fight. Here we have a hard and brutal tale of wandering in forests and acts of treason by the right-wing Polish underground, and on some occasions even by the left-wing one. Only a small portion of all these fighters survived to the end of the war.

We shall bring another example, from the center of the German occupation administration in Poland, Krakow — the second largest city in Poland and its ancient capital. In this city, an underground was organized, whose main leaders were members of the Akiva movement, for wherever this movement had a branch, the branch joined in the fighting. This was a movement of General Zionist youth. Its members acted in competition, and then in concert with another underground, one run by Hashomer Hatza'ir and Jewish communists. These people were careful not to involve the ghetto itself in fighting, since this might make all its inhabitants collectively responsible and thus cause the Germans to massacre all of them. Instead, they launched attacks on the Germans outside the ghetto. On December 22, 1942, this underground set off a bomb in a cafe in the center of town, the Ciganeria, and killed German officers; it set fire to German warehouses, and damaged railway lines. Its base was in the ghetto, but it carried out its operations outside it, until most of its members had been captured. This was another method of fighting.

On the other hand, there were disasters, like that of the Bialystok Ghetto, one of the last ghettoes in Poland, liquidated in August 1943. We should note here that the transports out of the Warsaw Ghetto began in the summer of 1942, and the Warsaw Ghetto uprising took place in April 1943. This was the time when most of the ghettoes in Poland were liquidated. In Bialystok, there was a head of the Judenrat who had strong connections with the

Jewish Reactions to the Holocaust

underground and covered up for it to some extent, but he was not part of it and opposed an open rebellion. Within this underground, which eventually united under the command of Mordechai Tannenbaum-Tamarow, there was a dispute, whether the members of the underground should escape to the forest or fight within the ghetto. Some of the people left for the forest, but the majority remained in the ghetto and conducted their fighting there. When, in February 1943, partial transports from the Bialystok Ghetto began, there was a dispute as to whether to have an open revolt or not. This was before different groups had united, and the group under the command of Tannenbaum decided to delay the revolt. Its calculation was that one had no choice but to sacrifice some of the people of the ghetto, in the hope that, as time went on, there would be larger quantities of arms available and fighting would be more effective, or that the Soviet army might be able to liberate the town by then. There are clues which seem to indicate that in that earlier stage, in February, the ghetto still supported the underground, whereas at the later stage, that of liquidation, it no longer gave it any support, since at the time of the first transport only one group rebelled, and that without any proper firearms.

In August 1943, the last transport from Bialystok took place. On August 16, a rebellion was started by the fighting groups, under the command of Mordechai Tannenbaum. After a day of open fighting, the rebellion went on for a few more days within the ghetto. These fighters were almost all murdered during the fighting, and only a small portion of them managed to cross over to the non-Jewish section of Bialystok and to establish contacts with those in the forest. These fighters remained in Bialystok and engaged in anti-Nazi activities, in helping the fighters in the forest, and sometimes in fighting side by side with them. A group of young women who remained in Bialystok after the rebellion, headed by Chajka Grossman, continued with anti-Nazi activities and maintained the vital contacts with the partisans in the forests.

The fighting in the Bialystok Ghetto is an example of another model of fighting. Every place was hell, and every hell was different from the hell next door, although there were some parallel traits,

Jewish Fighting

and mass murder was common to all. The tactics of the fighting reaction were different from place to place.

In the east of Poland, very different conditions prevailed. In eleven ghettoes in that area, there were Judenraete which took an active part in the revolt in one way or another. But in that large area, the number of the ghettoes was very much greater. In the northern part of that area alone there were about 110 ghettoes, and in its southern part another 70 ghettoes or more. Some of these ghettoes were allowed to remain relatively unimpaired by the Germans for economic reasons. In the northern area, there were 63 ghettoes which had organized groups planning resistance or a break-out into the forest, and another 30 ghettoes where there was some resistance, but we do not know whether it was organized. The great difference between the northern and the southern areas was that, in the northern area, Belorussia (White Russia), there were some primeval forests, and into these there was a large influx of Jews. It is estimated today that in the northeastern region of Poland — which is also known as Western Belorussia and is now part of the Soviet Union — about 25,000 Jews left for the forests. It goes without saying that many of them did not obtain arms, and we do not know precisely how many of them were still alive by the end of the war. We do know that in Eastern Belorussia — that is, that part which had always been within Russian, and later Soviet boundaries — there were about 7,000 Jews who came out of the Minsk Ghetto alone to fight in the forests. We are still in the dark about the units, and other pieces of information which would make it possible to add up the precise figures. But we do know that there were in that region tens of thousands of Jews who left for the forests in order to fight and avenge themselves. Some of them obtained arms and managed to fight, while some did not obtain arms. This caused terrible difficulties, since the Russian partisan units refused to take in unarmed Jews. Those who had no weapons were, in the best of circumstances, driven back, and it would be better not ask what happened in the worst of circumstances. In that area, there were partisan units — including some which were already under Soviet supervision, but mostly those which, at least in the beginning,

Jewish Reactions to the Holocaust

managed to escape Soviet supervision — which murdered Jews. Even in some Soviet partisan units, the attitude to the Jews was often antisemitic in the extreme. Thus, when a Jew reached a Soviet unit, his life was by no means safe, and he was faced with another struggle.

With all these provisos, one should point out that the Soviet partisan units did not make their appearance in those forests until a stage when most of the ghettoes no longer existed. That is, when the Jews were in need of partisan units, there were still none, and, when the units finally appeared there were no longer any Jews. This is another factor which minimized the number of Jews who were capable of being saved. One should add to this the fact that those forests, as distinct from the forests in Western Europe, are virtually East European jungles, full of huge marshes, where one does not see the daylight and there is no way of finding one's direction without a compass. One can die of starvation in such forests — and indeed, there were many who died there of starvation, especially those who had never lived in such areas. This made the situation even more difficult. There were very few wholly Jewish partisan units in the forests, since the Soviet command disbanded such units in Lithuania and Belorussia, and utterly refused to accept the proposition that the Jews constituted a separate nation which should have its own separate units.

Very few managed, with great difficulties, to survive until the end of the war. An especially well known case was that of the unit organized by the brothers Belski, who were not forest Jews but rather Jews from a village, and who organized around themselves a large group of fighters and non-combatants — over a thousand people — and carried on until the end of the war. There were also five units, under the command of Abba Kovner, which had left the Vilno Ghetto and were joined by Jewish fighters from Kovno, and these fought in the forests of Eastern Lithuania and West Belorussia. In this region, there were also the units of Dr. Yehezkel Atlas and of Djadja (Uncle) Misha. But such units, as we have said, were disbanded, or did not last until the end of the war, and they were under great pressure. Most of the Jewish fighters were part of non-

Jewish Fighting

Jewish units.

Jewish fighting was only a small part of the general Jewish reaction and could be regarded as marginal, since the tragedy of the huge numbers of Jews in the Holocaust was what counted — but what a marginal force! For what we have here was not only of considerable size, but represented an armed protest of the greatest significance.

We have already seen the considerable dimensions of Jewish fighting. One should, however, remember that this only started when the Jews realized that there was no alternative; that the Nazis were planning to kill all Jews; that their environment was far from friendly and in some areas even hostile and murderous. Let us take an example which will illustrate this clearly. In one of the small towns, a place called Tuczyn, the Judenrat was part of the resistance, and the uprising began under its leadership. On a certain day, the whole ghetto rose up in rebellion. People set fire to the ghetto, broke through the Ukrainian and German forces which surrounded them, crossed the river and reached the forest near the town. Many were murdered, but over 1,000 people certainly managed to reach the forest. Only thirteen of them survived. It was difficult to exist in the forest, because there were neighboring peasants who betrayed the Jews to the Germans, and because the Germans immediately organized a retaliatory action and entered the forest in search of Jews. The partisans in that area were far away, and it took many days to find them. Those who survived at the end were those who fought in partisan units and remained alive as part of those units — for, after all, many partisans were also killed by the Germans. This story seems to show that even in cases where the whole ghetto revolted and the forest was near, the chances of survival were very small.

There is another point which becomes clear if we simply read the literature about the Second World War. In most of Belorussia itself, of course, the advance of the Germans was very fast; but they were restricted in their advance when they reached Russia proper. The front became stabilized near the town of Bryansk, which was surrounded by marshes. Fighting took place north and south of

Jewish Reactions to the Holocaust

these marshes. There were German and Soviet soldiers on both sides, but there were no troops in the marshes themselves, since one could not maintain soldiers, supplies or anything else in that area, and it was impossible to conduct proper warfare in these marshes. Neither of the sides entered the marsh area. Thus a gap was created, the Bryansk Gap, which stretched over a considerable distance, and made it possible for soldiers and civilians to move between the Nazi occupied area and the Soviet area. The Soviets infiltrated partisans, supplies and arms through the gap. Jews and others, but especially Jews, soon came to know about this gap, and those of them who survived the first or second wave of murders organized themselves and set out for it. They crossed the marshes, sometimes with the assistance of Russian partisans, and reached safety. How many Jews were saved in this manner, we still do not know. Some Jews were saved by joining Soviet partisan units which were already under Soviet command, and reached the area of Belorussia through the Bryansk Gap. We are dealing here with a problem which has not yet been properly studied. But it appears that what we have here was a local phenomenon which had a decisive influence on events, and which would help us explain, at least to some extent, why in this area alone tens of thousands of Jews gave expression to their resistance to the Nazis in the most active manner and with weapons in their hands. This is not the case in the Ukraine, where there are no large forests, and where the population was far more hostile. The Belorussians — for reasons which we do not quite understand — were relatively less hostile to the Jews than the Ukrainians, and there were some cases of cooperation between Belorussians and Jews. Such cooperation was far more unusual in the Ukraine, where there are wide open spaces and the only way to survive was to hide. Where the population of such places was hostile, the fate of the Jews was sealed.

What one can say of Jewish armed fighting in this area of Poland and Eastern Europe is that it was very widespread, after the great wave of murders, and that it was extremely difficult, carried out as it was under terrible conditions and without much chance of assistance on the part of the local population. Among the motives for fighting, one can single out the wish to survive and to avenge oneself in the eastern areas, and revenge and the upholding of Jewish honor in western and central Poland. In eastern Poland and in the western part of the Soviet Union, the fighting was not carried out, as it was in the west and in Warsaw, by the youth movements, the communists, or similar bodies, but by Jewish youth who may perhaps have been organized earlier in some such bodies but lost their organized frameworks, and were now fighting in reaction to what had happened to their parents' generation and to the Jewish world as a whole. This was popular fighting, which tried to reach large masses, although it did not always succeed. The number of Jews fighting in these areas is impressive, and the whole image of this topic is in need of radical modification.

XIII.

Kovno, Vilno, Lodz and Minsk

We have already touched on the problem of the information available to Jews, both within the area of Nazi occupation and outside it, as to the Nazi plans and their execution. We have realized that information itself was not enough, and that the report that all Jews were being murdered was received with incredulity. We must not forget that we are living in the generation following the Holocaust, and that we now know that this was possible — indeed, that it happened. People who lived through the Holocaust had no precedent for such a phenomenon, and they could not know that it was possible — hence their reluctance to believe the reports reaching them.

A very clear reaction — the first of its kind, as we have pointed out — took place in the Vilno Ghetto, where a body of underground Jewish fighters was formed against the Nazis, because there was someone there — the writer and poet Abba Kovner — who, on the basis of incomplete information, nevertheless reached the conclusion that there was indeed a plan for the wholesale murder of the Jews, and since there was no way out, the only reaction was violent action. We have also pointed out that this was the reaction of young people. Those who had been brought up on European culture and had reached the middle or later years of their lives found it most difficult to accept these reports as correct. And once they began to understand this information more thoroughly and to believe it, their reaction was often shock and indecision.

Kovno, Vilno, Lodz and Minsk

This may be the place to return to the issue of the Jewish leadership. We shall touch here only on Eastern Europe after the beginning of the mass murder of the Jews — that is, after June 1941 — first, in areas of Eastern Poland and the Soviet Union, and later, from the beginning of 1942, when the plan for wholesale murder was put into operation, in the whole of Poland and gradually also in neighboring countries like Slovakia and Yugoslavia (where mass murder on a large scale started in late 1941). If we study the reaction of the Judenraete, we can discern a very broad range of individual approaches. We shall only bring here two examples from the same country, from two ghettoes which were very similar in the structure of their population, in their environment, and in the German forces carrying out the massacre. These are two cities in Lithuania, one of them the ancient capital, Vilno, and the other, Kovno, the capital of the country between the two wars. In both cities there lived very similar Jewish communities, and yet the reaction of the heads of the communities was very different.

In Kovno, a doctor named Yohanan Elkes was elected head of the Judenrat. He was elected to that position against his own will, after much persuasion, especially on the part of the local rabbis. He finally agreed to take up this hard task, although he could hardly have known what was to come. But already in the first days of German occupation of Kovno mass murders began, so, from this point of view, he was one of those who were soon forced to know what was lying ahead.

To speak of what happened in Kovno in general terms, it is clear that Elkes did all in his power to warn the population of the approaching threat of German actions, and he did not hide anything. He had important contacts with the local Jewish police force, which was one of the main bodies — if not the main body — of resistance to the Germans (unlike many other places, where the Jewish police cooperated with the Germans). For example, he gave advance warning, together with the Jewish police, of the German attempt to kidnap Jewish children and have them murdered. He established workshops in the city whose function was to employ the Jews, so as to avoid their murder as useless people. He used these

Jewish Reactions to the Holocaust

workshops as camouflage for people who engaged in underground activities. He helped people to leave the ghetto and reach the forests, which were very far from Kovno, in the most dangerous manner, in order to fight against the Germans in special units. Many people did, indeed, manage to leave Kovno in that manner. The sympathy of the Judenrat headed by Elkes for the underground was undoubtedly a positive factor, which upheld the relatively high morale of the youth which organized in the ghetto.

The negotiations Elkes held with the Nazis at the various stages of the ghetto's existence were honorable. He never yielded, never grovelled, knew how to press his point and how to try to insist, at least, on some things. This was a Judenrat which was devoid of the failings shown by some of the other Judenraete. At the same time, the Judenrat was required, on October 27, 1941, to issue "life papers" — official employment papers. It soon transpired that such papers were to save their holders — at least for the time being — while all the rest, who did not receive such papers, were in danger of immediate murder. There were terrible doubts and perplexities around. Was it right for the Judenrat to issue such papers, or should it refuse? Some members of the Judenrat maintained that one should hand back these papers to the Germans. On the other hand, there was a demonstration of craftsmen in front of the Judenrat building, demanding that these "life papers" should be issued by them. In the end, the opinion of Rabbi Abraham D. Shapira, who thought that the Judenrat was obliged to distribute these papers if there was a hope that part of the community would survive, carried the day. The Judenrat and its head Elkes did distribute the papers, and most of those who did not receive them were murdered.

These were very complex moral problems, and these people had to solve them, for better or for worse, according to their lights. But two points should be made. First, no leader of a community should ever have to be faced with such choices. Second, there can be no doubt that Dr. Elkes acted with impeccable honesty. In his own way, and according to his own understanding of the situation, he made the greatest efforts to save the population, even during the liquidation of the ghetto. The Kovno Ghetto was one of the few

Kovno, Vilno, Lodz and Minsk

ghettoes which existed until the summer of 1944, when one could already hear from a distance the shelling by the Soviet artillery which was approaching. It was only then that the Germans removed the last people from the ghetto and transported them to concentration camps in Germany. In his last encounter with the Nazi commander, Elkes courageously told him: "You know that you will face the death penalty after the war unless you save us now." His words did not help, but at least he tried. At the last stage, Elkes attempted to arrange a general escape of the Jews out of the ghetto. The attempt failed for technical reasons. We are faced here with the tragic figure of a true leader of Jews.

In Vilno, on the other hand, the man who stood at the head of the ghetto (there was virtually no Judenrat there, since the Judenrat set up in the beginning was officially disbanded in July 1942) was the man who had been head of the Jewish police in the first period, Jacob Gens. This man was not elected by the Jews but appointed by the Germans. Gens regarded himself as the man whose task it was to have the remnant of the ghetto survive until the time of liberation, and he was willing, after the liberation, to face any prosecutors in a Jewish court and justify his activities during the Holocaust period. He was prepared to take far-reaching steps in cooperating with the Germans. He turned the Vilno Ghetto into a "working ghetto," a ghetto engaged in production for the Germans. He believed that, in this manner, the Germans would not murder the inmates of the ghetto, since this would impair the German war effort. In this respect, his policy was not unlike that of Elkes in Kovno, Baraszh in Bialystok or Rumkowski in Lodz.

Gens' problem was that he went much further than that. He charged his policemen in the Vilno Ghetto to assist actively in the German murder actions in the region — for example, in the Oszmiane Ghetto. He sent his policemen there to collect a few hundred old people from the ghetto and to hand them over to the Nazis to be murdered, in full knowledge of what was about to happen. As Gens said explicitly to people in the ghetto, he did it because he believed that otherwise women and children would be taken; it was better, he though, to hand over the old people to the

Jewish Reactions to the Holocaust

Germans and save the others.

He really believed that by handing over some of the people of the ghetto to the Germans, he would save the rest. If he found out, he said, that it was true that all the Jews were being killed, he would then join the underground and go to the forest. He was a brave man, a former officer in the Lithuanian army, a member of Betar before the war, and married to a Lithuanian wife. He could have found a hiding place, but he did not exploit that possibility.

Gens did have contacts with the underground. This underground, which we have already described, had been formed early in 1942 at the initiative of the Zionist youth movements, and had some connections with Gens. It is true that there was a dispute between them, since the underground maintained that they should prepare for an uprising and he objected to this, but to a certain extent there was mutual respect between them, and Gens did, to some extent, cover up for the underground.

To some extent. For in July 1943, when there were probably less than 20,000 people left in the ghetto and the head of the underground was a young Jewish communist named Yitzhak Wittenberg, a Lithuanian communist was caught in the non-Jewish part of the city. This man told the Nazis that there was a Jewish communist underground man in the ghetto, and gave them his name. It is most likely that that Lithuanian knew nothing of the Jewish underground and had only heard the name Itzik Wittenberg. The Nazis ordered Gens to hand Wittenberg over to them. Gens convened a meeting of the commanders of the underground: he knew them all, and it was taken for granted by them that they came when invited by him. As they were sitting in his office, he had Wittenberg arrested by Jewish and Lithuanian policemen, who caught him and tried to take him out of the building and out of the ghetto. The underground people, who suspected that something was not quite in order, fell on the policemen and released their commander. Gens then appealed to the people of the ghetto, saying that now, on account of one man, the Nazis would come and murder everybody. The Jews of the ghetto rose up against the underground and supported Gens, saying: "Should we all die in one day?" On

Kovno, Vilno, Lodz and Minsk

that day, July 16, the underground was faced with a terrible choice: should they rebel? But in that case, the first clash would be not with the Nazis, but with the inmates of the ghetto. The alternative was to hand over their commander to the Nazis. In the end, the communist faction in the ghetto, a very small group of people, decided that Wittenberg had to give himself over to the Germans. Wittenberg, who had objected to this move, accepted the decision of his faction, and the faction accepted his decision to accept their decision. Wittenberg took poison with him, gave himself over to the Nazis, and before they began to torture him, took his own life. Gens came out of this struggle victorious.

In September 1943, Gens was ordered by the Nazis to appear at the Gestapo, and he believed that they were about to execute him. This happened at the stage when it was clear even to him that his policy had failed. He probably had an opportunity to escape, but he told his associates that he would not escape, for if he were to do that, the whole ghetto would be liquidated. He appointed his deputy as his successor, and instructed him to carry on his policies. He went to the Nazis in the full knowledge that he was not to return.

The question arises: What is the true role of a Jewish leader in such circumstances? There are some who believe that this is no question of Jewish leadership at all, for how can one speak of leadership in these circumstances? We are dealing with people who were virtually in prison or in the condemned cell, awaiting the death penalty, and one can hardly speak of leadership among such people. Yet, in the given conditions, this was still a leadership, whether it was elected or appointed, since it was responsible, to some extent, for the people of the ghetto. The difference between the behavior of Elkes and Gens, which we have just pointed out, reveals some of the perplexing problems we meet with when we come to examine this complex phenomenon of the Jewish leadership.

Jerusalem historian Dr. Aharon Weiss, carried out a very interesting study. He examined 146 Judenraete in Poland - or, to be precise, the behavior of their heads, since it is extremely difficult to investigate the actions of all the members of the Judenraete. He did this according to certain criteria, and specified the delivering of

Jews into the hands of the Nazis as an absolute moral limit which could in no way be transgressed with any justification. He took as test cases, according to this criterion, those who had reached this limit and did or did not exceed it. He restricted his examination to 146 heads of Judenraete serving their first term of office, since the Nazis often changed the head of the Judenrat after a fairly long period in office. This usually happened after the first wave of mass murders, and then a second Judenrat was appointed for a second, or even third, term in office. The result was surprising. According to documents and the testimonies of survivors, it transpired that 107 of 146 heads of Judenraete did not go beyond the limit of delivering people into the hands of the Nazis. That is, a very large proportion of heads of Judenraete during the first period do not fit the negative image of Judenraete prevalent in Israel and abroad. In Israel itself, Judenrat had become a dirty word, and heads of Judenraete even more so. It appears that things were not quite like that.

One should note that this statistic cannot lay claim to absolute accuracy, since it combines the heads of Judenraete of large communities with those of small ones. Rumkowski in Lodz, in charge of over 100,000 people even at the later stage, appears in this statistic beside a small Judenrat of a little township of a few thousand inhabitants. At the same time, both heads were in charge of a certain population. And the problem of the fate of a community was of necessity common to all the heads of these Judenraete, so that the analysis still has some validity.

Let us return now to the story of Rumkowski. We have the interesting testimony of a German, an opponent of the Nazis, who visited the Lodz Ghetto in the middle of 1942 on some pretext and met Rumkowski as well as the rabbi of the city and others. His testimony was published in Hebrew in Shaul Esch's book, *Studies in the Holocaust and Contemporary Jewry*, Jerusalem 1974, pp. 296-316. At that stage, Rumkowski undoubtedly knew that the Jews were being murdered. The inmates of the ghetto in general were not aware of this at this stage — or, at most, some were suspicious — but he knew. He still delivered people to the Nazis according to their demands, and with the permission of the rabbi of the community.

Kovno, Vilno, Lodz and Minsk

Like Gens, he believed that by handing over some people, he would save the rest, and he asked the German visitor whether he was doing the right thing.

The Nazis began to "thin out" the ghetto, and from early 1942 on, the transports to the death camps began. The most extreme measures came when the Nazis came and demanded the children. No one mentioned that they were to be murdered, but by then it was clear that if the Germans demanded children, it was not for the sake of forced labor elsewhere. Nobody said explicitly that the children were to be murdered – but it was quite clear to anyone who understood, and by that time many understood.

In the ghetto, as could be expected, powerful opposition arose to the delivering of the children. Despite this, the ghetto police and Rumkowski's supporters succeeded, in concert with the Germans, to kidnap the children and send them to their deaths. While this was going on, Rumkowski made it clear once more why he was doing this: "We deliver," he said, "one part of the ghetto into their hands so that another part may be saved." It was clear to Rumkowski that the war was to end in Nazi defeat. His view was that the only way left was to reach the end of the war with the young people who were capable of going through all its horrors, and then rebuild their families and the following generation. For that purpose, he believed that one had to take the line of submission to the Germans by handing over to them anyone they demanded, including children.

Toward the end of the war, in July 1944, the Lodz Ghetto was the only one left in the whole of what, before the war, had been Poland, and Rumkowski was still at its head. The reason for this was that the German authorities put pressure on the S.S. not to liquidate this ghetto, since they needed it as a source of supply for certain products which were made in the workshops and factories of that ghetto. At this stage, in July 1944, there were still about 69,000 Jews in Lodz, while the Soviet army was already advancing within Poland and liberating it. The Soviet army halted its advance in July 1944, at a distance of about 100 kilometers from Lodz, on the river Vistula. It stopped there, not because it had no intention of liberating Lodz. Its reasons were military and political, and had

Jewish Reactions to the Holocaust

nothing to do with the fate of the Jews.

A month later, in August, the final liquidation of the ghetto began. It lasted some weeks, and the Jews of Lodz were murdered in Auschwitz. In January 1945, the Red Army renewed its advance, and within three days its soldiers conquered Lodz. They found in it less than 900 Jews, who had been left there in August-September in order to clean up the ghetto and take away whatever was still left in it. The Nazis had not murdered these 900 Jews only because they had no time to do so.

We can ask ourselves a provocative question. Let us assume that, in July 1944, the Red Army had not halted on the Vistula, but had liberated Lodz in three days, as it did in January 1945. It would then have found in it tens of thousands of Jews, saved through Rumkowski's policy of turning Lodz into a terrible labor camp run for the benefit of the Germans. What would we have done in such a case? Would we have erected a memorial to him, as the only head of a Judenrat who succeeded in bringing about the liberation of over 60,000 Jews — or would we have condemned him to death, like Eichmann, as the murderer of children, the deliverer of people into Nazi hands, a Jewish war criminal? This is a tantalizing question. But when we speak of Jewish reactions during this period and of the treason of the Judenrat, we must apply ourselves to such questions.

There were others who behaved like Rumkowski, although one can say that he was probably the most extreme example. We will clarify this point by using another example, but from the opposite extreme. In 1941, the Germans invaded Russia and set up a ghetto in the capital of Belorussia, Minsk. At some stages, this ghetto included over 80,000 Jews, and it was the fourth largest ghetto in Eastern Europe. The Germans appointed a Judenrat in Minsk, but they could not make use of the former community activists, since in Minsk, which had been under Soviet rule, there had not, of course, been a Jewish community. As head of the Judenrat, they appointed a former official of the Minsk city council, a man named Ilya (Eliyahu) Mishkin, who was fluent in German. From the very first day, this Judenrat became the center of resistance against the Nazis. An underground arose in the ghetto under the command of Jewish

Kovno, Vilno, Lodz and Minsk

communists, and it established contacts with a communist underground (also under the command of a Jew) in the non-Jewish section of the city. The underground in the city was a failure; it was betrayed and disbanded; but the one inside the ghetto continued to operate, and later it even rescued non-Jewish fighters in the forests around Minsk as well as in the city itself. This underground, with the firm and efficient cooperation of the Judenrat under the leadership of Eliyahu Mishkin and his successor, also managed to smuggle out of the ghetto and into the forests, partly with the arms it had obtained, about 10,000 people. Eventually, both ghetto and Judenrat were liquidated, and as far as the final destiny of the Judenrat is concerned, there was no difference whatsoever between Lodz and Minsk. But there was a difference in the final destiny of the majority of the Jews, since Minsk, unlike Lodz, was surrounded by forests, and in Minsk there was resistance. Some of the Jews were saved by escaping to these forests; most of them fought, and some, at least, survived the Holocaust. The Minsk Judenrat is an example of the other extreme, of a purely accidental group of people who managed to organize Jews, or to help them organize themselves, in an armed underground, and induced the whole ghetto to help this underground. Each of these leaderships was called a Judenrat, but we have no right to include them in one simplified generalization.

In the Minsk Ghetto another event occurred, which also repeated itself in a number of places — including the Wilno Ghetto which we have already studied. When Mishkin was murdered, he was succeeded by Moshe Yaffe, who carried on his predecessor's policies of resistance to the Nazis. Meanwhile, the Germans tracked down the head of the ghetto underground, Hersh Smolar, and demanded that he be delivered into their hands. Even in the underground itself there were some who believed that if Smolar were to deliver himself to the Nazis, the ghetto would be saved from a calamity. But Yaffe was not of that opinion. He showed the Germans Smolar's identity card covered with blood, as proof that the man had been killed, and Smolar was saved. On July 28, 1942, 25,000 Jews were assembled in the square in the ghetto, and the Nazis ordered Yaffe to calm them down in preparation for their expulsion from the ghetto.

Jewish Reactions to the Holocaust

Instead, Yaffe told then to escape and hide. He was shot on the spot.

On this issue of the Jewish leadership, there are two opposing views. One of them, adopted by the great Jewish historian Raul Hilberg, maintains that the Judenraete were first and foremost tools in the hands of the Germans for executing their plan for the mass murder of the Jews. After all, even when a certain Judenrat worked, for example, at maintaining people's health, what did it achieve? Only that the Germans would have the Jews as their slaves until the time came for murdering them, and no more. Hilberg attaches little importance to the intentions of the Judenraete, and maintains that they were merely part of the Nazi murder machine. As against this view, there is another one, current especially among Israeli scholars, which maintains that one should take intentions into account as well. Hilberg is right in claiming that, from the German point of view, the Judenraete were, indeed, part of the Nazi murder apparatus; but from the Jewish point of view, they were the representatives of Jewish communities, and the problem of their behavior is a crucial moral problem. We have to investigate not only the actions, but also the intentions. In that case, we have to admit that the result — the murder of the Jews — is not what is decisive, since this is already known to us without any investigation. What we have to ask is how they behaved before they were murdered. What matters to us is not the fact of the mass murder, which is the basic premise of the Holocaust, but our own attitude to these people, whose part, flesh of their flesh, we are. From this point of view, Hilberg's attitude is only one part of the truth.

One can say that this spectrum, stretching from Rumkowski to Mishkin and Yaffe, included all the possible variations. In East Poland, with its large forests, we find yet another very different variant of these Judenraete (and they, incidentally, were not included in the specimen of 146 Judenraete mentioned earlier in this chapter). These Judenraete were never ordered to send Jews to their deaths. When the Germans wanted to murder people, they simply entered the ghettoes and took them away, and the Judenraete were not asked to cooperate. In this area, there were 11 communities whose Judenraete cooperated closely with the

Kovno, Vilno, Lodz and Minsk

undergrounds, where they themselves headed the resistance or were at least part of it. In two places, they were virtually the leaders of the rebellion, carrying the whole community along with them. Thus, if we have spoken of Judenraete which submitted to the Nazis, we have now brought examples of the exact opposite kind, while there were Judenraete in the middle which shared some of the qualities of each of these extremes. The obvious conclusion is that there is no room for generalizations.

XIV.

Western European Jewry

In our discussion so far, we have said little about Jewish reactions in the western countries during the Holocaust. In Denmark and Norway, the Nazis had ruled since the spring of 1940, and in May-June of that year, Holland, Belgium and France were conquered by them. The Jewish people who lived in those countries were thus under Nazi rule from the middle of 1940 until the end of the war.

In Holland, there were about 140,000 Jews, including the refugees who had arrived from Germany before the war broke out between the two countries — that is, before May 1940. The government in Holland was in the hands of a Nazi regent, one of the Austrian members of the party, like Hitler himself. This man, Artur Seyss-Inquart, called in the S.S. and maintained close cooperation between the occupation government in Holland and the S.S.

The Dutch government had escaped to London, and the routine administration was left in the hands of the secretary generals of the Dutch government offices, whose ministers were now living in London. According to international law, the Nazi occupation authorities had the right to dictate to these officials in all matters dealing with security or the interests of the occupying power. But according to international law they were not permitted to introduce any innovations which stood counter to the Dutch constitution or tradition. That was, at least, a legitimate interpretation of the situation. But these secretary generals virtually gave in to the Nazis throughout the period of occupation, and expressed no opposition

Western European Jewry

of any kind on any issue, including that of the Jews. When the Nazis began to segregate the Jews from the non-Jews, these officials gave it their full backing, although here and there they made a weak protest or a perfunctory gesture of dissatisfaction.

The large majority of the Dutch people not only opposed the Nazi policies, but many were willing to assist the Jews. Holland was the only country in which — in February 1941 — a general strike of the workers broke out in protest against the persecution of the Jews. This strike was stopped, in fact, not only through German pressure, but mainly because of Jewish submission. The Nazis exploited this strike for the establishment of a Judenrat in Holland.

This Judenrat, which was far from holding undisputed sway over the Jewish public, appealed to the strikers to stop their action, and thus brought about the end of this strike. At the same time, a group of Zionists and sympathizers was organized, headed by the president of the supreme court of Holland until the Nazi occupation, a Jewish professor named Lodewijk Visser. He attempted to establish a coordinating committee, whose aim would be to organize the Jewish population so that there would be no direct contacts between it and the Germans. If the Germans wanted anything from the Jews, they were to apply through the Dutch secretary generals. This was clearly against the policy of the S.S. which had set up the Judenrat, at whose head also stood two pre-war Zionist leaders, David Cohen and Abraham Asscher, both of whom were opposed to Visser. The Germans soon succeeded in doing away with his coordinating committee.

The Jewish leadership in Holland is one of two or three extreme examples of complete submission to the will of the Germans during the Holocaust. If one can speak of submission even before there was any need for it, it is certainly true in this case. On some occasions, the leadership gave in to Nazi instructions even before they had been issued. Here, too, the tendency was to save part of the Jewish population by this policy of submission to the Nazis. But the truth is that the Jewish public in Holland expressed signs of resistance as early as the summer of 1942, that is, during the first period of expulsions to the death camps, when the Jews were still unaware of

Jewish Reactions to the Holocaust

the aims of these expulsions. At the time, the Nazis were reporting from Holland to Berlin that the Jews were not presenting themselves for the transports. This can be explained in many ways, but the most important reason is that in Amsterdam there was a large Jewish working-class population — about 40,000 — porters, quay laborers, and industrial workers, who were well integrated into Dutch society around them, and they felt instinctively that something was not quite in order. In Holland it is a very difficult to hide, since the whole country is built on water, and there is no way of having basements. The problem was to find hiding places — but where? The country is flat, without forests and hills. Thus, the members of this Jewish proletariat were dragged to their deaths, albeit against their will. One cannot say that the Jews in Holland followed their leaders and gave in to the Germans. They tried to get out of the trap, but they did not succeed.

Yet out of these 140,000 Jews, about 25,000 managed to hide. In the given conditions, this is far from a negligible figure. About one third of these were betrayed or discovered by the Nazis, and at the end of the war only 16,000 remained. Most of those who were betrayed were betrayed by Dutch people, since about 10% of the Dutch citizens were Nazis or Nazi sympathizers, members or sympathizers of the Dutch Nazi Party. Here we have an extremely interesting question which cannot be answered. Ninety percent of the Dutch were prepared to stake their lives for the 16,000 Jews who were wandering from one place to another, since they had to change their places of hiding. Not only Jews went into hiding, but also Dutch laborers who faced expulsion to forced labor camps in Germany. The sympathy of the large majority of the Dutch people toward the Jews is by no means a mere legend. What is a legend, though, is that this was a unanimous sentiment, as it were, and as if no difficulties existed.

In Belgium, on the other hand, the situation was very different. Here, too, there were only a small number of Nazi sympathizers. The large majority of the Belgian population, with very few exceptions, supported the attempts to hide the Jews. It is a fact that in Belgium, over one half of the Jewish population — about 37,000 out of 66,000 — survived. This should be credited to the Belgians, more especially in the Walloon, French-speaking, part of the country, but also in the Flemish part. The head of the Catholic Church, Cardinal Joseph-Ernest van Roey of Antwerp, was Flemish. He came out in public against the Nazi policy and encouraged his followers in the churches to support the hiding of Jews. The initiative for hiding, disappearing, or escaping, came from the Jews themselves. Jewish communists and Zionists joined together in a committee, which was called the Committee for the Protection of Jews (CNDS), and was part of the general Belgian underground. At one stage, it was headed by a non-Jewish professor, and at all stages there was perfect cooperation with the Belgians. This committee engaged mainly in rescue, in the first place of children, but also of adults, and this developed into a nationwide network of concealment. When we speak of the Jewish reaction in Belgium, we can say that, unlike Holland, there were organizations here which represented the public at large.

In Belgium, too, there was a Judenrat. In the earlier stages at least, it cooperated with the Germans, and in the summer of 1942 it handed out announcements to Jews of their expulsion eastward. The Jews reported, since no one had any idea of the meaning of these expulsion to the east, and they believed that its aim was forced labor. But after the first two months the Belgian Judenrat began to be suspicious. The head of the Judenrat and some of its members were arrested by the Germans, and, when they were released through the intervention of the Belgian queen mother (who established a number of social aid programs in Israel after the Holocaust), they were not reinstated. A new Judenrat was appointed, which had no influence among the Jewish public. Thus, unlike Holland, the Judenrat did submit at first, but it stood up to the Nazis later. It was then virtually disbanded, with a mere skeleton left to deal only with matters of aid. Its activities were officially conducted under German supervision; but even in this skeleton Judenrat there were delegates of the Jewish underground, which in practice directed the Judenrat itself. Unlike Holland, there was in Belgium an armed Jewish underground. A small pioneer

Jewish Reactions to the Holocaust

Zionist underground in Holland escaped and reached France. It included a number of young women and men, especially members of the He-Halutz movement from Germany, who reached France with the help of Dutch friends. Some of them later crossed to Spain, and a few even reached Palestine in the midst of the war. In Belgium, on the other hand, an armed Jewish resistance was organized. The head of the armed communist unit which operated as part of the general Jewish underground lives in Jerusalem today, and the communism of these Jews was rather dubious. There was also a Zionist underground, which never reached the stage of open fighting, but was undoubtedly part of the armed Belgian underground. There were also Jews who joined the general Belgian underground as individuals. We have here a different reaction, which may be partly explained by the fact that the large majority of the Jews of Belgium — again, unlike the Jews of Holland — were in fact East European Jews, who had emigrated to Belgium between the two world wars. Only a small percentage of Belgian Jews were Belgian citizens, and the immigrants — mainly from Poland, but also from Germany and Rumania — were operating in a foreign country and were, perhaps, more sensitive to the persecution imposed on them. They reacted in a far more resolute manner.

In France, the Judenrat was a very strange creature, divided in two. One part of it operated in the northern part of France, which had been under German military rule since the capitulation of France in 1940. The other part represented the Jews of the south of France, which, until late 1942, was under the direct rule of the Vichy government and had no Germans in its administration.

The Judenrat in France cooperated with the Germans, but it also retained a certain measure of independence. When France was conquered by the Germans, there were about 350,000 Jews in it. Some tens of thousands escaped, and there were thus about 300,000 Jews left in the country. More than two thirds of these Jews were saved, thanks to a number of factors, not least of which was the self-organization of the Jews. Here, as in Belgium, Jewish self-organization encouraged the French to help. But it also went the other way, and French willingness to assist no doubt strengthened

Western European Jewry

the Jewish resolve to save themselves. There were a number of organizations in the country. While the Judenrat did submit to German demands, it did not, on the other hand, supply them with lists. Inside the Judenrat, there were clandestine sub-departments, and this means that one part of its activities were directed toward the Germans, while another part of its activities were held in secret. The clandestine departments engaged in non-armed resistance, in avoidance and in concealment. Most of the Jewish organizations active in France before the war began by acting within the Judenrat as semi-official departments, and went into action mainly after the great expulsion of the Jews from France to Eastern Europe began in the summer of 1942. As in other places, it was not clear at first what the purpose was of these expulsions.

In France, one should single out a few organizations, and first among them a health organization. Such organizations do not usually engage in underground activities; but Oeuvre Secours aux Enfants (OSE) did develop into one. In wartime France, OSE dealt mainly with children, and it regarded its task as being the concealing of children and smuggling them into neutral Switzerland and Spain. OSE activists, such as Mme. Andree Salomon, who died in Jerusalem recently, were active in this organization and helped in hiding 7,000 children through the offices of OSE and other organizations, including communist ones. They were so successful that we are not aware of a single case in which a child was delivered to the Nazis by a French citizen. There were cases in which children were discovered by the Nazis, but we know of no case of wilful betrayal.

These children were hidden by French peasants, and by Catholic and Protestant institutions. Among the Catholic institutions there were some which tried to take advantage of this situation and to have the children converted to Christianity. But one should note that this phenomenon was rather marginal, and that the Catholic and Protestant organizations as a whole, as well as the private individuals who concealed these children in France, usually did not exploit the situation. It is true, of course, that the ties created between these children and their adoptive parents created acute

Jewish Reactions to the Holocaust

problems of identity and relations after the war. There is no doubt that this rescue of children by French people of all sorts and conditions of life was one of the distinguishing marks of the history of the Jews in France during this period. The OSE organization made good use of this when it found an able and strong-willed Jewish youth in Lyons, Georges Garel and charged him with organizing this concealment network. Garel looked after the finances, the liaison women who visited the concealed children regularly, and the cover required in each place.

One should remember that at that time there was considerable sympathy in France for the pro-German Vichy government. This means that those people who gave shelter to the children often did so against their own political convictions, and yet they did not hand them over to French fascists who were actively cooperating with the Germans and were searching for Jewish children to hand over to the Nazis. At the same time, one should also remember that those Jews who were handed over to the Nazis during that period were usually arrested by French, not German policemen. Thus the people who sheltered these Jews acted in the first instance against the French authorities and only indirectly against the Germans.

Apart from OSE, Zionist organizations were also active in hiding children and others. There was also in France a rather unique Jewish boy scout organization, the E.I.F. (Eclaireurs Israelites de France) which was at first assimilationist with certain religious tendencies, traditional and typically French, which developed in time into a Zionist organization, and this organization also played a major role in concealing Jews. On the Catholic side, there existed an organization named Temoignage Chretien, which also concealed Jews. It was headed by the Catholic priest, Father Alexandre Glasberg, whom we have already mentioned, who saw himself as a Jew of the Catholic faith, and who felt it his duty to act for the rescue of Jews. Other priests were also active in this organization, whose center was in Lyons.

There was also an armed Jewish underground in both parts of France. The Jewish communist underground operated within the French communist underground, which was composed of people of various nationalities organized as a kind of Foreign Legion, and functioned mainly in Paris. The first groups in Paris which acted against the Germans were Jewish groups. Later on, the percentage of Jews in the armed section of the French communist underground acting against the Nazis far exceeded their percentage in the total French population. In the south there was also a Zionist organization, bearing the rather pretentious name of the Jewish Army. This was a small but forceful organization, born of the initiative of three men, one of them a supporter of Lehi in Palestine, the other a supporter of the Labor Party in Palestine, and the third, a French General Zionist, Abraham Polonski, who lives in Israel today. On the one hand, this organization maintained Maquis groups — that is, groups of fighting people — in the mountains of southwestern France, and on the other hand urban groups, which operated during the Allies' invasion of France as part of the general Gaullist underground. This organization was also active in smuggling Jews into Spain. All these actions of concealment and smuggling, and also indirectly the Zionist fighting activities, were financed by the Joint — that is, there were contacts with international Jewish organizations. One of the chief organizations engaging in all the various activities we have mentioned — concealment, armed resistance, and the like — was an organization of French Jews of Eastern European origin, headed by an outstanding Zionist, Marc Jarblum, who later immigrated to Palestine and lived the last years of his life there. This organization comprised many thousands of people, and provided the support system for a large proportion of these activities. Through it, money and people were channelled into the part of France occupied by the Nazis.

If we sum up Jewish activities in France, we find, once again, that it was quite different from what we have seen in Belgium and Holland. The Judenrat was different, the independent activities of the French Jewish organizations was extremely broad, and they also arranged for the mobilization of non-Jewish individuals and organizations.

In Italy, the situation was once again quite different. The Italian

Jewish Reactions to the Holocaust

Jewish population was very small, altogether about 40,000 people. They were confronted by the German murder apparatus virtually in the very last stages of the war in that country, in 1943, when the Nazis occupied Italy after the capitulation of the Italian government. The Nazis, with no support from the Italians, now fell on the Jews with fury. The assistance offered to the Jews of Rome by their neighbors, including both the Church and forces which were opposed to the Church, ensured that out of 8,000 Jews in Rome, over 1,000 were captured but 7,000 survived. In northern Italy, where the large majority of this small Jewish community was concentrated, most of the Jews went into hiding, with the assistance of ecclesiastical, communist, socialist and liberal forces — in fact, the various bodies of the entire spectrum of the Italian population were instrumental in concealing their Jewish neighbors. This is not to deny that there were here and there extreme Italian Fascists who supported Nazi policies, or people who refused to help out of fear. But when the anti-Nazi Italian underground arose in the north, the Jews had a considerable share in it.

In Western Europe, and to some extent in Southern Europe, Nazi policy was the same everywhere, and what was largely decisive was the reaction of the people on the spot. The Jewish reaction was also significant and raised the possibility of succeeding even in Holocaust conditions. The Jewish reaction, for its part, brought about a general, non-Jewish reaction, and these two sides become so interdependent that it is now difficult to decide from which side the first initiative came.

XV.

Jewish Reaction and Resistance in Other Countries

It appears that the reaction of the Jews in various countries was a result of the influence of a few factors, chief among these being the attitude of the local population, the nature of German occupation (military occupation; direct rule by the S.S. or the Nazi Party; rule by local collaborators), and the local tradition of Jewish leadership.

One of the most interesting phenomena in this period of catastrophe for the Jewish people was the stand taken by Rumanian Jewry. Between the wars, Rumania was an unstable country with a very strong antisemitic tradition. When war broke out, there were in it about 760,000 Jews, of whom about 300,000 lived in the areas of Bessarabia and northern Bukovina, which were annexed by the Soviet Union in June 1940. When Rumanian forces, accompanied by their German allies, broke into Bessarabia in June 1941 in order to reconquer these areas from the Soviets, an unbridled massacre began of the Jewish population. After well over a third of them had been massacred on the spot, a half, close to 150,000, were expelled, in the autumn and winter of 1941-42, into the area of southern Ukraine, which the Rumanian conquerors called Transnistria. The Jews were squeezed into ghettoes, labor camps, or poor villages, without any food or means of subsistence. Hunger and disease were rampant, and mass murders were carried out by German and Rumanian troops. A remnant was left behind in the town of Czernowitz in Bukovina.

Jewish Reactions to the Holocaust

The Rumanian regime, under the rule of the military dictator Ion Antonescu, regarded as its first target the getting rid of the Jews by means of massacre and expulsion. But the economic and social weakness of Rumania, as well as the contemptuous attitude of its German allies, made the Antonescu regime have second thoughts about its Jewish policies. At the time, Rumania had a Jewish leadership whose outstanding personality was the president of the pre-war Organization of Jewish Communities, the lawyer Wilhelm Fildermann. The Zionist movement and its youth movements were also active there. Fildermann was a typical representative of what in medieval times had been known as a Jewish *"shtadlan"* (lobbyist), with all the positive qualities of a *shtadlan*. He made use of any chink in the armor and exploited any opportunity for intervening with the authorities, and he demonstrated with uncompromising logic the senselessness of the anti-Jewish policies from the point of view of the Rumanian authorities themselves. By demonstrating unusual courage, Fildermann managed to make a major contribution to the survival of the Jewish population of "old" Rumania — that is, without those areas which were annexed for a time to the Soviet Union and Hungary — and most of the community was not murdered and stayed alive during the war. Owing to the particular nature of the Rumanian regime, a method of dignified and stubborn lobbying was employed here — a method which would have been doomed to failure in other places. This is not to say that Fildermann's intervention was decisive, but only that it contributed to the Rumanian decision, in August-October 1942, not to deport the Rumanian Jews to their deaths. The main factors for that decision were Rumanian mistrust and disappointment with Germany, and the desire not to cut off all possibility of future negotiations with the Western Allies. When, at the end of 1941, the Rumanians attempted, under Nazi inspiration, to disband the Jewish institutions and established in their place a "Jewish Center" ("Centrala Evreilor") — that is, a Judenrat (headed by a Jewish convert to Christianity) — the "Center" had no influence on Jewish life, and an underground headed by Fildermann continued to represent the Jewish population. Fildermann was arrested and sent

Jewish Reaction and Resistance in Other Countries

to Transnistria, but the authorities could not do without him, and they brought him back from his exile. Fildermann and his associates, as well as the Zionists, set up aid organizations for the survivors of the expulsion to Transnistria, and they even managed to return to Rumania the orphans among them before the Russians recaptured Transnistria.

A different situation, once again, prevailed in Greece. The large and ancient community of Salonika was in the German occupation zone, whereas the Jews of Athens enjoyed the moderate rule of the Italian occupation army. With the full collaboration of a Nazi Greek puppet government, the Nazis prepared, in the early months of 1943, for the expulsion of the Jews of Salonika to the death camps in Poland. The stand taken by Rabbi Koretz, the leader of the community, was similar to that taken by the heads of the Judenrat in Holland: he believed that there was no way of resisting the Nazis, and that he might save part of the community by total submission. The Jews of Salonika did not know anything about the death camps, but despite this a few hundred Jews escaped to the mountains and joined Greek underground units fighting against the Germans.

It is difficult to give a general picture of what happened in Yugoslavia after the Nazi occupation in April 1941. The Jewish population of Serbia was massacred in 1941. The Jews of Croatia — about 35,000 people — were subject to most brutal rule by Croatian collaborators, who massacred most of the Jewish community by means of inhuman torture in local camps. The survivors were expelled to Auschwitz. In the face of this campaign of annihilation, the leadership of the Zagreb community was completely helpless. The western part of the country was occupied by the Italians, and until the collapse of Italy in September 1943, the Jews of these areas were protected. Many of the remnants of Serbian and Croatian Jewry, as well as many of the Jews of the Italian zone which was conquered by the Germans in the autumn of 1943, joined the partisan groups of Josip Broz-Tito. According to figures published some time ago, they numbered over 6,000. Although no Jewish resistance movement was formed — there was, though, one Jewish unit, composed of those who had escaped from the camp run by the

Jewish Reactions to the Holocaust

Italians on the island of Rab — the part played by the Jews in partisan warfare was very considerable.

The rescue of Bulgarian Jewry posed some complex questions. About 50,000 Jews lived in that country, most of them — like the Jews of Greece — descendants of the Jewish exiles from Spain or of the ancient Jews of Byzantium. Hostility toward the Jews, who were mainly traders and craftsmen, was based chiefly on economic rivalry and religious hatred. Modern antisemitism had not yet penetrated into this country. Bulgaria was ruled by a fascist regime, which was supported by King Boris, and it was an ally of Germany, although it did not join the German campaign against the Soviet Union. The Germans had no difficulty in persuading the Bulgarians to deliver into their hands most of the Jews of Macedonia and Thrace, areas which had been annexed to Bulgaria from Yugoslavia and Greece in the spring of 1941. In March 1943, 11,343 Jews were expelled from these areas to the death camps, and we know of none who survived.

The situation was different in Bulgaria proper. An agreement between the Nazis and Alexander Belev, who was in charge of Jewish affairs, to expel the Jews to Poland, was actually signed in February 1943. The Jews were expelled from the capital, Sofia, and some of the men were put in forced labor camps. Jewish property was confiscated, and the first victims were earmarked for the death camps. But here, a resistance movement arose against the expulsion, and its origin was a Jewish initiative. The Jews of Kyustendil appealed to the member of parliament representing their area, Dimiter Peshev, who was also deputy leader of the House of Representatives, and he organized opposition to the expulsion. The underground Communist Party, the heads of the Orthodox Church, and even the king himself joined the opponents of the expulsion, for different and contradictory considerations. And indeed, the expulsion was not carried out, despite heavy German pressure. There is little doubt that in the spring of 1943, after Stalingrad, and while Nazi and Italian forces had been capitulating in North Africa, the Bulgarians did not wish to make things harder for themselves by participating in the massacre of the Jews. But in

Jewish Reaction and Resistance in Other Countries

the very same period, local supporters of the Germans collaborated in the murder of the Jews in Vichy France and in Slovakia, to give but two examples. We are not quite clear as to the motives of all those who participated in this Bulgarian drama, but is clear that the Jewish public was in no way passive, and that it was Jewish initiative which gave the first push to the opposition to the Germans on this issue.

XVI.

The Reaction in Palestine and the Slovakian Affair — The "Plan"

In our attempts to survey the rescue operations which were part of the Jewish reaction, we now turn to the beginning of 1943, the period of Stalingrad and of the British advance in the Western Desert after Alamein. It was now clear that Nazi Germany was to be defeated, but that this was still going to take some time, in the course of which the Nazis were likely to murder the remaining Jews of Europe. In Palestine, the full range of the Holocaust became clear only in this period. The reaction of the Yishuv was complete shock and despair, since the members of the Yishuv believed that the Nazis, in their retreat and defeat, would not leave a single Jewish soul alive.

The Jewish Agency for Palestine established a rescue committee headed by Yitzhak Gruenbaum, who had already been in charge of relations with the diaspora. This committee operated on the assumption that there was no real chance of rescue, and it was only acting to salve its conscience after the war and to be able to prove that it had acted for the saving of Jewish lives. In spite of this, the leaders of the Jewish Agency made efforts to achieve something, partly through this committee, but largely by circumventing it.

The Agency dispatched people to establish connections with the diaspora, and the most convenient place to send them to was Istanbul. It also began to take action for the dispatch of Palestinian parachutists to the diaspora. The experiment in Constantinople was

The Reaction in Palestine and the Slovakian Affair

of great importance. It was necessarily more or less an undercover activity, since the Turks did not, of course, consent to any Jewish mission — at best, they were prepared to allow the passage of Jews who held official immigration certificates issued by the British authorities. At the head of the mission stood Hayyim Barlas, a representative of the rescue committee. Two men in particular had connections with the diaspora — Menahem Bader and Venia Pomeranz (today Prof. Ze'ev Hadari). Their main preoccupation was the attempt to smuggle money into occupied Europe, especially by means of members of foreign embassies and legations, such as papal representatives, various agents, and the like. Bader and Pomeranz were active in Istanbul from the beginning of 1943, and were soon joined by additional agents, representing Agudath Israel, the Revisionists and other political bodies. They all attempted to act through this kind of direct contact, since there was no possibility of smuggling people from Istanbul into the Nazi-occupied areas. All the roads were blocked by the Turks, the Bulgarians, the Germans and the Russians. It was, however, possible to smuggle information and money. The Yishuv in Palestine collected sums of money, and for the small community of Palestine at the time — about half a million people — these were very large sums. Attempts were also being made to influence the representatives of foreign countries, especially the neutral ones, including the papal nuncio, Monsignor Angelo Roncalli, later Pope John XXIII. Bader and Berlas met him, and he did indeed intervene in favor of the Jews of the Balkan states. Through this channel, important news also reached Palestine, and we shall return to this later.

The other line of action was through the British army. There was no other way, since all attempts at a dialogue with the Americans and Yugoslavs, the Czechs and the Poles, were in vain. As part of the Allies' strategy, the British were responsible for the Middle East, and the only way of reaching Europe was through them. From the beginning of 1943, the Jewish Agency began to put immense pressure on Britain to make the dispatch of parachutists possible. But the first parachutists were sent into action only in September 1943, and into Yugoslavia, an area which was of no interest to the

Jewish Reactions to the Holocaust

Agency. The Jewish Agency was interested in reaching areas where remnants of European Jewry were still around, to Central and Eastern Europe, and not to that area of Yugoslavia which had already been liberated by Tito. But the British did not give their consent to this plan. With no Jewish army or air force in existence, there was no way of reaching Europe independently. Later on, parachutists were sent to Rumania. Here, bad luck combined with bad planning, since no one knew what to expect in that country.

The attempts were unsuccessful, not because of a lack of willingness on the part of the Agency or of the parachutists. On the contrary, very great efforts were made by organizations and individuals, but not everything attempted in a war is automatically a success. The British did not consent to send more than a very small number of people. Most of those parachuted in were caught on arrival, wounded, or unable to take action until it was too late.

Another attempt to save Jews in the Holocaust countries began with the expulsion of the Jews from Slovakia in March 1942, a process which continued until September. Of a population of 90,000 Jews in Slovakia, the Nazis expelled the majority — 58,000 — to Poland, mostly to Auschwitz. In Slovakia there was a Judenrat appointed by the Germans, and inside it there was an underground which called itself the Working Group. At the head of this body stood Gisi Fleischmann, the leader of WIZO and representative of the Joint in Slovakia, and Rabbi Michael Dov-Ber Weissmandel, representing the anti-Zionist orthodox in that country. He was the son-in-law of the spiritual leader of the ultra-orthodox Jewish community in Slovakia, Rabbi David Halevi Unger of Nitra.

These two, who were, incidentally, family relations, surrounded themselves with a group of activists, mainly Zionists, including Oscar Neumann, who was later the head of Judenrat. Representatives of this group replaced the existing Judenrat, so that a group which began underground was later to be officially at the center of things.

In June 1942, it occurred to Weissmandel that one might bribe the Nazis into putting a stop to the expulsion from Slovakia. They appealed, through a Jewish renegade, to the Nazi chief butcher in

The Reaction in Palestine and the Slovakian Affair

Slovakia, Dieter Wisliceny, and offered to bribe him. He accepted the proposal: (apparently) 50,000 dollars for stopping the expulsion from Slovakia. They had no such amounts of money in hand, but they immediately collected 25,000 dollars, and the expulsions were stopped for a while once half the bribe money had been paid.

The Jews undertook to pay the second half, but they did not possess that sum of money. They appealed to the Joint and to the Jewish community in Hungary. The Joint representative in Switzerland, Sally Mayer, could not transfer the money. In any case, it was necessary to raise the money, and it came from another source, from ultra-orthodox Jews in Hungary. The rest of the bribe money, 25,000 dollars, was paid before Yom Kippur 5703 (toward the end of 1942). According to Weissmandel, the expulsions from Slovakia had come to a halt; but in fact, there were still a number of expulsions before the second payment and one following it. Then, the expulsions stopped for two years. The question is whether the expulsions were stopped because of this payment or for other Nazi considerations.

It seems likely, despite the opinion of some scholars, that the expulsions were, indeed, stopped because of bribes, but not the bribes to Wisliceny; Slovak officials were bribed, and that was more important at that point. Of the $50,000, Wisliceny apparently put $30,000 into his own pocket, and gave the rest to his superiors. But the bribe he received made him less enthusiastic regarding deportations.

Another side of the same coin is that in 1942 Sally Mayer in Switzerland had no money. The whole budget of the Joint in that year, for its world-wide activities, was 7.38 million dollars. But Mayer could not transfer money to Slovakia, since the Swiss authorities refused to transfer abroad any money they received in dollars from the United States. In any case, the dollars remained in the United States, and the Swiss, had they agreed to transfer the money, would have paid out Swiss francs, not dollars.

Sally Mayer did not have the required sum of money; but even if he had had it, he could hardly draw it from the bank in the middle of the war and tell the bank manager that he was about to transfer it to Slovakia by all sorts of roundabout ways. Currency control in countries like Switzerland was most stringent, and no transfer of any large sum of money was possible. Weissmandel and others had been infected with the idea, whose ultimate source was Nazi ideology, that the Jews did indeed rule the world, and had unlimited opportunities to do whatever they fancied. Incidentally, it is interesting to find a similar view current among the younger generation in Israel today, who believe that Jews did not act during the Holocaust because they did not wish to act, although they were in a position to do things. This view is, of course, wholly erroneous.

A situation was created in which Sally Mayer was forced to dupe the Jews, and, while he pretended to represent the great and wealthy Jewish Joint Distribution Committee, the money he had in hand was extremely meager. To transfer black money in Swiss francs or in dollars officially from Switzerland to Slovakia in the midst of 1942 was more of a hallucination than a real possibility.

As soon as the expulsions were over, Weissmandel and his associates had another logical idea: if bribery had worked in the case of the Jews of Slovakia, one could try to apply the same method to the whole of European Jewry. They appealed to Wisliceny and proposed to him to stop the expulsions throughout Europe — in exchange for bribes, of course. This plan is now known as the "Plan."

Weissmandel, it appears, understood that the Nazis were not doing it for the money. After all, 50,000 dollars was a minute sum of money, utterly insignificant in the midst of a war. It was a sum of money which was expended in a matter of minutes of warfare. There had to be another reason. Weissmandel soon found out the reason: the Nazis apparently were seeking some connection with the United States. It seems that as early as the summer of 1942, while the German offensive in the Soviet Union was still going on and victory appeared to be within reach, it was already clear to Himmler that there was no way of winning the war. Thus he sought some options of possible contacts with the west. This was apparently done without Hitler's knowledge.

When Weissmandel understood — although, perhaps, not quite

The Reaction in Palestine and the Slovakian Affair

as clearly as we have set it out here — that some Nazi leaders were seeking some contact with the western world, he wrote a letter to himself. He did it on Swiss writing paper, which he had acquired on trips to Switzerland before the war, and on an old typewriter, of the sort that was still in use in Switzerland. He signed the letter "Ferdinand Roth, Representative of the Rabbis of the World." He thus fabricated the international Jewish conspiracy spoken of and described by the Nazis all those years. The letter stated that the rabbis of the world were willing to pay ransom for the rescue of Jews. He handed the letter to the Nazis. They checked it and saw that it was actually written on Swiss writing paper and typed on a Swiss typewriter. They saw no reason to doubt that the "Jewish world government" would address a letter to Weissmandel. This letter was probably a factor in this process, since the Nazis replied that they were indeed willing to take the ransom money.

Speaking of putting a stop to all expulsions from the whole of Europe was a serious affair. Negotiations opened in November 1942 and continued until August 1943. We shall not survey here all the various stages in these negotiations. At first the Nazis mentioned no sum, and Wisliceny said again and again that he had to consult Berlin. He did eventually go to Berlin, enquired, and came back with answers. At the end, the sum stood at two million dollars, which were supposed to be only a large advance for the stopping of all expulsions. Ten percent of this sum, that is, 200,000 dollars, were to be paid immediately, to make it possible to get down to realizing the new plan — that is, stopping the expulsion of Jews from Western Europe, Holland, Belgium, France, and the Balkans (which were only under partial German control). Poland and the Reich — that is, Germany, Austria and Czechoslovakia — were to be discussed later.

Where was one to obtain 200,000 dollars? Weissmandel addressed himself to Sally Mayer. For Mayer, this was a large sum, which he simply did not possess. Furthermore, he was opposed to the whole idea as a matter of principle, and he did not wish to assume the responsibility for such a step. He contacted the Joint leadership in Lisbon, and it referred the question to the United

Jewish Reactions to the Holocaust

States. The answer, as could be expected, was absolutely negative. It was a piece of Nazi deception, the United States Joint said. The Nazis were only trying to extort money and had no intention of giving anything in exchange. Besides, one could hardly transfer 200,000 dollars by "underground" ways. In addition, the United States government would object in principle to such ransom money and would not let these people emigrate, even if they were to be saved.

This was the answer received by Sally Mayer. He made his own decision not to disclose it to Gisi Fleischmann. Instead, he began by offering her alternative solutions of all sorts. He would muster 200,000 dollars, he said, but not for immediate payment, but only to be paid after the war, on the assumption that these Nazis, once they had capitulated, would require money abroad. He would safeguard the money in the United States. He also told her to collect the money now, in occupied Europe, in dollars, on the assumption that those who gave her the money now would receive it back after the war. Mayer was attempting to find alternative ways, while he had no money or any chance of obtaining it from the United States.

Gisi Fleischmann hardly understood, and began to complain. At that stage, Mayer transferred the money he had in hand, a far smaller quantity — 90,000 francs, and all in "black" money. If he was caught, it would be a catastrophe. He was not afraid for his himself, for he was a Swiss citizen. The danger would lie in a complete stoppage of his work and of the activities of the Joint. But he took the risk and transferred the money.

Weissmandel and Gisi Fleischmann also appealed to Istanbul, and the Jewish Agency representatives there passed on the information — not as a recommendation, but as a demand, written in the firmest terms. Bader and Pomeranz were delegates of the Histadrut (the Jewish Trade Union Movement in Palestine) and of the Kibbutz movement. They therefore appealed in the first instance to their own organization, the Histadrut, and demanded money. Their demand reached the Jewish Agency; Sharett had his doubts, but he eventually decided to pay. The Agency began by transferring to Istanbul 50,000 pounds sterling (then 200,000

The Reaction in Palestine and the Slovakian Affair

dollars), and the first 15,000 pounds sterling were transferred from there to Slovakia. This means that at least the leadership of the Yishuv responded to the demand. But collecting the money took much time, and its illegal transfer to Istanbul caused immense difficulties. At the end, the money seems to have reached its destination. It appears that it was not delivered to the Nazis, since in May and June they began to raise doubts concerning the plan. At first, Wisliceny told the Working Group of Weissmandel and Gisi Fleischmann that he had to make further clarifications of the whole business, and then, in August, he told them that the plan was not being cancelled, but was being postponed temporarily.

We know that the plan was reported not only by Sally Mayer, but also by the World Jewish Congress. The reports reached Aryeh Leon Kuborwitzky, Nahum Goldmann and Aryeh Tartakower — the men who were conducting the business of the World Jewish Congress in New York. To the Jews of the United States, their representatives and their leaders, this appeared to be an attempt at extorting money, made by some petty Nazi official in Slovakia, not even by the German government. We now know that this was not quite the case. Eichmann himself approved of the plan, and since he was not in the habit of taking such decisions on his own authority, one may be virtually certain that he had obtained Himmler's approval. What exactly were Himmler's reasons in attempting to send such feelers to the Americans through the Jews, and what were his reasons for calling off these negotiations in 1943? These are questions which are still open, and no answer has been forthcoming so far.

The question arises whether opportunities were missed. One must understand that the information about the Holocaust had by then been received in the outside world, and from the beginning of 1943 any attempts by the Nazis to send such feelers appeared, at least officially, to be acts of camouflage and deception. Precisely because one now took seriously the reports of the Holocaust, one could hardly believe in the possibility of negotiating with the Devil himself.

Here we have a most unfortunate psychological inhibition. People who were in Europe, such as Gisi Fleischmann, overcame it, and so, probably, did those in direct contact with these people, such as Bader, Pomeranz or Mayer. The difficulty became greater the further away one moved from the Nazi purgatory. When we reach the story of Hungarian Jewry, we will meet with the same phenomenon in a far more pronounced manner.

XVII.

The Mission of Joel Brand

The attempt to bribe the Nazis to stop the expulsions from the whole of Europe (which, as we have mentioned, was referred to by those who were trying to bribe them as the European Plan), had its sequel. In 1943, the country closest to Slovakia from which money and aid could be obtained was Hungary, which had not yet been occupied by the Nazis. Hungary was, it is true, an ally of the Nazis, and had even taken part in Germany's war against the Soviet Union. But it was not under Nazi occupation, and the Jews of Hungary lived in a twilight situation, so to speak. For the Jews, this was a situation of relative unease, but not yet a Holocaust. The Jews of Hungary were also convinced that there would be no Holocaust in their country, since the Russians had begun to advance in 1943. The end of the war seemed to be on the distant horizon, and there was a reasonable chance that Hungarian Jewry might get through the war without being seriously affected. That is not to say that during this period, before 1943, Hungarian Jewry was in no way harmed. In 1930 and 1939, discriminatory laws were enacted against the Jews, and these affected them economically and socially. As early as 1940, Hungarian Jews began to be conscripted into labor units in place of military service, and when war broke out in 1941 between Hungary and Russia, these became forced labor units. The Jews, of course, possessed no arms; their clothes were marked with yellow stripes, and they wore military caps. They were transferred mostly to the eastern front, and the large majority of these Jewish men were killed

Jewish Reactions to the Holocaust

in minefields, or died of hard labor, lack of nourishment, or in mass murders perpetrated by the Hungarians and the Germans. But if this was the case, we can ask ourselves why a massive resistance movement did not arise in Hungary. We should remember that there were hardly any men left among the Hungarian Jews, and without them one cannot speak of massive resistance. Between 16,000 and 18,000 Jews from the northeastern part of fascist Hungary — which had been part of Czechoslovakia in the past, an area called Carpatho-Russia — and from northern Transylvania, were expelled to the Ukraine in the summer of 1941 and were murdered near the city of Kamenetz-Podolsk by German S.S. troops, assisted by the Hungarians.

In any case, although the men were in labor units, and there was severe discrimination against the Jews, the Jewish communities continued to exist, there was freedom of movement, and there was, more or less, enough to subsist on. This was the situation until early 1944.

At the end of 1942, a Zionist Committee was set up, headed by a Zionist leader named Otto Komoly, and his deputy, Dr. Israel Kastner (who was known in Hungary as Reszoe Kasztner), with a group of activists. At first, this was a coalition of Zionist movements, but later on, Komoly and Kastner became the people who took the real decisions in this group. The members of this committee assigned themselves the task of smuggling Jews from Poland into Hungary, where the situation was still relatively good. The man who engaged in this smuggling, Joel Brand, a former communist, had already arrived in Hungary in the 1930's. He was a highly talented man and was moved by a strong desire to save people. At the same time, he was an adventurer and a man of somewhat unstable personality — but certainly a hero from the Jewish point of view.

The Nazis began to suspect, with good cause, that the Hungarians were about to stop their cooperation in the war, and on March 19, 1944 they entered Hungary. Together with the Nazi occupation troops came Adolf Eichmann with a special unit, whose aim was the wholesale murder of the Jews of Hungary. Eichmann

The Mission of Joel Brand

began to prepare the measures for the deportation of the Jews to Auschwitz, with the keen support of the antisemitic Hungarian regime. A Judenrat was established, consisting of terrified people who tried to find some way of introducing order into the new situation. This Judenrat was composed mainly of people of liberal religious views, known in Hungary as neologues, and of orthodox Jews. The members of the orthodox minority, just as much as those of the neologue majority, were assimilated Jews who were Hungarian patriots, and, of course, extreme anti-Zionists. The Judenrat also contained a small and rather insignificant Zionist representation. The underground council, the Aid and Rescue Committee run by Komoly and Kastner, was not included.

With the German occupation, Wisliceny — the man who had conducted the negotiations concerning the bribes in Slovakia — also arrived in Budapest. He came with a letter from Weissmandel to the heads of Hungarian Jewry, asking them to conduct negotiations with him for the rescue of the Jews of Hungary in exchange for bribes, as had been done with success in Slovakia two years earlier.

Wisliceny came with this letter to the leader of the Hungarian Jewish orthodoxy, Baron Phillip von Freudiger, head of the Orthodox Jewish Office. Freudiger exploited this bridgehead, eventually rescuing himself and a group of people associated with him, since he did not believe in the possibility of any large-scale actions in Hungary. Anyone who could save himself should do so, and that was that.

Wisliceny appealed to other people, including Kastner, whose name he had received from the Zionist Working Group in Slovakia. He met with him, and began to negotiate the paying of bribes in return for preventing the expulsion of Hungarian Jewry. He promised not to expel the Jews, and in exchange demanded and received bribe money. The Nazis did not fulfil their promise. As early as their first conversation, the idea of emigration to Palestine was raised by Kastner. He was thinking of an initial figure of 600 people, but Wisliceny believed that this was too small a number, and if one was speaking of emigration, he should be thinking of a

Jewish Reactions to the Holocaust

few thousand people. Wisliceny "quit the game" immediately after the first conversation, and Eichmann took his place.

Today, it is quite clear that Eichmann stood behind Wisliceny, and that behind Eichmann stood Himmler. Hence it is obvious that, from the Nazi point of view, these negotiations were not to be left in the hands of a minor official such as Wisliceny. Kastner was rather inconvenient to the Nazis as a partner in these negotiations: he was far too independent and firm. They required someone simpler and more naive — someone, say, like Joel Brand.

Brand was invited on April 25 to his first meeting with Eichmann, who told him: "Go wherever you want and negotiate." At first, they spoke of merchandise, and then of lorries. At the end, they came down to 10,000 lorries for a million Jews, not only from Hungary, but from the whole of Europe. The Germans were prepared to release them, but only to the west, not to Palestine, where they had an obligation to the Mufti of Jerusalem, head of the Palestinian Arab national movement, not to let any more Jews enter.

Brand accepted the offer and brought it to his friends Komoly and Kastner. They were not happy about Brand conducting the negotiations, not because they did not rely on his loyalty and willingness to act, but they did not regard him as the most suitable person for conducting political negotiations. It was clear to them that this was a matter the success of which depended on the intervention of the Allies. But in the end, it was not the committee, but Eichmann, who determined who was to be dispatched.

Brand arrived in Istanbul on May 17, 1944. He did not come alone. He was accompanied by Andor-Antal (Bandi) Grosz, a double agent and a very interesting personality. The main mission was, in fact, put in the hands of Grosz. He was entrusted with it, not by Eichmann, but by Eichmann's superior, since Eichmann was only a Gestapo man. The commander of the S.S. Security Service, the S.D., in Hungary, Otto Klages, charged Grosz with the central task, which was to be negotiations with the Americans, and, in case the Americans were inaccessible, with the British, for establishing peace between the S.S. and western powers. Hitler was still in power, but Himmler had heard that there were plans for the

The Mission of Joel Brand

generals to rise up against Hitler. Himmler did not know who was to carry out the assassination attempt; he was unaware of the technical details, and probably did not wish to know them. But he did know that there was a plot against Hitler; he knew who the people were who were involved in it, and he was awaiting the result. If the result was to be Hitler's removal, the incompetent heads of the army were unlikely to stand up to the well-organized S.S., with its huge combat units inside Germany itself. The S.S. would then take over in Germany, and he, Himmler, would conclude his own separate peace with the west — provided that someone was now to prepare the ground. This was the task entrusted to Grosz.

Thus, the two of them, Grosz and Brand, arrived in Istanbul. The central mission was that of Grosz, but Brand's mission was also of great importance. It was a secondary mission, whose aim was to effect the breakthrough to the Americans by way of the Jews, in case the mission entrusted to Grosz was to fail.

Negotiations began. But in Istanbul there was, after all, only the Jewish Agency mission. The Jewish Yishuv in Palestine was the first to learn of the arrival of a messenger from purgatory with the message: Help! It is a matter of 10,000 lorries. Get worldwide aid. Brand, who was extremely naive, actually believed that the Jewish Agency for Palestine had the power to array the whole free world to the support of the Jews of Europe. In fact, it was even impossible to bring Sharett to Istanbul, since the Turks, who understood what was going on, were still neutral, and were not willing to risk a rift with Germany. Thus they were not prepared to allow a representative of the Jewish Agency to enter Turkey for the sake of such negotiations. The British were unwilling to accept Grosz and Brand, since this would be interpreted by the Soviets as holding negotiations with the Nazis. They made it clear that they had no intention to negotiate with these envoys, and that they were to return to Hungary forthwith. Their fate was of no interest to the British authorities.

The Jewish Agency mission in Istanbul was under heavy pressure. How could it allow the two envoys to be returned empty-handed? The emphasis was on Brand, since Grosz was a spy and a Jewish agent for the Nazis. Brand, on the other hand, was a man who was ready to risk his life, an idealist by all accounts. To let him return to Hungary would mean giving up the only chance of negotiations. What was more, this would mean abandoning him, his family and his friends. But there was no choice. It was May 26-28, 1944, and the Turks were going to return Brand to Europe in a matter of a day or two.

The writer Amos Elon published a book in Israel which claims to describe these events. Elon is an outstanding writer, but in this case he made a fundamental mistake, and as history this book is a distortion of events. Elon pictures Brand as a man who was under immense pressures, who did not quite know what was happening to him, but wished to return to Hungary at any price. The Jewish Agency envoys are described in this book as having abandoned Brand to his fate, while the exact opposite is true. The envoys tried to avoid his return to Hungary at any price, knowing that if he were to return, he would be murdered. Brand himself was unwilling to return, and he was right not to wish to return without an answer to Eichmann's proposal. Contrary to what has been asserted on various occasions, as if the Jewish Agency expelled him from Istanbul and handed him over to the British authorities, the situation was just the opposite. The British were not prepared to meet him, and the Turks were pressing for his return to Hungary. Brand and the mission in Istanbul were against this.

At the end, when it seemed that there was no alternative, Bader persuaded Brand, in a dramatic all night conversation, to be a hero and to return. He promised to do his best to make sure that Brand was not executed on his return to the German occupation area. They wrote up an agreement, ostensibly by the Allies — but it was clear that this would be of little avail to him, and that he would fall into the clutches of Eichmann.

At the very last minute, just as the Turks were about to make Brand cross back into Hungary, the British changed their minds. They were now prepared to meet Brand in Syria. A sigh of relief was heard. The mission was on, and there was someone to speak to. Brand went to Syria with a British promise that he was to return as a

The Mission of Joel Brand

free man. But the British did not fulfil their promise. They took him to Cairo, and although they maintained that they would eventually let him return to Hungary, he was put under strict surveillance, together with Grosz.

What was the attitude of the representatives of the western powers, and of the Jewish Agency for Palestine, to this mission? The Jewish Agency took the mission very seriously. What had taken place in 1943 made Sharett treat the whole matter in earnest. He interviewed Brand in Aleppo, near the Syrian border, and, surprisingly enough, won the support of the British High Commissioner for Palestine, who was not prepared to be the man who would undermine a rescue mission — as he himself explains in one of our documents. Not for an excessive love of the Jews — that was not one of Sir Harold MacMichael's "vices" — but he was not prepared to be responsible for the loss of human lives. He therefore assisted in enabling Sharett to fly to London. The time was the end of May, and at the beginning of June the Allies' invasion of France was to take place. The British had other things on their agenda beside flying Moshe Sharett from Cairo to London. But they flew him. Not only MacMichael, but also Lord Moyne, who was in charge in Cairo, was not willing to be an obstacle in the way of a rescue mission — and Sharett was dispatched.

A remark is in place here. Somewhere in the book of memoirs dictated by Joel Brand, it is alleged that Lord Moyne said to him: "One million Jews? Where shall I put one million Jews?" The members of Lehi (the Stern Group), who were later to assassinate Lord Moyne in Cairo, and some historians, have seen in this an expression of the inhumanity on the part of Lord Moyne, who is alleged to have left the Jews to their fate. What they have not noticed is that Brand himself, in a footnote in the same book, writes that he later found out that it was not Lord Moyne at all. He had met with a certain Englishman who said to him: "A million Jews? What shall we do with a million Jews?" But this man was not Lord Moyne (see Joel Brand, *A Mission for the Condemned*, Hebrew version, Tel Aviv 1957, p. 156 — English version: Alex Weissberg, *Advocate for the Dead*, London, 1958).

Jewish Reactions to the Holocaust

When Sharett came to London and presented the case, the British were already aware of this mission. They had received information from their own sources, and they opened negotiations. Their approach was: One is not to close the gates. We cannot afford, after the war, to be told that we had a chance of saving human lives and did not save them. But the British were also apprehensive of the Americans, and found it necessary to inform them.

When the Americans were informed, their first response was that one had to tell the Russians. Here, the British position was different: if one were to tell the Soviets, the proposal was doomed to failure and the mission would be ruined. It was clear to them that the Russians would oppose the whole project. Thus, the British were willing to assist — although it is still far from clear how or to what extent — while the Americans were insisting that the Soviets should be informed, and the Americans soon did so. As could be predicted, the Soviet response was entirely negative. No negotiations with the Nazis, on any issue whatsoever, were to take place. (Incidentally, the Soviets were putting out feelers to the Nazis, at that very moment, in Sweden.) Their solution was to win the war, then all the victims of German Fascism would be saved.

At this initial stage, the western powers found themselves in a quandary concerning the proper response to the mission. What decided the issue was the interrogation of Bandi Grosz in Cairo. On the morning of July 13, the minutes of Grosz' interrogation reached the British government. They realized that the Nazis were really aiming at separate peace talks, and the Jewish issue was only a means to that end. The British government received the information from Cairo and decided that no separate talks were to be held with the Germans. They made a distinction between Brand and Grosz. Brand's mission was regarded as a proper rescue mission, whereas Grosz' was a Nazi provocation, and they were not prepared to have anything to do with him.

At this point, the positions were suddenly reversed. The British were now insisting that no negotiations were to take place. If anyone wished to send Brand back into Hungary, he was welcome to do so, but without any message. This would imply, of course, that

The Mission of Joel Brand

he would be killed on his return there empty handed.

The Americans, on the other hand, now believed that one should not close any opening. One could, of course, hold no negotiations about Eichmann's concrete proposal, which had been conveyed by Brand — but perhaps one might be able to negotiate in some other manner. The War Refugee Board set up half a year earlier was now beginning to press for anything possible to be done to save the victims, provided this did not damage the war effort. This was the situation in July 1944, as Brand's mission had proved a failure.

XVIII.

The Kastner Train

We have noted that the mission of Grosz was to have brought about a meeting between senior American officers and representatives of the S.S. in order to discuss the possibility of a separate peace agreement.

A question immediately arises: separate peace between the S.S. and the western Allies? Where was Hitler, and where was the German state machinery? As we have noted already, Himmler knew that there was opposition to Hitler in Germany, and, even if he was not privy to all the details, it was clear to him that this opposition might take control of Germany, or at least try to do so. But Himmler was also certain that his well-trained S.S. forces were to be the new rulers of Germany. It is now clear that Himmler was looking for ways — with or without Hitler — to jump off this headlong war against the whole world, and to carry on fighting the Soviet Union with the cooperation of the west. In order to achieve this, one needed to establish some contacts, and that was the purpose of Grosz' mission, which was to fulfil a major task in this context.

We have seen that the British decided that Brand could be sent back, but without bringing any answer with him. The Jewish Agency was unwilling to have Brand sent back in such circumstances, for it felt that that meant sending Brand to his death. It informed the British authorities that it was only prepared to have Brand returned if some message was to be passed through him, which could form a basis for negotiating with the Nazis about putting a stop to the

The Kastner Train

murder of Jews.

The Americans, on the other hand, persevered, even after July 13, in their policy, according to which no possibility of contacts with the Germans was to be ignored, since the very existence of negotiations, whatever was to be discussed in them, was likely to preserve the lives of potential Jewish victims of the Nazis. The Americans were thus prepared to establish some form of contact with the Germans, although this was contrary to agreed Anglo-American policies. At the American end, support was being given to the idea formed in the War Refugee Board headed by John Pehle, who believed that one should find a mediator who was neither American nor German for conducting these negotiations.

The Germans were also extremely interested in these negotiations, for their own reasons. The first person to receive an offer to cross over to the Nazi occupied zone in order to hold negotiations was Menahem Bader in Istanbul. The offer was passed on to him by a member of the German consulate there. Bader, of course, could not simply get up and go. He was too well known, and it was inconceivable that he would simply board a plane and fly out. As the holder of a Palestinian passport, he required some form of permit. Bader asked Ben Gurion for such a permit. Ben Gurion applied to the British. Their answer was that this was entirely out of the question.

The Germans next proposed — on the advice of Kastner in Budapest — that the head of the Joint in Portugal, Dr. Joseph J. Schwarz, conduct the negotiations. Schwarz passed on this request to the American authorities, who answered on the next day that this was out of the question, since Schwarz was an American citizen. But the formulation of this answer already hinted that, if the man proposed was not an American or a British citizen, or a citizen of any other Allied state, one might be able to talk.

At this stage, Kastner made the proposal that perhaps the most suitable man was the Joint representative in Switzerland, Sally Mayer, who was not an American or a British citizen, but a citizen of neutral Switzerland, and at the same time represented the Joint. This was possible from the American point of view. Discussion now began between the Joint, the State Department and the WRB, in order to investigate the possibility that Sally Mayer might indeed be capable of conducting the negotiations opened by Brand. From this point of view, it would be possible to maintain that Brand's mission had not been a failure, but merely that its first stage had failed, mainly because of Grosz, but also, perhaps, because of the fantastic nature of the proposals which Brand had brought with him.

We will stop here for a while — we will return to Sally Mayer in our next chapter — and concentrate on a completely different issue, namely on what was happening in the meantime in Budapest, which Brand had left just as the transports had begun to roll to Auschwitz.

These transports, organized by Eichmann and his Hungarian collaborators, began on the night of May 14, and on the 15th the first train left. From then until the beginning of July, 437,000 Jews from the provinces were expelled to Auschwitz. It has been maintained that the Jews of Hungary were murdered because they did not know what was awaiting them, and therefore they did not resist or escape. This claim cannot in any way be substantiated. On the contrary, one may claim that the Jews of Hungary received information, but they did not digest the significance of this information. Hungarian soldiers and their officers, who had witnessed the murder of the Jews in the Ukraine, came to Hungary on leave and told their stories. Some remnants of the Jewish labor units in the Hungarian army, who had also served in the Ukraine — about 5,000 broken and dejected men — also returned to Hungary in 1943 and described what they had seen. Refugees from among these Hungarian Jews, who had been expelled to the Ukraine as early as 1941 to be massacred there and had somehow managed to escape back into Hungary, brought back their own tales. All through 1943, the B.B.C. reported these facts, in Hungarian as well as in other languages. It did not report them very frequently — not every day or every week — but things were reported, heard and absorbed. There were also thousands of Slovak Jews who managed to penetrate into Hungary. In addition, probably close to 2,500 Polish Jews managed to escape the mass murders in Poland and to reach Hungary, in 1943-4. They settled in the larger centers and

The Kastner Train

told their stories. All these were sources of information. But, as we have already pointed out, there is a very wide gap between a piece of information received and between what is absorbed and digested by those receiving it. Thus, when the transports of Jews out of Hungary began, most Jewish communities needed no Kastner or anyone else to tell them what was going on. Information had been available for some time: what was lacking was awareness.

Kastner himself has been accused of withholding this information from the people of his native city of Cluj, on the border of Hungary and Rumania. This city is only about 12-13 kilometers from the Rumanian border, and, had the people of Cluj known, they might have escaped. But it has now emerged from an extremely interesting study written at the Hebrew University of Jerusalem, that in a Rumanian border town not far from Cluj, Turdea, there existed an organization for smuggling Jews out of Hungary into Rumania, an organization run jointly by the ultra-orthodox and Zionists, which was thus acceptable to Jews of all descriptions. Parallel to it, there also existed in the city of Cluj itself a Jewish rescue organization, consisting of some outstanding members of the community. This organization attempted to persuade the Jews of Cluj to escape to Rumania, warning them that what was at stake was a question of life and death. But only very few were to be found who were willing to cross the border. One can understand those who later claimed that they had not known. Forty years have elapsed and those people who possessed the information but rejected it are now claiming that they had no knowledge. It is true that they had no knowledge of Auschwitz, but only of a total and wholesale murder of the Jews of Poland. Here we are put in a serious quandary, since those who can remember this period today are utterly convinced that they had no knowledge then, and we are hardly in a position to accuse them. One should not raise this issue as an accusation against anyone, but merely as an explanation to a phenomenon which we discover anew time and again in dealing with the reminiscences of those who survived the Holocaust. People are reluctant to remember some of the facts, since such reminiscences would be frustrating, horrifying, or both. Thus, the main problem of Hungarian Jewry during the expulsions was not lack of information, but the reluctance to accept as a fact that expulsion to Poland spelled death. This is also why the people were so prone to believe the diversionary stories spread by the Germans.

The Hungarian Judenrat, which was itself submissive to all the dictates of the Germans, had a sub-department, whose task was to warn the Jews of the provinces about the terrible threat of death involved in the expulsions. This office was manned by members of the youth movements — the whole spectrum of them, from the socialist and secularist Hashomer Hatza'ir to the religious Bnei Akiva. Envoys of these youth movements went out to the transit ghettoes which had been set up in Hungary for the few weeks remaining until the expulsions, but people were reluctant to believe them, and they were expelled, on the pretext that they were spreading panic around. Thus, the Jewish public was finding it difficult to absorb the information concerning the Holocaust, which had descended on it so suddenly. The Germans entered Hungary on March 19; the expulsions began on May 15 and ended on July 9. This was a very brief space of time, during which it was extremely hard to adapt oneself to the unpalatable truth. We emphasize once more: these facts are not cited here as an accusation against the victims, but as a denunciation of the murderers. Those who study these facts nowadays should direct their hostility toward the murderers and accord the victims their sympathy.

Kastner was obviously far from being an angel, but he was a man of unique talents. He was an extremely ambitious man, motivated by a most powerful drive to perform great actions, some of which he carried out very well, and some of which were rather dubious. Like all those around him during this period, he wanted to save people: there can be no doubt about that. In order to break through this trap of total murder, he formulated a plan with Eichmann, according to which a few hundred Jews were to be allowed out initially; in the end, there were over 1,680. They were to be sent by a special train from Budapest to a neutral country.

This train left Budapest at the end of June. It was representative of the whole spectrum of Hungarian Jewry. The ultra-orthodox put

The Kastner Train

Rabbi Joel Teitelbaum, the violently anti-Zionist and anti-modernist Rebbe of Satmar on this train. It carried neologues and orthodox, refugees and children, members of the youth movements and Zionists. The list of people who travelled on this train had been compiled by the popular and admired head of the Rescue Committee, Otto Komoly — the representative of the General Zionists, who won the praise of everybody — by Kastner, and by some others.

What was Kastner's chief motive in organizing this train? It appears that his motive was to create a precedent. In the midst of the war, in 1944, the Nazis were to send a train full of Jews outside the boundaries of the Reich. The implication of this would be that the principle of total murder had been breached, and this might get the Nazis nearer to stopping the mass murder and to sitting at the negotiating table.

On this train, Kastner saved his own family and friends. This is often raised as an accusation against him. But could he be sure that this train was really going to cross the border rather than end up in Auschwitz? After all, the Germans had deceived the Jews on many previous occasions, and Kastner was well aware of this. Indeed, when this train reached one of the Austrian stations and the people were taken out for a shower — for a real shower — at a time that rumors of the gas chambers had already become widespread, panic took hold of them. They suspected that they might be driven to a death camp, and Rabbi Joel Teitelbaum sent a telegram, asking to be released from the train. At the end, in fact, the train did not reach a neutral country like Spain, as the Nazis had promised, but the transit camp of Bergen-Belsen, and its passengers had to be rescued from the camp later. There is reason to believe that Kastner put his own family on this train in order to demonstrate his trust in the Nazi promise, and his belief that this time the Nazis would keep their word.

It is tempting to think what people would have said of Kastner had his gamble proved unsuccessful and had the train ended up in Auschwitz.

This issue of the rescue train raises serious problems, of course.

Jewish Reactions to the Holocaust

On the one hand, it appears as if those saved were mainly eminent and distinguished people. This is true in itself, although many on this train were ordinary people, refugees and the young. On the other hand, one can regard this — and it seems that this is the right attitude — as an attempt to break through the barrier of wholesale Nazi murder. The behavior of Kastner, Komoly and others can be explained against the background of their frantic efforts to save Jewish lives. Komoly attempted to do this by means of what was called "the Hungarian Line." He tried to save Jews through negotiations with the Hungarian government, but was unsuccessful. He did manage to contact various people; but even if that had some marginal effect, no real consequences were apparent. Kastner tried to carry on the negotiations for the sake of which Brand had been dispatched to Istanbul. He tried to carry on from where Brand had left off and to save in any way whatever could still be saved.

It was precisely at this time that the youth movements, and chief among them the pioneering youth movements, began to organize, not against the policies of Kastner and Komoly — although they had no faith in those policies — but along parallel lines, engaging in illegal activities. They smuggled over 4,000 Jews from Hungary into Rumania, and a few thousand other Jews from Hungary back into Slovakia. They called this movement "Tijul" ("Excursion" in Hebrew) and the movement of Jews into Slovakia "re-Tijul," since these people had previously escaped from Slovakia into Hungary and were now returning to Slovakia. They engaged in a large scale forgery of documents — not just documents of personal identity, but food rations and other types of documents. They set up workshops, in which they forged documents not only for Jews, but for the pathetic and miserable Hungarian anti-Nazi underground, which was so weak that it was wholly dependent on Jews, on pioneering Zionist youth, to supply it with documents. In the midst of the tragedy, this was a piece of comic relief.

What remained in Hungary in July was essentially Budapest Jewry alone.

To continue our story, we now pass to our next subject, the

The Kastner Train

bombing of Auschwitz. When we discuss rescue attempts by the free world and the reactions of the free world to the Holocaust, we arrive here at what appears to be a climax in the whole process, but which was, in fact, largely an accident. For this idea — to bomb the camps and the railway lines leading to them — had never before occurred to anyone. Was such a thing at all possible from a technical point of view? It now appears that it may have been, from the end of 1943, for at that time the airport at Foggia in Italy had been adapted for American bomber planes whose range was sufficient for bombing Auschwitz and the railway lines leading to it. On May 16, 1944, Rabbi Weissmandel, whom we have already met on a few occasions, sent a letter from Slovakia which reached Istanbul and Switzerland. It was addressed both to the Zionists and the ultra-orthodox. He spoke not only in his own name, but in the name of the whole working group in Slovakia, Zionist and orthodox alike. His message was that now that the trains were beginning to travel from Hungary to Auschwitz, it was time to bomb the railway lines as well as the camps.

By sheer accident, this news was passed on to the United States by Yitzhak Gruenbaum, the Zionist leader in Jerusalem, and by Yitzhak Sternbuch, an ultra-orthodox Jew in Switzerland, on the very same day, June 2, 1944. The immediate demand was: "Bomb the railway lines!"

Gruenbaum also passed this demand on to Ben Gurion, Goldmann and Weizmann. It began to be raised through all these channels, both by Agudath Israel and by the various branches, departments and prominent personalities of the Jewish Agency. It was included in the demands of the Jewish Agency when it insisted in London that Brand be returned to the Germans with some proposal to hold negotiations. Among the demands of the Jewish Agency on this occasion there were two which appear to have had equal weight: a. to appeal to Stalin to join this initiative; b. to bomb the railway lines leading to Auschwitz. This was based on the message of Rabbi Weissmandel, which included details of all the various railway lines which ought to be bombed.

The demands reached the British government, and something

Jewish Reactions to the Holocaust

quite unbelievable happened. The foreign secretary, Eden, treated this demand with considerable sympathy. But it transpired that the British only had night bombers. These bombers were capable of reaching the eastern areas of Germany. There was also now a new war plane used by the Allies, the Mustang (P-51) which had the proper range for accompanying the bomber planes, but carrying out an accurate attack on a camp or on a railway line was simply impossible at night. This meant that one would have to apply to the Americans, once the British Air Force had given its approval.

Eden passed on the proposal to Churchill, who answered in the affirmative: "Get anything out of the Air Force you can, and invoke me if necessary." Eden contacted the British minister of aviation, Sir Archibald Sinclair, who was a great friend of the Zionist movement. Sir Archibald did not understand the technical aspects of such an operation, and he referred the proposal to his military experts. They reported back to him: a. They could not launch such an operation since they had only night bombers; b. They had no plans of the camp. The long and short of it was that this proposal had to be referred to the Americans, and even to do this, one needed maps of the camp.

Sinclair passed this reply to Eden, who scribbled on it a mordant remark: "He wasn't asked his opinion on this; he was asked to act." This was where the matter rested, since the Foreign Office officials had decided to undermine the whole project. The prime minister had given his approval; the foreign secretary had given his support — but the civil servants in the Foreign Office were holding everything up. They supplied no maps, nor did they contact the Jewish Agency or the Polish Government in Exile in London, which also possessed maps, to ask for them. They simply left things as they were.

Two months — July and August — elapsed, and, whenever the Jewish Agency applied to the British government and asked what was being done about bombing the railway lines and the camp itself, it found itself up against an incomprehensible wall of silence.

XIX.

The Bombing of Auschwitz

On June 6, 1944, the Allies invaded Europe, and fierce battles raged in Normandy. The question of bombing the railway lines leading to the Auschwitz death camp was laid aside. The Holocaust of European Jewry was regarded by the British, including those who favored the proposal to bomb the railway lines to Auschwitz, as only one of many questions raised by the war. This was the seed of this particular tragedy.

It was only in August 1944 that the problem was raised again on the British side, when a relatively new official at the Foreign Office checked his files and discovered that the Foreign Office had not yet replied to the request of the aviation ministry to supply plans of the death camp at Auschwitz. The British contacted the Jews and asked them whether they were now prepared to give up the idea of bombing Auschwitz or were still insisting on it. The representative of the Jewish Agency in London was thunderstruck, and replied that of course there was no intention on the Agency's part of renouncing the plan. The British claimed that they had information that the expulsions from Hungary had stopped. It was, in fact, true that from July 9 onward there were no more expulsions from Hungary to Auschwitz. On the other hand, people were now being shipped to Auschwitz from various other places in Europe. The Agency stood firm. It did not know, it said, which deportations had been stopped and which ones were still going on; but the Nazi murder plan was still in force, and the camp had to be bombed. The Jewish Agency

Jewish Reactions to the Holocaust

supplied the plans. A peculiar situation now came about. The Jewish Agency supplied the plans to the RAF; but the RAF was not prepared to carry out the bombing, since its bombers were suited only for night actions. The matter, therefore, had to be referred to the Americans. On September 1, 1944, the secretary of the British cabinet gave his final reply in a letter to Weizmann: He was sorry to inform him that the British were unable to bomb the camp.

Meanwhile, the request was also referred to the Americans. They weighed the possibilities, and on July 4, 1944 — that is, a month and a half before the British reply, the deputy secretary of aviation, John McCloy, sent a negative answer; the Americans were not able to carry out the bombing for technical reasons. Behind this refusal there is a simple fact: the WRB, headed by the pro-Jewish John Pehle, whom we have mentioned already, did not address itself with a clear demand to the American air force, through the department of aviation. It merely passed on a Jewish request, and Pehle made it clear that he was not dealing with a military issue and had no intention of putting pressure on the military arm. He left it to the discretion of the air force, and, if it was to find good reasons for carrying out the operation, it should do so.

It should be noted here that, in the America of July 1944, Pehle could not yet comprehend the reality of Auschwitz. In April 1944, two inmates escaped from Auschwitz and reached Slovakia. They carried with them a detailed plan of the camp, and told the full story of what was going on inside it, including the gas chambers and the number of those murdered. At the beginning of May, two other Jewish prisoners escaped. This was already after the plans for the expulsion of the Jews of Hungary to Auschwitz had been made known to the inmates by their torturers.

These people also escaped to Slovakia, and there, a detailed report of their stories was taken down in writing. These reports reached Budapest and came into the hands of Kastner, the orthodox (Freudiger), and the Judenrat, and later reached Switzerland. The Czechoslovak representative at the headquarters of the International Red Gross in Switzerland, Jaromir Kopecky, one of Jewry's greatest friends, passed on this report to all the Allies. In an

The Bombing of Auschwitz

abbreviated version, his report also reached the British government. On June 24, the telegram lay on Churchill's desk, and on July 11 wrote: "There is no doubt that this is probably the greatest and most horrible crime ever committed in the history of the world." What was one to do, Churchill asked Foreign Secretary Eden. This ties up with what we have already said concerning Churchill's willingness to authorize the bombing of Auschwitz.

But the Auschwitz report did not reach the United States until the beginning of November 1944, nearly half a year later. Thus, when Pehle received the names of the camps in June, they did not mean much to him.

The American deputy secretary of aviation, McCloy, refused to deal with this matter. If we ask whether the Americans were in a position to bomb the camp, the answer must be positive. Moreover, they had already dispatched reconnaissance planes, from England and from another base in the south of Italy (we have already mentioned the airport at Foggia) to the whole area of Upper Silesia, where the Nazi concentration camps, including Auschwitz, were located. They made aerial photographs of all these places in an attempt to discover those locations where synthetic fuel was being produced. They did discover such a location, about 13 kilometers from Auschwitz, at Monowitz, which was part of the concentration camp, but not the part containing the gas chambers. The death camp was also included in these aerial photographs, but it did not interest the Americans. The United States Air Force was only interested in the factory — which was, indeed to be bombed — but not in the murder camp.

On September 13, 1944, the camp at Auschwitz was bombed by mistake. Bombs hit the death camp, and some S.S. men and Jewish inmates were killed. But, as we have said, this was not a planned air raid. The Americans managed to bomb a place so remote from their bases since they had reached an agreement with the Soviets to bomb targets on their way from Britain and Italy to the Soviet Union. The Soviets prepared a convenient base for them in Poltava in the Ukraine, and American planes flew in that direction, bombing military targets on their way. This makes it clear that by then the bombing was possible. All the claims about technical difficulties preventing the bombing the camps were mere empty words, since no difficulty existed.

The next, and obvious, question is: What then prevented the bombing of the camps? Was there some antisemitic calculation at work? An examination of the documents shows that there was no such consideration, and that the whole issue was never discussed from that angle. The Americans had been requested by a body which, in their eyes, was purely civilian, to bomb a certain camp, where people who were civilians were being persecuted by the Nazi regime. It was not a military target. Since, despite the large number of planes in their possession, their means were limited and they wanted to end the war as soon as possible, their line was that anything which diverted the means of combat from purely war aims into what were not purely war aims was to be rejected.

In January 1944 — that is, half a year before it had received the Jewish request to raid Auschwitz — the American high command made a decision that, as a matter of principle, no American means of combat were to be diverted for civilian purposes. The plan to bomb Auschwitz and the railway lines leading to it fell victim, not to some antisemitic or anti-Jewish plan, but to a fossilized routine which could not understand that the supreme aim of the war — not just from the Jewish point of view, but also from that of the Allies — was to dislodge and undermine the most horrifying tyranny which had ever blighted the face of the earth. When one was faced with this, it was impossible to say that the war aims were purely military. Where it was possible to save the lives of hundreds of thousands of people — and it does not matter who these people were — the Allies should have expended any means of combat, regardless of the consequences, on this task; for the moral considerations of millions of people who had joined the forces and were now fighting were based, whether in a somewhat hazy or in a more clear manner, on their conception of this war as a struggle against the very embodiment of evil.

But this was not to happen. To this story of the attitude of the great powers and the free world, including the Jews, to the

The Bombing of Auschwitz

Holocaust, we must now include another episode, a Palestinian one. The time was June-July-August and, perhaps, also September 1944. The Jewish Agency had been putting uninterrupted pressure on the British, with whom it was in constant touch, to enable the Jewish Yishuv in Palestine to assist the Jews of Europe. The concrete proposal put forward by the Jewish Agency throughout 1943 and in early 1944 was to parachute some people into Europe — but this time, not just a few dozen selected parachutists to this place or the other, but a large number of them. Eventually, it came down to 500 people, to be recruited mainly out of the Palmach, the striking force of the Haganah, who were to be parachuted into the Voivodina area, between Yugoslavia and Hungary, an area which was now intermittently in the hands of Tito's partisans. (In Palestine, people were not quite aware of the fact that the Voivodina area was not the most suitable for partisan activities — but this should not concern us here.) From this area, the Palestinian parachutists were to spread out in order to carry out two functions: to fight against the Nazis in general, and to support those Jewish concentrations which still existed — and one should remember that in Palestine it was far from clear at the time what had remained and what was already gone — in Poland, Slovakia, Rumania and Hungary.

This proposal was passed on to Churchill through the mediation of his son Randolph. It was authorized by Churchill and delivered to the Allied high command in Italy to be carried out. In May 1944, Reuven Shiloah, one of the central figures and the one of the most brilliant members of the political department of the Jewish Agency, went to Italy as the Agency's representative, to clarify the technical side: how the parachutists were to be recruited, how they were to arrive, what training was necessary, and what the mission was to be.

At the end of some complex negotiations with the heads of British Intelligence and with the Royal Air Force in Italy, an agreement was reached, according to which people were to be recruited in Palestine and dispatched to Italy, whence they were to be parachuted into Yugoslavia. This was a very serious plan. The number of volunteers agreed on — 500 — was the only figure of which the British were prepared to speak, and there was no other

Jewish Reactions to the Holocaust

way of Palestinian Jews to reach the diaspora. There were already soldiers from Palestine serving in the British army, but they did not get to the front, since the British would not allow them to do so.

June was now over as was July, and the British aid in recruiting the men, transporting them and training them was not yet forthcoming. Shiloah, who was already accustomed to the vicissitudes of British policy toward the Jews, "smelled a rat," and with some difficulty managed to reach Italy in August to find out what was amiss. After some negotiations, in the course of which he was sent back and forth from place to place, he was informed that orders had arrived from London to have the whole plan called off. The Foreign Office had intervened, and due to considerations related to British Middle East and Arab policy, it had been decided not to put the plan into practice. The Jewish Agency had believed that it had at last reached a breakthrough, since one was dealing here not with the Middle East, but with Yugoslavia, Poland, Rumania and other European countries. But in the end, even this project failed.

At the same time, another proposal made by the Jewish Agency was now lying before the British government: to recruit a large Jewish unit from among the Palestinian Jewish soldiers who were already serving in the British army and from new recruits, and to send it to the front to fight under a Jewish flag. When Churchill found out that he could not withstand the pressures of the Foreign Office, he brought the matter to a cabinet meeting and struck the table with his fist. Until now, he said in effect, you have blocked my way. There has always been a majority in this cabinet against any pro-Jewish proposal. Now I insist that either of the two proposals be carried out. One can now say that the establishment of the Jewish Brigade in September 1944 and its location, at the very last moment, on Italian soil, where it managed to participate in the fighting during the last weeks of the war, was some form of compensation for the failure of the plan for parachuting 500 people into Europe. The Jewish Agency's demand for the establishment of the Jewish Brigade had a double motivation: a. to establish a right for the Jewish people to claim its share in postwar Palestine on account of its combat in the front (and this was what the British feared); b. to participate in the battle against Hitler, as a concrete expression of the assistance which the Jewish Yishuv in Palestine could offer the battle against the arch enemy.

Until the last minute, September 1944, the British refused. It was only then, under great personal pressure from Churchill, that the decision to establish the Jewish Fighting Brigade was accepted. Its flag was blue and white, and its soldiers carried a badge on their sleeves with the legend "Jewish Brigade" (in English only). The members of the brigade went through the appropriate training and were at last sent to the front.

Final preparations were now being made for the period following the war. In 1944, when there were already Jewish units from Palestine in Italy — the southern part having already been occupied by the Allies, while the northern part was still in German hands — a joint committee was established of all the Palestinian units in the British army in Italy. This body, which consisted of members of the Jewish Brigade, transport units, ATS units and the like, was named the Diaspora Center. Its task was to deal, after the war, with Holocaust survivors, but it had already begun its task in the midst of the war. This body was to play its part in the gigantic struggle which was to bring Jews into Palestine after the war in all different ways.

The brigade, together with other units, was trained in Italy. This training was most lengthy and thorough, and at the end the brigade was finally able to engage in actual fighting in Italy, in the spring of 1945, near a river named the Senio. Even an Italian, if he were to be asked for its location, would only know it if he had lived in the vicinity, in the northern Po Valley. Here, once again, the tragedy affecting the representatives of the Jewish Yishuv in Palestine throughout the war repeated itself. There was no lack of good will, courage or readiness to fight, and, at this stage, even training and heavy weapons were at hand; but the brigade units were stationed in a section of the front among various Indian, Yugoslav and other national units. They undertook an offensive in a narrow salient, entered the front line twice, were taken out, returned, and finally took part in the last offensive against the German army which was now totally broken. They entered and accepted the capitulation of the Germans, and were then stationed in northern Italy, near the Austrian border.

We naturally tend to be preoccupied with the problem of the Yishuv, the Jewish community in Palestine. What did it do and what could it do during that period? Could one have any complaints against the Yishuv and its leadership? Of course, one can point to cases of negligence — but these cases, just as the possibilities of action, were rather insignificant. It was a small community of about half a million Jews in Palestine, and it had no outlet for its feelings of anger.

In January 1944, the revolt of the Irgun Zvai Leumi broke out in Palestine, to a large extent as a reaction to news of the Holocaust. Those who have read the internal press of the IZL — and there are already historians who have studied this field — believe beyond a doubt that the decisive factor behind the outburst of indignation which brought about the IZL Revolt were the reports of the Holocaust. The aim of the revolt was to do something for the Jews who were being murdered in Europe. But was one single Jew saved as a consequence of the IZL revolt? The IZL continued with its anti-British struggle for the balance of the war, and this was the tragic aspect of the revolt. After all, the British were fighting against the Germans, and one can maintain that, by fighting against those who were fighting the Nazi enemy, the IZL gave indirect help to the Germans. Can one avoid such a conclusion?

There were no practical ways of rescue. Between the Yishuv and the diaspora stood the sea, the British army, and the total lack of means for doing anything concrete to help. There was no way of sending messengers, or even individuals, to Europe. Even to travel to Turkey, one required a British visa from Palestine. In order to cross over from Turkey to the Nazi-occupied countries, one had to break through an area dominated by the Germans. There was no way of crossing the border between Turkey and Bulgaria or Greece. The border was sealed by the war. To those who read the documents and listen to the descriptions and testimonies of those who were involved, it becomes quite clear that impotence and rage were the dominant moods of those days. This feeling of impotence is far less intelligible to us with a Jewish State of Israel of the 1980's. In order to understand what happened then, one has to recapture the mood of the time, and this is hard for us to accomplish, although Israel's strength is not all that great even today, and the options it has are still limited. But today at least Israel is in possession of means which were simply not there forty years ago.

That is not to say that one should turn a blind eye to the cases of negligence that one can clearly point to in the activities of the Jewish institutions and of the Jewish public in Palestine at the time. We speak here mainly of the manner in which people behaved in their everyday life. What was happening in Europe brought about some ceremonial reactions, but it would be difficult to say that the awareness of the Holocaust was translated into the language of everyday behavior. We have already explained the psychological inhibitions behind this kind of behavior. It would also be hard to say that the Yishuv institutions gave a leading and instructive example in this case. What is more, the main efforts of the Yishuv and its institutions were centered on themselves and their political future, and so were the internal political struggles. The divisions and the scuffles between parties and factions occupied the center stage. The psychological inability to face up to what was happening in Europe is clearly obvious. Even after all those dozens of years, one cannot help being hurt by seeing the front page headlines in the Palestinian Jewish press of that time, which go into ecstasies about some local party-political affair, while the murder of the Jews of Europe is reported only in the inside pages.

There is no doubt that the Yishuv and its institutions took some action. Much effort was put into the futile attempts to break the wall of indifference surrounding the Holocaust. It is likely that this was as much, or nearly as much, as one could do in the circumstances. But even such a conclusion would not release us from the task of being critical of the attitudes and approaches prevalent, and this field is still wide open to future research.

XX.

Too Little, Too Late

Beside the attempts by the Jews of Palestine to assist the Jews of Europe by internal adjustment and through self defence and the Jewish Brigade, the activities in Istanbul of the envoys of the Jewish Agency, of the Histadrut and of other bodies, went on.

The little assistance that one could offer, especially to the Balkan area, indeed came from Istanbul. The small Jewish Yishuv in Palestine provided finances, and, although these were insufficient and meager in quantity, it was significant that funds were supplied. These funds were then transferred, by means of messengers, to areas under German occupation. In 1944, these activities were renewed with increased vigor, especially since the possibility arose once more to engage once again in Aliyah B, an activity which had almost entirely ceased since 1942. Early in 1942, the boat Struma was sunk by a Soviet submarine in the Black Sea, after the British had refused to let its passengers enter Palestine, and all those on board except one person were drowned. In 1943, a few small boats, with a few dozen people, managed to arrive in Palestine. But one could hardly think of immigration in large numbers. The Black Sea was swarming with Soviet submarines and with Rumanian and Bulgarian men of war, and the whole thing was simply impractical.

In 1944, the possibility came up once more. The Rumanians began to change their policy. They now realized that the war was taking a turn against them, and they were looking for a way of reconciliation with the west. One expedient way was to stop their

Too Little, Too Late

oppression of the Jews. They were now retreating from the Soviet Union, taking with them the remnants of the Jews of Bessarabia and Bukovina who had been expelled to Transnistria. In this area, large masses of Jews expelled from these Rumanian provinces had met with death by starvation, disease and murder at the hands of Rumanians and Germans. Those who had survived succeeded largely in returning to Rumania.

The problem was that one could not transport large numbers of people out of Rumania, either by sea or by land. Nevertheless, the Rumanian agreement to allow the emigration of the Jews in early 1944 was a breakthrough. Aliyah B of the Haganah, operating from Istanbul through its envoy there, began to organize this immigration, and the first boats, especially the two boats the Maritza and the Mefkure, began to call at Istanbul. In July, the Maritza was torpedoed by a Soviet submarine and sank, with all the immigrants on board drowning. The Soviets mistook it for a Rumanian boat — that is, an enemy vessel. Aliyah B was not stopped because of this, and continued until Rumania withdrew from the war in August 1944, and even increased afterwards. This was one type of activity. There were also some successful attempts to smuggle out Jews who were hiding with the Greek partisans, and to bring them through the Aegean islands to the Smyrna area in Turkey, in order to transfer them to Palestine. About 600 Jews were saved in this manner by Aliyah B.

But the major, and most dramatic by far, was the activity of the parachutists, which we have already mentioned. We are speaking here of no more than 34-35 parachutists, a few of whom were not even parachuted in at all, and reached their destinations only after the battles were over. Apart from one subsidiary group which joined the American forces, most of the plans of these groups were made together with the British, since there was no alternative. The aim was two-fold: a. to assist in the general war effort, whether by establishing contacts with Tito's Yugoslav partisans as part of the general British efforts to do so, or to free Allied pilots captured by the Germans, who were to be liberated in one way or another by these Palestinian envoys and then return to their task; b. to help the

Jewish Reactions to the Holocaust

Jews organize armed resistance.

Some of the these young people reached Yugoslavia, like the parachutist Peretz Rosenberg and a few others. They wanted to reach the Jews and had the ability required to do so, but the conditions of the war made it impossible for them to achieve their aim. Rosenberg, for example, served as a radio operator in Tito's headquarters, and was therefore tied to his broadcasting set. Here and there, meetings with Jews took place, but formal Jewish activities were out of the question in the circumstances. Dan Laner, for example, was parachuted into the border area between Yugoslavia and Austria. He took part in partisan warfare in that area and even entered Austria; but he met no Jews, since there were no longer any left there.

Similar things happened to other parachutists. Among those sent to Rumania, one was unlucky enough to fall on a roof and break his leg, while another landed in the wrong place and fell into the hands of a Rumanian unit which took him captive. Some arrived in Bucharest, but these were already the last months of the war. They went into frantic action at once and did the best they could. They tried, for example, to smuggle out of Rumania Allied pilots who were incarcerated in prisoner of war camps. They even managed to organize Jewish resistance in Bucharest, in case the Germans were to enter the Rumanian capital and attempt to take the Jews away with them. This resistance never went into action, since Rumania had meanwhile dropped out of the war. The tables were turned: the Rumanians were now defending Bucharest against the Germans, who did not succeed in returning to it.

In Hungary, the poetess Hannah Szenes reached the Hungarian border and was immediately caught and was later executed. Peretz Goldstein and Joel Palgi arrived in Budapest and were caught in a tragic situation. The Germans were aware of their presence there, and in order not to endanger the Zionist committee in Budapest itself, they surrendered themselves to the Germans. Goldstein was murdered in one of the German concentration camps. Joel Palgi managed to escape and to return to Budapest, where he was active during the last phases of the war. Being alone, though, there was not

Too Little, Too Late

much he could do. He joined a group of young people who were concealing children and engaging in large scale rescue activities. But he was now "tainted," and could not come into the open, or he would have been caught immediately. Another case was that of Enzo Sereni, who was parachuted into Northern Italy, was caught and murdered.

What we do have here is a mixture of "too little," "too late," and sheer bad luck, which reached its most extreme form in Slovakia. Haviva Rajk and some of her friends managed to arrive in the country. At the time — August-October 1944 — there was an anti-Nazi rebellion in progress in Slovakia. The young people reached the area which had been liberated by the rebellious Slovak army. There were Jews in this area, and Havivah Rajk took charge of these Jewish refugees. But the liberated area could withstand German pressure only a few weeks, and was then recaptured. Havivah and some other parachutists went into hiding in a partisan camp in the high mountains. One day, at dawn, Russian soldiers who had defected to the Germans came across this camp. These were traitors, Vlassovites, named after their commander, an ex-Soviet general who had changed sides. They spoke Russian, and the Jews of this camp mistook them for Russian soldiers who had come to liberate them. They came out in joy and met with gunshots. Those who survived were captured. Havivah Rajk and almost all her friends were executed by the Germans, to whom they had been delivered. One of them, Hayyim Hermesh, who now lives in Israel, succeeded in escaping. He went on fighting in the Tatra mountains in Slovakia until the end of the war.

To the question as to whether these people fought and performed acts of supreme courage, which can serve as an example for future generations in Israel, the answer is unequivocally: yes. But did they succeed in their aims? That is very doubtful. Once again, it was too little, too late, and one can add to this extremely bad luck. Seven of the parachutists died. The rest did what they could. They were the spearhead of a relatively large army, with hundreds or thousands of members of the Yishuv in Palestine who stood behind them; but they never reached their destination, and were powerless to do what

Jewish Reactions to the Holocaust

they had set out to do.

There is another story, which took place earlier, but which fits into the general picture we have drawn here, of rescue attempts by external forces. The story begins inside occupied Europe. It is the story of a rescue attempt, not by Jews, but by Danes, and it is now well known in Israel. In October 1943, the Germans were about to transport the Jews of Denmark — altogether, less than 8,000 people — to the death camps. They failed to do this because the Danes saved the Jews. The Danes knew what was about to happen, since some Germans living in Denmark at the time passed this information into Danish hands. These Germans had clearly been influenced by the atmosphere of rebellion surrounding the Danish resistance movement and encompassing the whole Danish population, which was now beginning to fight against the Nazis. The Danes saved all but a few hundred of the Jews of Denmark and transported them to Sweden. Sweden also absorbed a small number of the Jews of Norway — the very few people who managed to escape through the long border between Norway and Sweden.

The attitude of neutral Sweden toward the Jews had not been particularly sympathetic until this period; but after the beginning of 1943, when the whole world realized that Germany was on the retreat and that, even if this was not yet the beginning of the end the Germans were bound to be defeated sooner or later, Sweden also began to change its tune and showed more flexibility in the rescuing of lives. When the Danes approached the Swedes in October 1943 and asked them to take the Jewish refugees from Denmark, the Swedes opened their gates without hesitation — although, in 1943, the Germans still had it in their power to conquer Sweden. This was a risk, showing some willingness to take chances and make sacrifices.

At the same time, the Swedes also began to engage in negotiations with the Germans for the rescue of various groups which were under German occupation. This concerned, first and foremost, Scandinavian citizens: Norwegians and Danes, who had been captured as prisoners of war and put in concentration camps. The Swedish Red Cross was the main initiator of this operation in

Too Little, Too Late

early 1944.

This ties up with our next issue. When negotiations with the Germans came to a standstill after the failure of Brand's mission, both the German S.S. men and some Americans were still prepared — albeit with many reservations — to continue the negotiations for the rescue of Jews. The obvious aim of the S.S. was to establish contacts with the United States through these moves to rescue Jews, with the ultimate aim of holding separate peace talks. The documents in our hands have provided us with incontrovertible evidence that this was the situation by the summer of 1944.

It all began with some meetings in Budapest between Kastner and a new person dispatched by Himmler to Hungary, in the first instance for the purpose of economic negotiations. This man was Kurt A. Becher, a Nazi officer, who lives in Germany today in great affluence. Becher was undoubtedly a war criminal, and in 1941 he served in units which massacred Jews in the Soviet Union. On behalf of the S.S., he confiscated the factories of Manfred Weisz, the largest industrial complex in Hungary. This complex belonged to an assimilated Hungarian Jewish family, many of whose members had already become Christians. The family now had to purchase its freedom by selling its factories — that is, by virtually having them confiscated by the S.S. Becher was in charge of this confiscation.

Through his contacts with the Weisz family, Becher came to meet Kastner in person. This was of some importance since, as early as July 1944, when the transports from Hungary stopped, Eichmann had left Hungary, at least for the time being. Now, negotiations were conducted not only through Eichmann, but through this new individual, with direct access to Himmler — Kurt Becher. Here we can be perfectly certain that the contacts were with Himmler himself.

Becher was seeking, in Himmler's name and with the assistance of Kastner, a distinguished Jewish figure abroad who could negotiate with him. Kastner, as we remember, suggested Sally Mayer, the Joint representative in Switzerland. Mayer was contacted and asked if he would be willing to act as mediator, and he agreed — but of course, he could not do this as merely a private person, and had to be authorized to do so by some public body. He applied to the Joint and received a negative answer. The Joint regarded this as a political issue, in which it ought not to intervene. Mayer was told to ask the American embassy or the Swiss government, since, as a Swiss citizen, he was not allowed to carry out such activities without the permission of the authorities. In 1944, a Swiss citizen could not meet with a German without the supervision of the Swiss police, and any attempt to do so was a criminal offense.

Mayer turned to the WRB, which had a representative in the American legation in the capital, Berne. It was headed by Roswell D. McClelland, a devout Christian, close to the Society of Friends, (Quakers), which already had a record of rescue operations of Jews in Europe. In the code language used by Sally Mayer, this man was referred to as "Hanukkah." Mayer was an orthodox Jew in the Western European style, close to Zionism without being a Zionist himself. He addressed himself to McClelland, who was willing to contact the United States and ask whether he, Mayer, might be authorized to conduct the negotiations.

In America, the proposal was investigated by the WRB, and the answer given McClelland on August 21, 1944 was that it was willing to allow Mayer to meet representatives of the other side, but that he was not to offer money or merchandise — that is, any kind of ransom. He could negotiate in order to draw out the issue, on the assumption that, as long as the negotiations were being continued, the S.S. would not murder Jews.

Mayer received this telegram a day after he had already met with S.S. men, but he had already known its contents beforehand. On that day, August 21, he met with four people of "the other side" — as the Americans so elegantly put it. The meeting took place on a bridge, since the Swiss did not allow the men to enter the country. The four were Kurt Becher, accompanied by two other S.S. officers, and Kastner, who was to mediate between them and Sally Mayer. Mayer was not allowed to appear as an American or as a representative of the Joint, but only as a Swiss citizen representing a Swiss organization for Jewish refugees. He was thus tied and

Too Little, Too Late

restricted on all sides, especially since he had been instructed not to tell anyone about these contacts. Nevertheless, Mayer applied to the Swiss authorities and asked the senior police commissioner in Switzerland what he was allowed to offer as a Swiss citizen.

This man, Dr. Heinrich Rothmund, told him that he was permitted to hold any negotiations, but any Jew liberated by him through bribery would be prevented from entering Switzerland. He was not to offer money or merchandise. But as soon as he reached the border, Mayer was told by Kastner that the only possible basis for holding negotiations was through the offering of goods or, in the worst case, money. If Mayer had no money or goods, there was nothing to negotiate about.

The two sides stood on the bridge between Switzerland and Austria at St. Margarethen and conducted the negotiations standing on their feet. When the Nazi demand, that the Jews could only be liberated for merchandise, was brought up, Mayer gave them a positive answer, in defiance of all the instructions he had been given. He asked them to inform him what sort of merchandise they required, and incidentally, as it were, he told the Nazis in the sternest of tones that, as long as they continued to murder people, there was no place for negotiations. They were to stop the murder immediately, not only in Hungary, as Kastner had requested, but in all parts of Europe which were still in Nazi hands in August 1944.

The Nazis were impressed by Mayer's approach, and Becher's report to Himmler was coached in the most positive terms. The Nazis believed that they were negotiating for goods and money, while Mayer knew that he had nothing to offer. Thus began the negotiations, as a result of which many of the very few survivors in Europe were to be saved.

XXI.

Negotiations with the S.S.

The negotiations which began in August 1944 continued until February 1945. They had their ups and downs, and Kastner participated in all the stages. A reading of the documents shows that, as a result of these negotiations, Himmler instructed his men in Budapest not to transport the Jews of that city to Poland. One is thus entitled to say that the survival of the Jews of Budapest is related — to say the least — to the negotiations of Sally Mayer.

On August 21, and again in December, the train organized by Kastner and mentioned above arrived from Bergen-Belsen on the Swiss border, bringing the people in two convoys. This was Mayer's condition for opening the negotiations and for carrying on.

The Nazis brought to the Vienna area, for their own purposes, 15,000-17,000 Jews from the Debreczen area in Hungary. These Jews were brought there with their families — a very rare thing in itself — and they were kept alive, while being employed in various kinds of hard labor. Keeping these people alive also became, as time went on, a condition for the negotiations. Toward the end of the war, at the beginning of 1945, the possibility of keeping alive Jews who were still in the camps also became part of these negotiations. Thus, Mayer tried all the time to divert the negotiations from the demand for merchandise, as the Nazis wished to have it, to other possibilities — ransom for money, and, later, the transfer of Jewish funds to the Red Cross, so that the Red Cross could keep alive the Jews of the various camps who still remained in Germany.

Negotiations with the S.S.

Mayer broadened the object of the negotiations, which was originally the Jews of Hungary, to include all Jews in Nazi occupied territories. At the end, he was even trying to negotiate with the S.S. not only about Jews, but even about non-Jewish forced laborers who had been enslaved in all the countries of Europe and made to work for the Germans. His aim was to give the negotiations the broadest possible background, and thus to have the Red Cross take an interest in the fate of all prisoners, not excluding the Jewish ones.

It is possible that these negotiations also made their contribution to Himmler's decision to stop the murder in the gas chambers of Auschwitz. This was probably an instruction given orally by Himmler. The murder was stopped at the beginning of November. Murder by gas was replaced by another policy, namely gathering together all the Jewish survivors of the various camps and leading them in a death march to those camps which still remained under German rule, either in order to serve the Nazis as a labor force for building fortifications — at the last minute, in 1945 — or as one way of continuing the massacre, not only of Jews, by new means. Large masses of Jews and others found their deaths on those marches. They died of the cold and of plagues or merely of fatigue, and those who lagged behind were invariably shot to death by the S.S. men.

Beside Mayer, there were others in the free world who made attempts to rescue Jews. The Va'ad Hatzalah (Rescue Committee of the American Rabbis), which was represented in Switzerland by the brothers Sternbuch, and especially their sister, Rachel Sternbuch, recruited for this task a Swiss statesman, a former supporter of the Nazis, who was now seeking an alibi as a rescuer of Jews. His name was Jean-Marie Musy. Musy and his son Benoit came to Germany and held parallel negotiations with Himmler for the release of Jews.

Some of Himmler's men held negotiations with Musy and some with Mayer. Himmler was the head of all these groups, and he was frantically attempting to establish a lifeline to the Americans.

On November 5, 1944, Mayer succeeded in having the Nazi Becher meet the representative of the WRB, McClelland, in Zurich. This was the first meeting between a German and an American during the whole period of the war. The common ground was the rescue of Jews. Had the Soviets known of it during that period, they would no doubt have made this into a major issue. The WRB and McClelland were taking an immense political risk in order to assist Mayer in his negotiations. But Mayer was deceiving the Americans as well, as he kept negotiating based on goods and money, contrary to the specific instructions he had received. What was more, he even purchased tractors in Switzerland and handed them over to the Germans, in the hope that this would oil the wheels of his negotiations. This was done without the knowledge of his American sponsors. Besides the negotiations of Musy and Mayer, other negotiations were also taking place at the same time, conducted by S.S. men in Sweden. They were held with the local representative of the Committee for Refugees, Ivor Olsen, an American of Swedish extraction. These negotiations extended even further, and were joined at the end of 1944 by Count Folke Bernadotte, the Swedish representative of the Red Cross. At first, Bernadotte negotiated for the release of Swedes and Danes, but in the last stages of the war he also engaged in negotiations for the rescue of Jews. All these initiatives were only an expression of the wish of the S.S. to save itself at the last moment from the collapse of Germany by concluding a separate treaty with the west.

We have already seen that, in Hungary, the transports to Poland stopped in July 1944. Until October, all was relatively quiet. The Hungarian government was headed by General Geza Lakatos, who sought to make peace with the Allies and to take Hungary out of the war. His attempts were unsuccessful. The Jews, who were now all concentrated in Budapest, felt that a constant threat was hanging over them, and they made efforts to be rescued.

Two attempts were made, which later meshed together. One was made by Moshe Krausz, the representative of the Zionist religious party, Mizrachi, in Budapest, who entered the Swiss legation and contacted Vice-Consul Charles Lutz, a former Swiss envoy in Tel Aviv and friend of the Jews. From his location in the Swiss legation, Krausz persuaded the Swiss authorities to offer assistance, and Lutz endorsed this cause enthusiastically. The first concrete proposal

Negotiations with the S.S.

was the issuing a few thousand permits for emigration to Palestine. At first they spoke of 7,800 permits, and later of 8,700. There was also a debate whether these permits were to be issued to individuals or to families.

On July 18, Horthy declared that he accepted the idea of allowing some Jews to leave Hungary. The Germans, of course, did not let them go, but these permits became the basis for widespread attempts to rescue Jews. The method used by the Swiss legation spread to other neutrals, who were now issuing documents testifying that the bearers were under the protection of foreign countries and were destined to leave Hungary.

The other attempt was made by the Swedes. A member of one of the best known and most highly respected families in Sweden, Raoul Wallenberg, arrived in Budapest in July, with Jewish money supplied by the Joint and with close political contacts with the WRB. He engaged in issuing permits for entry into Sweden to Hungarian Jews.

On October 15, 1944, a fascist government headed by Ferenc Szalasi seized power in Hungary and began to assault the Jews. Jews were murdered on the banks of the Danube and their bodies were thrown into the river. Jewish men and women were hunted out and sent to the Austrian border in a death march, to build fortifications. Eichmann made his appearance in Hungary again to supervise these operations. This time, the purpose of the Germans, who had commissioned this work force, was really to build fortifications on the Austrian border. The Nazis marched these masses of Jews, men and women of all ages, some of them unsuited for such labor, and, in the terrible circumstances of this forced march, death took a large toll. Those who reached the Austrian border were so exhausted that they were of no use to the Germans, and some of them were returned to Budapest.

The Jews attempted to evade this march, and one of the main ways for doing this was by using the documents of foreign legations and embassies. The Swiss legation issued the greatest number of such documents, with the second highest number being issued by Wallenberg, who supplied about 4,500 such forms. Wallenberg was one of the few foreign envoys who personally saved people put in impossible circumstances, and he did this at great risk to himself.

But the official papers were not sufficient, and the Zionist youth movements joined forces and produced tens of thousands of forged documents in their workshops. It is to the credit of the Swiss, Wallenberg, the Portuguese, the Spaniards and the Vatican, as well as the International Red Cross, that they were all made fully aware of what was going on, and assisted in this. But those who did the real work and expanded it into a mass action were the underground youth movements, who also established children's and adults' homes and attempted to obtain the patronage of some legation or embassy for each of these homes. Children were usually placed under the patronage of the Red Cross. But even this did not always help.

The Hungarian fascists did not always recognize such documents. They often arrested and murdered people who held these documents, regardless of whether they were real or forged. Nevertheless, the large majority of those who were protected by such self-produced papers — the number is estimated today at 40,000 or more — were saved. This action was based, as we have said, on the activities of the foreign legations and the Red Cross in Budapest. It was begun by Krausz, Lutz and Wallenberg. News of the operation spread in the neutral countries and in the west through internal memoranda or diplomatic correspondence. In 1944, people were already fully aware of what was happening to the Jews in Europe. In this new situation, various neutral governments, even the governments of Spain, Portugal and the representatives of Tangier, were prepared to take action, even if it was only symbolic. They were no longer hiding behind a great power which was doing nothing. What they achieved was not much, but it was something. The representatives of these countries made their appearance and contributed to saving the Jews of Budapest for the second time (the first time was when their expulsion to Poland was prevented). They made their contribution to rescuing them from the fascist Hungarian government of Szalasi, which ruled the country from October 15, 1944 until the liberation of Budapest by the Soviets in

Negotiations with the S.S.
January and February 1945.

When the war was over, about 200,000 people were liberated from the Nazi concentration camps. If we estimate the number of people left to be saved, we must admit that these were only a small remnant of what had been there before. In addition to this figure, there were those who managed to hide during the war and those who, like the Jews of Budapest, were saved from the camps. But the vast majority of European Jewry had been massacred by the Nazis.

Thus, when we speak of the attitude of the outside world — Jewish as well as non-Jewish — our first conclusion must be that the rescue operations were few and far between, and that they were mostly unsuccessful. Our next question must be whether it was possible to save the Jews.

It seems that, once mass murder came into operation, the concrete possibilities of rescue were very small. It is very doubtful whether the picture would have been very different even if the Vatican, Britain, the United States and all other such forces had acted to try to prevent of the massacre. The Nazi murder machine, once it began to work, could not be stopped with the means at the disposal of the free world at the time. But we must add some provisos to this statement.

It was possible to save the Jews of Europe earlier, before it came to mass murder. And, although it is difficult to believe that once it started there was a way of rescuing large numbers, some parts of European Jewry could still perhaps have been saved. We have been brought up in a civilization which maintains that he who has saved one life is like unto one who has saved a whole world, and here there were millions of worlds to be saved. For each of these worlds, a supreme effort should have been made. We are not speaking here of mere numbers — another hundred, another thousand, another ten thousand. Each additional individual saved would have made, from our point of view, an essential difference to the whole picture. This, in any case, is how things *ought* to have happened. But things almost never happen the way they ought to.

We are therefore led to our third question: Were those

Jewish Reactions to the Holocaust

possibilities of rescue available used to the full extent? The answer is, unfortunately, that they were not fully exploited, as we have seen from some of the stories told in previous chapters.

Were there nevertheless some attempts which succeeded? There were, indeed, some. One can recall the few and rather meager success stories, like the activities of the Japanese consul in Kovno, Sugihara, who saved 2,400 Jews and brought them to Japan; that of Aristide de Susa Mendes in France, who issued thousands of entry visas into Portugal; the Joint's actions of smuggling money into occupied areas to save lives; the attempts to escape from France to Spain and Switzerland; and the rescue attempts made by righteous gentiles throughout Europe.

One should also recall what we have described in our earlier chapters — that in Belgium, France, Italy, Denmark and Bulgaria, the majority of the Jews were saved. This was largely the result of a sympathetic attitude on the part of most of the population. But there were also countries like Holland, where a large majority of the people were extremely sympathetic to the Jews, yet only a relatively small number of the Jews in the country were rescued. Those who did help the Jews drew support, to a greater or lesser extent, from external influences, and from the hope that the Nazis would eventually be defeated, despite the untold sufferings of the various conquered populations at the time; and that after the final victory, the time of reckoning would come and the question would arise: What have we done for our Jewish fellow citizens?

What did the Jewish Yishuv in Palestine, and the Jewish people as a whole do? This question is of special importance to those in Israel. What could the Jewish people do? One should again underline a fact we have already mentioned: the utter impotence of the Jews. This, although an objective factor, is very difficult for us to comprehend today. Israeli Jews now live in an independent state, with its own army, navy, air force, diplomatic service, and an ability, however restricted, to put pressure on other countries of the world. Such a potential was simply not there during the Second World War, and we must get used to this fact of Jewish political helplessness during the war and accept it for the fact it is.

Negotiations with the S.S.

Could more have been done, despite the helplessness? The answer is that it could. Can we point to concrete cases where more could have been done? Certainly. Did these cases of negligence have their source in ill will, or even in sheer incompetence? The answer is no. Where there was the shadow of hope — as in the case of Brand, of the parachutists, or in similar cases — people went into action. These actions did not succeed, not only because of objective difficulties, but also because the Jews themselves did not quite comprehend the meaning of Holocaust, of wholesale massacre, even when they already "knew" of it in 1942 and thereafter. The huge dimensions of the Holocaust are incomprehensible to us even today, and they were even less comprehensible to the Jews of the period. They wrote and spoke about it as if they understood, but the true significance of it eluded them.

Having considered all these facts, it is, perhaps, advisable to try to understand the actions of the generation of our parents, the people who lived in that period between 1939 and 1945 and took whatever action they took, from the point of view of that generation and that period themselves. We should not project into the realities of those times what we know today of the Holocaust. We should stop accusing and begin to understand. We must see things through their eyes. To the extent that they understood what was happening, they attempted to act. They acted in a number of directions, with hardly a chance of success. They might, perhaps, have acted differently, trying, for example, to raise more money, or by pressure on governments in exile. Although such governments were themselves in financial straits, the Jews might at least have transferred money through the help of these governments to the Holocaust areas.

There was one avenue of rescue — exploiting the wish of some Nazi leaders, especially in the last phase of the war, to reach the possibility of negotiations with the western powers and to use the Jews as part of an exchange. But in order to make use of this willingness to let the Jews go, the western powers had to alter the political and moral order of priorities which they had established, and for this they were not prepared.

Jewish Reactions to the Holocaust

The simple truth is that ways of rescue were very few. We have tried to investigate these ways, and have found one ray of light in the general darkness: those few people, individuals and groups, whose assistance in the right place and at the right time leave us some hope for the survival of a more humane world. One should mention again the consuls in Kovno and in France, or such individuals as Mayer and Brand, Kastner and Weissmandel, who attempted to act in the right place and at the right time. The measure of their success was small, but at least they made the attempt.

XXII.

As Sheep to the Slaughter?

From our attempt to sum up the whole issue of rescue, we pass now to our last issue, and will attempt to sum up the Jewish reaction in the Holocaust countries themselves. We have already pointed out that one cannot make generalizations concerning Judenraete. We have brought examples of Judenraete which were fully submissive to the Nazis — especially in Poland, where Lodz is a good example. For Western Europe, we used Holland as an example, and for southeastern Europe, the example was Budapest. We have also brought examples of Judenraete which offered wholesale opposition to the Nazis, like that of Minsk. We have also seen Judenraete which were somewhere between these two extremes — whether they were more inclined toward resistance, as in Slovakia or in France, or toward the other side of the spectrum, but without full submission to the Germans. It is clear from all these examples that the Jewish leadership during the Holocaust adopted different approaches and different strategies. We have seen similar phenomena among the Jewish public at large. There were Jewish social organizations whose general tendency was to oppose the Nazis or to organize resistance activities. We have seen one such organization — OSE — in France; another one in Poland — the Joint and all its branches — and another in Slovakia and Hungary, with the youth movements there.

But what, in the end, was the reaction of the Jewish public in general, and how did it stand up to the Holocaust? Here we are faced

Jewish Reactions to the Holocaust

with a difficult problem, since this is a matter for long and voluminous research, and we are only in the initial stages of this work. One should also add that the testimonies we have are of different kinds and point to various types of reaction. Let us have one example. In Denmark, we remember, almost the whole of the Jewish community, the large majority of which lived in Copenhagen — a rather small community of under 8,000 people — was rescued. The people were rescued by Danes, not by Jews. This implies that Jewish action played a very small part in this case. It is possible that what we have here is a Jewish failure of nerve in the face of harassment and persecution.

We also meet with a similar phenomenon in some other places. At the other extreme, we find in most ghettoes in Poland a powerful drive to remain alive, which involved active, unarmed opposition to Nazi policies. The more the Nazis hardened their attitude and their policy, the more determined was the Jewish reaction not to give in but, on the contrary, to find ways of getting around Nazi restrictions.

In such cases, what we witnessed was an active Jewish reaction. One must not use the term "passive resistance" here. This resistance was in no way passive but rather extremely active — although it was unarmed — and we have seen why this was so.

Another Jewish reaction was the one we met with in places where the Jewish public opposed a Judenrat which acted submissively. In Holland, for example, we have seen that the general instinct of the Jewish population told it to go into hiding, while the Judenrat collaborated in all the preparations for expulsion.

In order not to have to gild the image excessively, one should also point out that in many ghettoes in Eastern Europe, the Jewish police were virtually an arm of the Gestapo inside the ghetto. On the other hand, there were places where the Jewish police were the focus of resistance. In numerous places in Eastern Europe, the Nazis recruited agents at some stage from among the Jews, and these agents, in return for promises of saving their lives or of money, were prepared to collaborate by uncovering hiding places, acting against the underground, and similar activities. In the ghettoes, there was a

As Sheep to the Slaughter?

great deal of corruption and social tension.

The picture is thus hardly uniform, and things take more than one direction. But if we are to be asked about our general impression of Jewish behavior, we can say that it was far from a general picture of submission. And here we come to the issue of the concentration and death camps, not only because there was armed resistance to the Germans in some of these camps — and we have already touched on this — but also because in these camps, which were created in order to destroy man's humanity, we meet with some exceptional phenomena. It is true that in these camps, where Jews were at the very bottom of the ladder, many Jews broke down and were prepared to risk the lives of others, or even to betray them, for a slice of bread, or even for the mere promise of a slice of bread or a better place of work. In the circumstances of a concentration camp, this was natural behavior, since such a camp was created for making people break down. Nevertheless, there were in these camps many examples of preserving one's human dignity. Such phenomena stand out and they may, perhaps, give us some hope for mankind in general.

We find such phenomena in all the camps. Collecting the details of such stories is a process which will take much time. We now possess thousands of testimonies, and one has to sift through them and check them. But altogether, it is already clear to us today that this phenomenon existed. Even if such cases were in a minority, they are far more significant than the majority.

There was one type of Jewish reaction in the camps which found its expression in maintaining the laws of religion. We have many testimonies on this issue. We also have evidence of cases where people did not keep the commandments of the Jewish religion or abandoned them, but kept the norms of human morality. We have examples of people who followed in the way of this or that ideology, be it Zionist, communist, or humanist of this or that sort. A man who held on to some ideology found it, no doubt, easier to maintain his psychological resistance to what the Nazis planned for these camps.

All this raises the major question which comes up in every

Jewish Reactions to the Holocaust

discussion of the Holocaust, whether among soldiers, schoolchildren, or even students, and usually finds its expression in the slogan "as sheep to the slaughter." This slogan is of special interest, since it seems to be used only among Jews. About twenty million Russians, Ukrainians and other Soviet citizens died at German hands — far more than all the Jews who were murdered in the Holocaust. Has anyone in the Soviet Union ever asked the question, why most of these millions went as sheep to the slaughter? Has anyone raised this question concerning the 2.5 million Russian prisoners of war who were murdered by the Nazis without, of course, offering any resistance? Has anyone raised this question concerning three million non-Jewish Poles who were murdered, or many thousands of people of all nationalities who opposed the Nazi regime? We have not come across the question of whether these people went like sheep to the slaughter in any book of history, speech, or any other document written by people who were not Jews and which deal with the tens of millions of people killed in the Second World War. This is a peculiarly Jewish question. It is, so it appears, an expression of self hate and of a demand put to ourselves to be superhuman; heroic, as it were, in a manner which is far from being natural.

But the fact that this question is raised, and it is raised in a violent, and sometimes even in virulent fashion, requires some answer. The answer, so it seems, is to be found only in the uniqueness of the Jewish attitude of undermining and over-criticizing ourselves, at the same time that we forgive others. What is even worse, when we speak of "sheep to the slaughter," we no longer imply that someone murdered these people, but that he slaughtered them like sheep or cattle. By saying this, we no longer refer to those sons and daughters of the Jewish people who were murdered as human beings. Thus we virtually condone the Nazi argument, since the Nazis, too, did not regard the Jews as humans. The mere expression "sheep to the slaughter" depicts the Jews, not as human beings, but as a herd of animals, and it depicts the murderer as a butcher.

It seems to me that those who use such expressions are doing an

As Sheep to the Slaughter?

injustice, not only to the Jewish people murdered in Europe, but also to themselves. By doing this, they identify themselves — of course, without being aware of this and with no intention to do so — with ideologies with which they would be shocked to be identified.

Having noted all these reservations, one still has to ask the question and to answer it. The people who were taken to the places of murder were usually surprised and shocked. Immediately after the German invasion of the Soviet Union, people throughout the country — hundreds of thousands of them — were led to their deaths without being prepared for this in the least. They had not even imagined that this was a likely intention of the concentration of Jews. The Germans used excellent camouflage: they claimed that these people were being led away to places of labor — and some, indeed, were actually led to labor. This was used as a proof that the others had also been taken to do some work, while they were led to be murdered. Here we have an extremely interesting story. It is the testimony of a Slovakian Jew named Filip Mueller, who spent two and a half years in Auschwitz as a forced laborer in the gas chambers. He published his reminiscences of this period, where he tells everything he saw with his own eyes during two and a half years. He saw a large part of the Jewish people led to its death. There is one thing which you will not find in his story: Jews kissing the feet of the S.S. men, grovelling, or begging for their lives. Did such things never occur? Filip Mueller maintains that they never did. In any case, he never saw such things happen. People were in shock, of course. People sang, people prayed, people did all sorts of things — but to grovel and ask for mercy from the Germans, that was something they did not do. If there were such cases, they were isolated ones.

Thus, we are not dealing here with a herd. This is not the behavior of a herd. These were human beings who were caught up in an event which they could not comprehend, and they reacted like human beings in such circumstances. The question one asks is, how does a person behave when he has been trapped in a situation in which death is inescapable? What are his reactions? One must enquire of the psychologists as to the mechanisms which defend the mind of

Jewish Reactions to the Holocaust

someone in this situation, and soften this blow of being driven toward the inevitable. How do such mechanisms work? This is even more important when we deal with large numbers of people being together in such situations. Each of them can say: "This is unlikely to happen to each and everyone of us, and therefore I have some chance." This prevents people from acting in any manner exceptional to that of the group in which they are included.

We add to this the fact that the Nazis exploited the ties of family among the Jews who were led to their deaths. Take, for example, a young man, who had the strength to resist, to jump off a train, and the like. But he was with his family. To abandon it might mean that he would never see these people again; that he was leaving his mother, his father, his brothers and sisters in the hands of the Nazis, while he, young and strong as he was, could support them in their last moments. We have testimonies of survivors who have said: Had I not been separated in some way or another from my family, I would not have survived, since I would have regarded it as my duty to go with the rest of them.

We should add another argument here: Those people who were led to their deaths were surrounded by guards, usually armed with automatic weapons. But it was not only that they were surrounded by Nazis and collaborators, but they were also in the midst of a population which was mostly hostile, and this is a crucial point. When one has nowhere to escape to safety, what are the alternatives open to oneself? We have a considerable number of testimonies about people who escaped from the places of mass murder — mostly in Eastern Poland and Western Russia, where murder was carried out not in camps, but near the places of residence of the victims — but they were not rescued, since their neighbors betrayed them.

In this context, one should mention another fact. We have numerous photographs of Soviet prisoners of war being led away, at a time when it was already clear that Russian prisoners of war had little chance of surviving in the German camps. What is interesting in these photographs is that we see in them large crowds of prisoners marching in Russia, still surrounded by the fields and

As Sheep to the Slaughter?

forests of their own country. They can easily escape. They are guarded by very few guards who are clearly seen in those photographs — 8-10 guards on horseback armed with guns and nothing else. Can anyone maintain that such a crowd, a whole Soviet division, could not break away and escape? At least some could have saved themselves. But what was at work here were psychological mechanisms, and these apply to Jews just as they apply to French, Russians, Blacks, Japanese, Chinese — to human beings in general. This issue should, perhaps, be investigated in an objective fashion, including the reactions of people from other nations.

All in all, this relationship between the behavior of Jews and of non-Jews during the Holocaust still requires a proper investigation. After all, although the Jews were the main victims of Nazi policy — as a body, although not in numbers — violence against local populations occurred throughout Nazi occupied Europe. One can mention the example of Yugoslavia, where a mass murder of Serbs took place. How did people behave when Tito was organizing his partisan units in a bloody campaign in which huge numbers of civilians were killed? Did they behave like the Jews, or in a different manner? Here we have an unequivocal answer. There is no question here of any other behavior: they reacted just like the Jews. There are certain differences between the reaction of various nations — for example, between the Czechs and the Slovaks. Czech resistance was practically restricted to talking, and little real action took place. The Czech underground required help parachuted from England in order to assassinate Reinhard Heydrich, the Chief of the S.S. Police, who was also the brutal governor of the Czech parts of Czechoslovakia, in May 1942. This was the one single operation carried out by the Czech underground against the Nazis until the Czech liberation. The rebellion against the Nazis in Prague broke out virtually on the last day of the war. In Slovakia, on the other hand, there was an attempt to start a national rebellion against the Nazis in the summer of 1944. Thus, one cannot deny that there were some differences between the various nations. If we now try to fit the Jews into this spectrum, they were undoubtedly in a far more

Jewish Reactions to the Holocaust

active part of that spectrum than the Slovaks and the Czechs. The reaction of the Jews in the first stages of the war was that of evasion and of preserving life. But once it became clear to them that the Nazi aim was murder, there was, wherever the possibility existed, preparation for self-defence, rebellion, partisan warfare in the forests and resistance. We meet with very interesting cases of Jews refusing to cooperate with the Nazis even when there was no longer any choice.

I shall mention here what happened in Sachsenhausen, a concentration camp in Germany. The young Jews imprisoned in it were told that they were to be led away to Auschwitz, and what went on in Auschwitz was, of course, well known in Sachsenhausen. The Jews had no weapons in their hands, not even primitive weapons like swords or daggers. In October 1942 they fell on their guards with their fists, in full view of the other inmates. If we take this example — and there are others of the same kind — we realize that this is a different type of reaction from the Czech or Slovak pattern we have mentioned.

Thus the general problem of Jewish reaction must be discussed as part of a more general and wider problem, that of the general reaction of the various nations of Europe to the Nazis and their actions.

As to the concentration camps, the minority which did not behave as was expected is what matters. The reason for such a statement is that, as a matter of principle, in the Nazi system of government everything was meant to apply to everybody without exception. This is why it was known as a totalitarian system: it had to include the totality of those ruled by it. The aim of the concentration camps was to have everyone break down and behave according to the standards fixed by the Nazis. In principle, it would have been enough to find one person — and even more so a Jew, since the Jews were at the bottom of the scale — who did not answer to these expectations, to justify one in maintaining that the whole system had failed. In fact, the system was defied not by one person or by a hundred persons — nor even by a thousand or by ten thousand — but by many more people.

As Sheep to the Slaughter?

From this point of view, it is legitimate to say that the Nazis failed. They did not succeed in destroying man — and in our case, in destroying the Jew — either as a human being or as an individual who was also a Jew. They may have succeeded with the majority — these are, of course, things which we cannot now measure. But they failed with a large minority. This is of interest not only to Jews, but to mankind in general — for, if the Nazis did not succeed in breaking everyone in such optimal conditions, it appears that there is still some hope for the human race.

As to the specific Jewish issue, we can now say: this nation, most of whose members attempted to evade the persecutions in the most unlikely circumstances, and which fought for its life in the only way open to it, without arms, without a government or any army, and without anyone to parachute supplies and arms to it; this nation, in whose Judenraete — that is, councils appointed by the Germans — we find all colors of the spectrum; this nation, which organized armed resistance in all the countries of Europe, and in numbers which were quite considerable; this nation, which, even when being marched to death reacted with what can only be termed human behavior — this is a nation whose offspring can easily identify with it.

What was the connection between traditional Jewish moral values and this Jewish reaction? That is an issue which has not yet been investigated. One remembers that in Poland, for example, one third of the Jewish people or more were adherents of Jewish religious law and of Jewish tradition, while the remaining half or two thirds were either not observant of the commandments and of Jewish tradition, or only partly observant. But they had all grown in a traditional background, and the age-old traditions of the Jewish people exercised an influence even on those Jews who were not observant — together with general human ideals derived from socialism, liberalism and other such ideologies. One should examine these various influences and the way they were integrated by the Jews with their own traditions. Let us take, for example, the Bund in Poland. This was a socialist, anti-Zionist Jewish party. The language its members spoke and wrote was Yiddish. They regarded themselves as alien to Jewish history and rejected it, but at the same time they were also a product of that history. They accepted the ideals they believed in in a way unique to themselves, which was unintelligible to the people around them. Here, too, we seem to have something which is specifically Jewish, which should be investigated in terms of its influence on the behavior of these people.

We are the followers of this path and the successors of these people, whether we like it or not. All Jews, whether they were born in Morocco or in South America, or are the descendants of Jews who emigrated from Europe to Israel or to any other country, were Hitler's target; and the fact that the Jews of Poland were murdered is only an accident, since the Jews of Poland were simply near at hand. The long term influence of the Holocaust, and of the Jewish reaction to the Holocaust on us, is something we have all been living with and will continue to live with for generations to come.